ADMINISTRATIVE USES OF COMPUTERS IN THE SCHOOLS·

American Systems Computer Institute, Inc.

Harry P. Bluhm

University of Utah

with contributions by Charles C. Cummins

PRENTICE-HALL, INC., *Englewood Cliffs, New Jersey 07632*

Library of Congress Cataloging-in-Publication Data

BLUHM, HARRY P.
  Administrative uses of computers in the schools.

  Bibliography
  Includes index.
  1. Computer managed instruction—United States.
  I. Cummins, Charles C. II. Title.
  LB1028.46.B64   1987   371.2'0028'54   86-25335
  ISBN 0-13-008467-0

Editorial/production supervision: Susan E. Rowan
Cover design: Photo Plus Art
Manufacturing buyer: John B. Hall

Apple is a registered trademark of Apple Computer, Inc.

IBM Personal Computer is a registered trademark
of International Business Machines Corporation.

*Dedicated to Louise
and to Gary, Carolyn, Beverly, Kenneth, and Colleen—
for their love and confidence.*

Printed in the United States of America
10 9 8 7 6 5 4 3 2 1

ISBN 0-13-008467-0 01

PRENTICE-HALL INTERNATIONAL (UK) LIMITED, *London*
PRENTICE-HALL OF AUSTRALIA PTY. LIMITED, *Sydney*
PRENTICE-HALL CANADA INC., *Toronto*
PRENTICE-HALL HISPANOAMERICANA, S.A., *Mexico*
PRENTICE-HALL OF INDIA PRIVATE LIMITED, *New Delhi*
PRENTICE-HALL OF JAPAN, INC., *Tokyo*
PRENTICE-HALL OF SOUTHEAST ASIA PTE. LTD., *Singapore*
EDITORA PRENTICE-HALL DO BRASIL, LTDA., *Rio de Janeiro*

CONTENTS

Part 3
Administrative Computer Software

FOREWORD

As society moves on a steady course with the involvement of technology and information management, the impact on the educational setting is quite evident. Although computer processing made its first appearance in the educational community in the 1960s, public awareness of its effects remained relatively unnoticed until the early 1980s. With the advent of the microcomputer, the general public had an opportunity to become cognizant of the computer's potential. As if overnight, there has been an explosion of interest in computers, and education, as well, has been swept into the world of computers and the related informational technology.

This book is directed to educational administrators and boards of education as they handle their responsibilities and duties specifically related to the impact of computers on school business and the instructional process. Generally, the resource allocation to computers in education has been substantial. Educational leaders should understand the extent to which computer technology can assist the educational functions, and resource allocations should be wisely placed. This book covers many aspects of computer applications in the educational setting.

Although the cost of computer equipment has decreased in recent years, expenditures have increased dramatically in the school districts and colleges. Also, an increasing number of administrators, teachers, and other employees are becoming involved in the use of this equipment. The challenge of managing this proliferation is addressed for the reader.

Most school administrators and lay citizens have had limited experience in managing and planning educational computer facilities and activities. At the same time, understanding and careful planning in computer usage will pay large educational dividends for our students and will avoid unwise and inefficient expenditures in computer related ventures. This book should serve as a valuable aid in the ongoing task of improving and enhancing education.

CHARLES C. CUMMINS
Data Processing Manager
Utah State Office of Education

PREFACE

This book is for the school superintendent, building principal, business manager, educational administrator, school board member, district/school computer coordinator, teacher, student, or lay person who wishes to become familiar with computers as an administrative tool. It can be used as a textbook in an educational administration course emphasizing computer technology in education, as an introduction to the nature and scope of administrative computing, and as a resource reference for school officials.

The book seeks to present readers with a realistic account of how a viable computer information system can enable administrators at both middle and top management levels to effectively manage the educational enterprise. The uniqueness of the book is that it (1) discusses the computer information system from an applications-oriented view, (2) recognizes the role of mainframe and minicomputers as well as microcomputers in processing information, (3) addresses the functions of the data processing systems, the management information system, and the data support system, (4) acknowledges that computer growth goes through a series of stages before maturity is reached, and (5) stresses the importance of planning and policy making.

There are four parts to the book. Part One introduces the reader to the purpose and benefits of a computer information system, computer competencies for administrators, and the stages and types of growth a computer system undergoes before maturity is attained. Emphasis is placed on the need for the computer resource to be controlled and evaluated while determining which side of the house (business or educational) should have direct responsibility for administering the resource.

Part Two discusses how the computer can be a management tool for administrators. This is done in terms of instructional and instructional support applications. The former includes computer-managed instruction and computer-assisted testing. Instructional support applications pertain to the administrative office, business operations, and such educational functions as grade reporting, attendance accounting, scheduling, and standardized test scoring. Cost-effectiveness was advanced as a criterion to apply before the adoption of any of these applications.

Part Three deals with software issues and choices confronting school officials regarding instructional and instructional support computer applications. Software evaluation/selection, user training, costs and cost effectiveness, piracy, and the privacy and security of data files are major issues discussed. The merits of general purpose, task specific, and integrated software programs are examined as types of software that might meet specific purposes.

Part Four outlines the role of district/school computer policy in managing the computer resource. This is done in the context of examining aspects of policy formulation, factors affecting computer policy, and policy approaches. One technique, policy analysis, is applied to such issues as computer acquisition, maintenance, location, and networking to illustrate how it can be employed to formulate policy.

ACKNOWLEDGMENTS

Encouragement and assistance were received from many sources while preparing the manuscript. In particular, I wish to express my thanks to the following: Howard Sloane, University of Utah, who gave purpose, direction, and meaning to the book; Charles Cummins, Utah State Office of Education, in giving focus to the book and in assisting with chapters 2, 4, and 5; John Allen, Granite School District, Salt Lake City, who offered valuable suggestions on managing the educational and instructional programs; and Cecil Miskel, Dean of the Graduate School of Education, University of Utah, for his encouragement and support.

Special acknowledgment and thanks go to Edith Syphers and Debbie Jolley, whose professional skills in word processing and organization helped bring the book to fruition. Special thanks also to Susan Willig and Shirley Chlopak of Prentice-Hall.

HARRY P. BLUHM

1

THE COMPUTER: AN ADMINISTRATIVE TOOL

THE IMPACT OF COMPUTERS IN THE SCHOOLS

Computers are a fact of life in education. Commencing in the 1950s, many schools began using them to do administrative data processing. Early applications included student scheduling, grade reports, budget accounting, payroll, and inventory listing. Administrators found that by having computerized and centralized data they were better able to make decisions pertaining to fiscal matters, staff, and students. Information-reporting requirements necessitated by the increasing demands of federal and state agencies and accrediting bodies gave further justification for introducing computers into the schools. Computers are well suited for information-processing tasks because of their speed, accuracy, and ability to store large quantities of information in an accessible form. As school systems have grown in size and in the scope of their activities, computer technology has provided the mechanism for administrators to keep abreast of increasing demands for current and documented information.

In the early 1970s instructional applications of computers, such as computer-assisted instruction, computer-managed instruction, and computer-assisted testing, were being implemented in the schools. The focus on computer-assisted instruction was to help classroom teachers instruct students, with the goal of improving achievement. Computers were used to illustrate problem-solving techniques, teach lessons, introduce new materials, and provide drill and practice. Well over 1 million students were exposed to computer-assisted instruction on a regular basis. Computer-managed instruction served to manage the instructional process by assisting teachers in diagnosing instructional needs, testing and monitoring student achievement, prescribing learning activities, and/or generating instructional materials. Computer-assisted testing proved an aid to teachers in developing, administering, and scoring tests.

A revolution occurred in the schools with the introduction of the microcomputer. In the 1980s schools began buying hardware and software for both instructional and administrative purposes at a phenomenal rate. Their use has been estimated at 95% instruction and 5% for administrative and counseling and guidance applications (Gangel, 1983). Over 1 million microcomputers are being used by 15 million students in school classrooms throughout the nation. Secondary schools dominate in ownership, with 80% owning one or more microcomputers compared to only 62% of the elementary schools (Market Data Retrieval, 1984; Fifteen Million Students in U.S. Use a Million Computers; 1986). By 1990, experts predict there will be 2 million computers in the public schools (Sturdivant, 1984). Despite this optimism, others feel the microcomputer boom is slowing down (Technically Speaking, 1985a). The expected annual growth rate in the sale of personal computers between 1986 and 1990 is projected by Sofsearch, Intl. at 5.4%. If this figure is correct, by 1986 the computer boom may be behind us (Peterson & K-Turkel, 1984a). According to a study by Talmis, a market information and consulting service, a temporary plateau in the sale of microcomputers to schools will occur around 1987. They contend this will happen when nearly all school districts own at least one microcomputer lab with twenty to thirty machines (Compuview, 1983). Regardless, schools across the country are still buying microcomputers, but with more caution. They are seeking to buy machines that will keep them at the top of the line for at least a few years (Chion-Kenny, 1985a).

In the rush to computerize the classroom, education computing has become a multimillion-dollar industry. During the 1984–85 school year, district hardware costs were $390 million (Computers, 1985). On the assumption that the number of microcomputers will continue to increase in elementary and secondary schools, Grayson (1984) has estimated that by 1987 schools will spend $2 billion annually on computer equipment.

The expansion of microcomputers in the classroom gave rise to computer literacy instruction. In a practical sense, *computer literacy* can be defined in terms of the competencies administrators, teachers, and students should acquire about computers and their applications. To ensure that these competencies are taught, twenty-five states and the District of Columbia have mandated some form of literacy requirements (Reinhold & Corkett,

1985). Colleges and departments of education, in seeking to meet the needs of preservice and in-service teachers and administrators, have instituted computer literacy courses. Institutions in thirty-one (57%) states were reported as offering computer literacy coursework for student teachers, while twenty-four (44%) states had institutions offering such courses in an administrative preparatory program (Abernathy & Pettibone, 1984). According to a recent survey by the Department of Education's Office of Educational Research and Improvement (OERI), approximately 90% of the nation's teacher training institutions gave their students some training in computers during the 1983–84 school year. Virtually all of the schools had plans to initiate or increase their offerings over the next two years (Computer Courses, 1986).

The computer has had a profound effect on education, precipitating conflicting points of view. Cornish (1984) contends it may have the most significant impact since the creation of the book due to these benefits:

- *Expert Instruction.* Quality prepared learning programs, being individually interactive, enable students to have their own private tutor.
- *Self-testing.* Students can keep testing their own performance until their level of aspiration is attained. Teachers assist in this process by motivating them to achieve up to their potential.
- *Instant Feedback.* When an error is made, students can obtain immediate feedback rather than having to wait a day or week on homework or class test performance reporting, as is typical in a traditional classroom.
- *Control of the Pace of Education.* Instructions can be repeated easily until mastery is obtained if a student has difficulty learning content material.
- *Convenience.* Data can be provided for a learner whenever and wherever wanted, since a human tutor is not needed.
- *Continual Education.* Computer-assisted instruction can be lifelong, with no need to enter a classroom or leave one's home (p. F16).

Teachers using microcomputers report that the greatest impact of the machine has been on the social organization of learning rather than on increased student learning. This appeared to be manifest through students (1) working more independently without assistance from teachers, (2) having an increased enthusiasm for learning, (3) being assigned to work at a level more appropriate to their achievement, and (4) answering one another's questions (Becker, 1983).

Because the microcomputer revolution has been so swift, Benderson (1983) wonders whether computers will be relegated to the pedagogical junk heap in a few years along with teaching machines, programmed learning, and the new math program. School board members, parents, legislators, and interested citizens concerned about computers in education have been asking educators such questions as: At what school level should they be emphasized? What priorities should be placed on their use? Have they been used appropriately? Has their use been beneficial or harmful? Increasingly, school officials have had to address these issues.

The likelihood exists that new and innovative computer technology will continue to impact schools. For example, communication with a computer through speech is becoming a reality. Video disks and a microcomputer have the potential to provide an individualized interactive experience for students by accessing instant frames of learning for them. If educational computing is to be a continuing force in the school, educators and the community must build upon the strengths of the technology, minimizing the limitations in the process.

COMPUTERS, A HELP IN MANAGING SCHOOLS

School systems are complex social organizations with many people fulfilling specialized tasks. At the district level is the superintendent of schools, who is responsible for every aspect of the system, including instructional and business operations. Some of the specific duties carried out by these administrators include providing educational programs for staff, making recommendations to the board of education on all personnel, planning both current and long-range programs and improvements, and evaluating the effectiveness of the entire academic program. At the local level are the building principals. They are responsible for buildings and grounds, supplies and equipment, staffing, curriculum, scheduling and registration, and the supervision of students.

The management and operation of today's schools have become increasingly difficult. Economic and social factors have affected schools adversely. Rising costs, dwindling enrollments, demands for accountability of staff and programs, and constant requests from regulating agencies for information and reports have compounded administrators' responsibilities. Confronted with the tasks of keeping schools operating within the boundaries of goals and expectations set for them and the financial resources available, administrators have turned to computer technology and computer-based information systems.

School business administrators were among the first to recognize how the computer could assist them in accounting for funds, processing payrolls, and maintaining personnel records. Computer technology, though, has implications for all aspects of the educational system, including facilities, equipment and supplies, instructional programming, and student records. Superintendents and building principals have come to recognize that computers are ideally suited to process information that can be used in making management decisions. Table 1.1 illustrates typical administrative and student-related functions that can be addressed by a computer.

TABLE 1.1 Computer-based Administrative and Student-related Applications

ADMINISTRATIVE				STUDENT-RELATED	
FINANCIAL	PERSONNEL	EQUIPMENT/ SUPPLIES/ FACILITIES	OFFICE	STUDENT RECORDS	INSTRUCTIONAL/ CURRICULUM
Accounting	Demographics	Inventories	Textual Material, e.g., correspondence, memorandums, newsletters, directories	Attendance	Computer-assisted Instruction
Budgeting	Assignments	Lists, e.g., textbooks, keys, lockers, etc.		Grades/GPA	Computer-managed Instruction
General Ledger	Certification	Room Locations and Capacities		Registration	Scheduling
Salary Schedule	Health	Room Assignments		Demographics (student and family)	Class Lists
Cost Analysis	Payroll Check and Deductions	Utilization	Files, e.g., memos, inventories, lists, etc.	Health	Staff Assignments
Purchasing	Tax Information and W-2 Reports	Maintenance Scheduling		Tuition and Fees	Computer-assisted Testing
Student Finances		Energy Utilization Control	Mailing Lists and Labels	Graduation Requirements/ Progress	Homeroom Lists
				Class Schedule	Study Hall Lists
				Extracurricular Activities	

School officials surveyed regarding the impact computers have had in operating and managing their school districts stated that computer use freed personnel from clerical tasks; enabled accurate financial, student, and personnel records to be maintained and accessed; permitted flexible scheduling of classes; reduced the time period between the end of a term and the distribution of student progress reports; allowed decentralization of budgetary development and control due to personnel having accurate, relevant, and detailed budget information; ensured cost savings in developing bus routes; and enabled research studies to be conducted to predict student enrollments and to make planning and curricular decisions (Hansen, Klassen & Lindsay, 1978).

Decision making is considered the most important function of administration. Daily, demands are placed upon principals and superintendents to make a variety of decisions. At the school level, decisions typically center on student and faculty concerns. District administrators are frequently confronted with transportation, budgetary, or school boundary decisions; they often must justify to critics or concerned citizens decisions made about curriculum reform.

A fundamental step in decision making is the collecting of relevant (free from bias) and repeatable (the same when viewed by others) data (Griffiths, 1959). An assumption made about decision making is that the decisions made are no better than the information upon which they are based. If an information system is lacking, an administrator is forced to rely upon incomplete data or the opinions of his/her subordinates and associates. If the information shared is biased, poor decisions may result. The implication is that if the goal of administrators is to make sound decisions in managing schools, then a total information system should be established.

A SCHOOL COMPUTER-BASED INFORMATION SYSTEM

A computer-based information system is intended to provide information needed by users in the conduct of their business. As a first step in the establishment of a system, the administrator should identify what these needs are and who the users would be. Is information, for example, wanted only on the day-to-day operations of the schools? In addition, are data needed to help monitor and regulate the day-to-day operational events? Further, should information be had to plan for future events such as remodeling or building new facilities, hiring additional staff, and so on? Hussain (1973) provides a model which reflects the vertical relationship of informational requirements to the different user levels of the administrative hierarchy (see Figure 1.1).

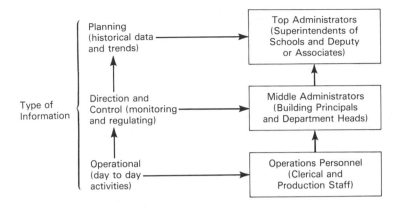

FIGURE 1.1   The Vertical Relationship of Informational Needs to Users on Different Administrative Levels.   Adapted from Hussain, K. M. (1973). *Development of Information Systems for Education* (pp. 107–108). Englewood Cliffs, NJ: Prentice-Hall, Inc.

Operational information is the factual reporting of the current operations of the schools. Specific types of reporting could be done daily, weekly, monthly, and/or annually. Data would be collected on student progress, attendance, grades, classroom usage, scheduling activities, and so on. The information may be compiled by hand, but the use of a computer materially reduces the time required to input the data and prepare reports. Though operational personnel are responsible for the processing and reporting of this level of information, middle administrators such as building principals and heads of large school departments will be the users of the produced reports and lists.

Building principals, though, need to monitor and regulate the operational activities in their schools. This is done to optimize performance consistent with the objectives of the school. Operational information provides facts that can be used to compare desired performance with actual performance. When exceptions are noted, remedial or corrective steps can be taken. Examples might be: Do expenditures exceed budget? Are faculty grading practices too lenient or too strict? Is class size above recommended standards? Are teaching loads equitable? Analysis of data dealing with these types of events enables principals to have the facts necessary to make decisions respecting the control and direction of their schools.

Top administrators such as school superintendents need information to study relationships, make projections, assess the different components of the school district, and do short- and long-range planning. Data are also essential for public relations purposes to meet the information needs of the PTA, interested citizen groups, pressure groups, and for conducting bond elections. Planning information may be used by superintendents and their administrative staff to define objectives and establish district strategies to attain these objectives. Operational, direction, and control information is used to accomplish planning purposes, though outside information may also be collected relating to state, regional, or national trends. Judicious use of planning information enables superintendents to resolve problems that can't be corrected at the operational or control level, to address variables that seem to have a major effect on district goals and plans, and to improve the learning environment.

The interrelatedness of the three information levels to the administrative hierarchy and internal and external sources of information is shown in Figure 1.2. It should be recognized that a dependency exists between users and their information needs and the forces that impinge on the school organization. Externally, social, community, political/legislative, and

FIGURE 1.2   The Interrelatedness of the Three Levels of an Information System to the Administrative Hierarchy and Environment Sources.   Adapted from Hussain, K. M. (1973). *Development of Information Systems for Education* (p. 121). Englewood Cliffs, NJ: Prentice-Hall, Inc.

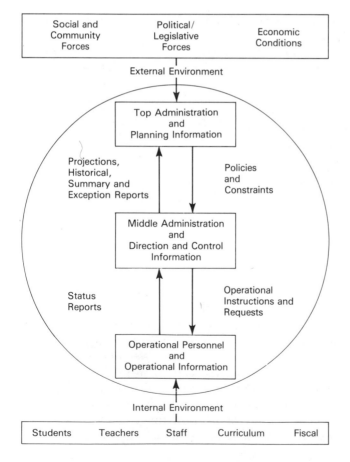

economic conditions operate to influence school policy and programming. Social and community forces may be represented by pressure groups and concerned citizens who want either special concessions or changes in the school.

Political/legislative forces operate to affect bond issues, budgets, and appropriations. Economic conditions such as recession and inflation serve to erode budgets, with a resultant effect on the salary schedule and funds for equipment and supplies. Internally, the informational system compiles and processes data on students, teachers, staff, curriculum, and sources of revenue. Decisions school administrators make are dependent on a functioning informational system that provides quality data. If successful, internal organizational needs can be met and effectiveness achieved in coping with external forces or conditions.

ATTRIBUTES OF AN INFORMATION SYSTEM

Hussain (1973) states that the attributes of an information system are timeliness, accuracy, relevancy, and completeness. Timeliness of information is important to school administrators if they need to answer questions regarding students, faculty, and building utilization. Timely information means knowing the number of students enrolled totally and by class, what the daily attendance is, the number of teachers in each department, those students on the honor roll or those failing, which students have not completed graduation requirements, and the number of classrooms that are underutilized. Timely information means having a staff and faculty directory that lists current names, addresses, and phone numbers. To produce timely information, costs are incurred. The administrator needs to weigh costs against benefits in producing these reports. Factors to take into consideration when making the choice, "Do we need this information or is it too expensive to prepare?" are the effect had on parents and the institutional image.

Accuracy means the data compiled are error free. Accuracy is essential in financial accounting and should exist in making grade and scholastic computations and in keeping student records. Unfortunately, errors occur in these records which may adversely affect the student. Every effort should be made to reduce errors and improve accuracy. The types of errors that may occur are input errors, incorrect processing rules, improperly followed or poorly designed procedures, and equipment or processing breakdowns. Inherent in the information system should be procedures to detect and reduce such errors.

Completeness refers to having all relevant information that is needed by an administrator to resolve a problem. This may not be possible in all instances due to the many internal and external variables operating in such a complex institution as a school system. Further, it may not be economically feasible to compile and maintain all the information that is desired. Time constraints, too, may be restrictive. Limits may have to be set as to what constitutes a "complete" information system, perhaps in the form of a compromise between resource constraints and information requests. The determiner, though, is collecting relevant information that is directly related and applicable to the problem being considered.

Problems dealing with relevancy are the keeping of obsolete, "nice-to-have," and unrefined, unusable information, and having too much information. When confronted with the whole array of information that a computer can generate in terms of charts, analyses, predictions, and simulations, the administrator can be overwhelmed and immobilized. Campbell, Corbally, and Nystread (1983), in lamenting this dilemma, state that the surplus of data may hide what is important and relevant. They contend that it is the administrator, not the director of the computer service, who is responsible for determining what information would be relevant and helpful.

ELEMENTS OF A COMPUTER INFORMATION SYSTEM

A computer-based information system, as shown in Figure 1.3, involves hardware, software, and the people who input and utilize the produced data. The computer and its peripherals, such as a letter-quality printer, are the hardware or physical devices that support the data-processing functions. Because of its high speed, the computer can perform with ease such processing operations as calculating, sorting, and classifying data. These

FIGURE 1.3   Elements of a Computer Information System

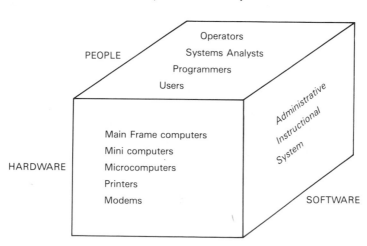

operations are carried out according to instructions telling it what to do. The term *software* is used to reflect these instructions, which may be in the form of commercially prepared or custom-written programs. Instructional and administrative software programs (Chapters 8–11) are available to schools.

The computer may be a large mainframe computer or a minicomputer typically used in a central location like the district office, or a small microcomputer housed in the principal's office. The mainframe is a large computer that can operate at an ultra-high speed and store millions of bytes (units) of information. It has the ability to support several users performing a variety of tasks at the same time.

The minicomputer is more compact in size than a mainframe; it is limited as to the number of tasks it can perform simultaneously. It has the capability, though, to service a number of terminals hooked to it under what is known as a time-sharing arrangement. Mini and mainframe computers have been used heavily to perform school business applications such as inventory control, accounts payable, accounts receivable, payroll, and cost analysis. They have also been used to meet student services applications, particularly grade reporting, scheduling, and standardized test scoring.

The microcomputer, which school districts have been buying in record numbers, is a small but complete computer with an input unit like a typewriter keyboard. Output data can be viewed on a display monitor and printed using a dot matrix or letter-quality printer. The microcomputer is generally used by a single user. Though it has less memory than a mini or mainframe computer, microprocessor technology advances have permitted more memory and the networking of the machines to each other and to a central processing unit.

People involved in a computer information system are the consumers or users of the processed data; programmers, who write the software programs; the operators of the equipment, particularly in a mainframe or minicomputer facility; systems analysts, who are specialists in the design of an information system; and maintenance personnel, who service the computer hardware. Direct users in the schools are administrators, teachers, counselors, and students. Administrators, as we have seen, use information from the system to manage the school and plan for the future. Teachers and counselors use information to advise students and monitor their progress. Students use information on courses and their academic status to make educational and vocational plans.

Parents and school board members are indirect users of the information system. Parents, being concerned about their children's progress, want information on grades, course offerings, and the completion of graduation requirements. School board members need information from the administrative staff to help them make policies and allocate funds.

TYPES OF COMPUTER INFORMATION SYSTEMS

For each informational level in the administrative hierarchy an information-processing system has evolved. An interrelatedness exists between these components, as reflected in Figure 1.4. To provide information on the current status of the schools, data-processing systems (DPS) are established. The management information system (MIS) is a decision tool for building principals. Decision support systems (DSS) become the mechanism to help superintendents make planning and strategy decisions.

Underpinning the entire computer information system are the data-processing systems developed. By data processing we mean the process by which data on personnel, programs, and activities of the school are collected; assigned meaning; communicated to administrators, teachers, counselors, students, and parents; and stored for future use. In the process the data go through three stages—input, processing, and output, as shown in Figure 1.5. *Input* is the preparing of the information to be entered into the computer. In the *processing* stage the computer performs certain functions such as classifying, sorting, calculating, comparing, and summarizing the data. *Output* refers to the records and reports produced that contain meaningful information for the user.

FIGURE 1.4 A Total School Computer-based Information System Showing the Vertical and Horizontal Interrelationships

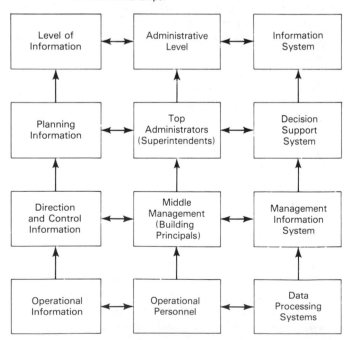

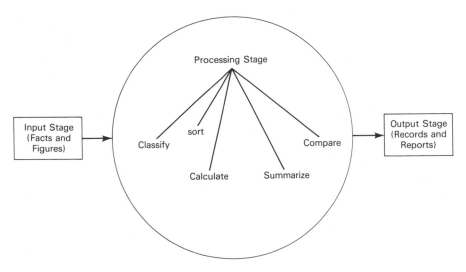

FIGURE 1.5   The Data-processing Cycle

The purpose of a data-processing system is to produce periodic output documents which provide a snapshot look at the current operational activities of a school. The processed information may be filed, stored, and retrieved to support the management functions of the school organization. An effective DPS provides the data needed in the form desired at minimum expenditure. A number of data-processing systems would be developed in the schools, with each providing data about a particular activity such as payroll, personnel, scheduling, purchasing, and grades.

A student information data-processing system is illustrated in Figure 1.6. Information on student attendance, academic performance, course schedule, and so on would be entered into the computer. Data files on grades, attendance, scheduling, and testing would subsequently be established. Reports required by the principal and his/her staff to help administer the school would be produced as needed. Possible questions these reports should be able to answer are: What is the average daily membership of our students? What was the mean reading comprehension score of our eighth graders? What students made the honor roll this term? When a data-processing system is operational we have the beginnings of a management information system.

A management information system (MIS), in the strictest sense, is not a computer system. Its purpose is to give additional meaning to the output data produced from the data-processing systems. This is done by reviewing the results of longitudinal or historical data and the day-to-day operations of the school to identify situations that require special concern or decisions. The administrator may procedurally compare actual performance

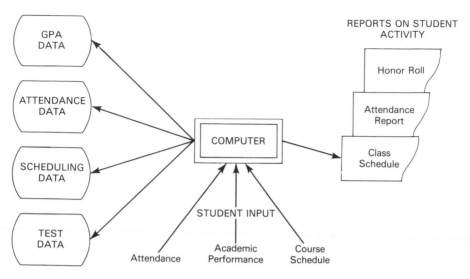

FIGURE 1.6 Components of a Student Information Data-processing System

with past or projected results or look at the relationships that exist between given school variables. When exceptions occur or things are out of line, the administrator would be better prepared to make needed decisions regarding corrective action. Administrators are confronted daily with the need to make decisions regarding the performance of others (control) and the desired direction school programs should attain. A functioning MIS provides them with the information necessary to determine which of several alternative courses of action is best. It also may assist administrators in determining which variables need to be controlled to facilitate better management or to increase school productivity.

Figure 1.7 depicts the components of a management information system. The historical summaries generated from the data-processing files furnish the analytic reports which can be scrutinized by administrators, counselors, and department chairpersons. School administrators would be able to formulate a plan of action to handle problem situations such as the following: How can violations of state and federal guidelines for educating the handicapped be resolved? How can unreasonable faculty-student ratios in given courses be reduced? What bus routes should be changed to meet population shifts within the boundaries of the school or school district? Can funds be found to bring staff salaries in line with those of their counterparts in school districts of similar population?

Available to school administrators are data-based management systems or DBMS. They are software programs designed to integrate and report information (Chapter 10) in a timely and cost-efficient manner.

Decision support systems (DSS) utilize projection and simulation procedures to predict trends and simulate the future state of school districts based upon the assumptions and conditions furnished by superintendents and their administrative staff. To accomplish this, the data support system utilizes not only the output generated from the data-processing systems and management information system, but relevant outside information. An effective DSS assists superintendents in determining long-range goals and envisioning and planning for the district organization and functions of the schools in the future. Spreadsheet software programs (Chapter 11) have been developed for microcomputers. They may be used in a DSS to provide administrators with details about the effect economic conditions may have on a district budget.

To facilitate planning in the decision support system, computer planning models might be developed. A computer planning model is a computer-based representation of all or part of a school district's current or prospective operation or its economic environment or both. One type of model that might be developed is a forecasting model. Its purpose would be to provide predictive data on K–12 enrollments, tax revenues, and other variables that would be used to determine future building, transportation, and staffing needs. A computer planning model may not be either feasible or practical for a school district. School administrators need to determine if such a model would be useful. In making the decision, consideration must be given to these concerns: Technically, is it possible? That is, does the district have the personnel, equipment, and data base necessary to develop a model? Economically, is it worthwhile? Would costs expended to develop and implement the model be prohibitive based on expected out-

FIGURE 1.7 Components of a Management Information System

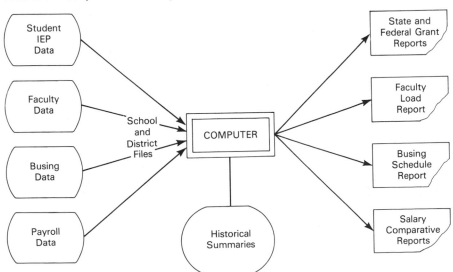

TABLE 1.2 Examples of Educational Problems by Level of Information and Type of Computer Information System

LEVELS OF INFORMATION AND APPLICABLE COMPUTER INFORMATION SYSTEM

Information Areas	LEVEL 1 OPERATIONAL DATA: DATA-PROCESSING SYSTEMS	LEVEL 2 DIRECTION AND CONTROL DATA: MANAGEMENT INFORMATION SYSTEM	LEVEL 3 PLANNING DATA: DATA SUPPORT SYSTEM
Faculty, Staff, and Students	Comprehensive statistics of teacher and student background.	Relationships among factors such as nature of training, age, assignment, class load, etc., and teacher retention in the system.	Decisions made pertaining to instituting teacher retention procedures, with predictions made to plan future staffing using the retention outcome data and census data.
	Longitudinal data on student achievement, dropout, health, etc.	Relationship between factors in school achievement and factors in student health or environmental background.	Prediction of students' success in school using longitudinal data, followed by experimental interventions with an analysis of the outcomes.
Curriculum and Instruction	Number of students enrolled in various curriculum tracks.	Relationships between students' high school curricula and later academic and work careers.	Decisions made pertaining to revamping the guidance program to better assist students who choose curricular courses that would enhance educational and career goals.
	Storage and retrieval of data on student performance in different instructional settings, e.g., individualized instruction, open classroom, large groups, small groups, etc.	Relationship between student performance and instructional settings.	Determination of which instructional environments should be supported in the schools.

16

Budget and Financial Support	Statistics on school costs of budgeted categories.	Determination of overruns in any of the categories.	Projections made on budget allocations based on overrun figures and revenue forecasting.
	Longitudinal data of assessed evaluation and data pertaining to the proportion of the district's income going to education.	Relationship between financial support and various evidences of school productivity.	Determination of how the educational dollar can best facilitate school productivity.
Facilities, Equipment, and Supplies	Cost statistics on all aspects of school maintenance and construction.	Relationship between costs expended to maintain old buildings versus construction of new facilities.	Determination made as to whether district funds should continue to maintain or replace old facilities.
	Longitudinal data on equipment and supply allocations by school enrollments.	Relationship between equipment and supply inventories by size of school enrollment.	Determination of equipment and supply allocations based on projected school enrollments.

comes? And will district and school administrators accept and use it, recognizing they would have to be educated how to use it?

Table 1.2 illustrates how, at each informational level, each of the three computer information systems would focus on sample problems. The data-processing system(s) generates the raw data that feed in to the management information system (MIS). The MIS focuses on relationships among the data or, where discrepancies occur, between expected and actual outcomes. The data generated by both the data-processing systems and the management information system are used in the data support system to make planning decisions based on projections and simulations.

CONCERNS ABOUT COMPUTER INFORMATION SYSTEMS

A problem inherent in data-processing systems that feed principals and superintendents managerial and planning information is that the data are too detailed in some areas and not detailed enough in others. Further, the data may not be packaged in a format conducive for planning. In large school districts or state-run systems, well-defined data-processing systems exist which support operational and managerial control activities. In small districts this may not be the case. A problem that may result from well-oiled and smoothly operating systems is that administrators can be overwhelmed from having too much information, which has the same effect as having no information. Other concerns that seem related to data-processing systems are the emphases placed on the data base and cost considerations. If the former exists, clerical and routine reporting requirements are accented to the exclusion of management data. As to the latter, though a DPS may make for productivity, these gains may be offset by excessive costs incurred in setting up and operating the system.

A number of problems have been identified with the management information system and data support system. A fundamental concern is the lack of experience by some school administrators with computers, their applications and system design. To make an MIS work, principals need to approve and be involved in its development. Further, they need to be familiar with the various data-processing systems operating within their school or on the district level which provide input for the MIS.

Too few superintendents, it seems, are aware of the benefits of a data support system as they make policies and allocate resources that affect the future of the district. Even if they wished to utilize such a system, information needed for planning frequently doesn't exist or is not in a format easy and convenient to use. As a consequence, superintendents need to be the catalysts in establishing data support systems.

Caution should be exercised by school administrators to not exclude information not entered into the formally structured computer-based information system. As Hentschke (1975) has indicated, there are times when important data for management decisions could not and should not emanate from the information system. Gardner (1965), in examining the impact of the computer in decision making, reinforces this point. He contends that top managers may find that a computer information system may make them less dependent on firsthand experiences. Processed data, he infers, may be too massaged once the raw data has been sampled, screened, condensed, compiled, and coded. What the administrator receives is statistical information spun into generalizations and crystallized into recommendations. The net result may be that certain kinds of information that managers need have been systematically filtered out by the system.

BENEFITS OF A COMPUTER INFORMATION SYSTEM

A computer information system, if it is to prove its worth, should reduce time expended on clerical or paperwork tasks, produce accurate information, ensure generation of reports when needed, and facilitate the decision-making process. A computer system, it is said, can result in time savings. This is true only if the time expended to input and process the data is less than the time that would be devoted by a person doing the task by hand. If this occurs, secretaries and administrative staff may be freed to do other tasks. The microcomputer, used either as a stand-alone or linked to a mainframe computer, permits administrators to do this. A microcomputer has the capability not only to access student, faculty, and financial information, but it may be used to keep track of appointments and obligations, record notes on conferences and meetings held, produce interoffice memos, and execute selective or mass mailings to students and school patrons. The judicious use of a single microcomputer by a principal, it has been postulated, could save up to 200 hours—or the equivalent of 25 eight-hour days—in a school year (Give Computers to Administrators First, Researcher Urges, 1984). The time gained can help principals be more accessible to students and staff as they seek to upgrade the educational program.

Middle managers responding to a special Harris survey (Business Monitor, 1983) conducted on how computers are remaking the manager's job reported the following: (1) 91% believed computers increased their productivity; (2) 84% believed they were able to increase the number and variety of responsibilities they can handle; (3) 51% indicated they have not mastered the operation of the machine themselves. Managers who used the computer reported they have become more analytical and now asked better questions to get better answers. The implication seems to be that information is power, and those who master its acquisition have an edge.

Accuracy and timeliness, we have found, are two attributes of a computer information system. Accuracy is essential in financial accounting and in computing the scholastic standings of students. Principals may face angry and hostile parents and students if, by error, computed GPAs may deprive the students of a scholarship or cause them to be placed on academic probation. Personnel, too, would be upset if their payroll checks showed a shortage. It has been found that a computer system compared to a manual system produces more accurate student, personnel, and financial records.

A computer system has the potential to provide information to administrators that is timely if it is consistently updated and readily retrievable. Problems, though, can occur with a central computer system when building principals desire reports unique to their school. This may necessitate the writing of a special software program, with a resultant time lapse. This limitation, however, can be offset if the principal has a microcomputer with the appropriate program software to use for generating specialized in-house reports.

Respondents to an extensive survey (Hansen, Klassen & Lindsay, 1978) on the impact computer information systems have had upon school and school district administration said computer use facilitated more effective resource management, better decision making, better long-range planning, and more time to work with people. Larger school districts and those that used computer services had greater computer use and impact. Overall, most of the impacts or benefits mentioned were at the operational, directional, and control levels of the information system.

WHAT THE SCHOOL ADMINISTRATOR SHOULD KNOW ABOUT COMPUTERS

Principals and superintendents, as the educational leaders in the schools, need to be computer literate if they are to be in the forefront in having computers used effectively for instructional and administrative purposes. As Estes and Watkins (1983) state:

> We believe it is a clarion call for administrators to become literate—sufficiently literate to be able to ask those who program information to do it in a way that will enable them to answer the necessary questions; sufficiently literate to know the full range of capability of computers so that they can plan to use them for access to information bases, teleconferencing, automatic data transmission and receipt after hours; data base management, scheduling, word processing; and sufficiently literate to strategically increase the computing capabilities of their schools (p. 29).

Unfortunately, too many administrators are naive regarding computers in general and microcomputers specifically. Colleges of education have yet to remedy this deficiency, according to a survey of forty leading universities (Training Lack, 1985). Only one in three institutions was offering any course for school administrators on high technology. Further, one out of five universities was not even thinking about adding such a course in the years ahead. Efforts, though, have been expended trying to determine in what areas the administrator should be literate (Noonan, 1983; Serabian, 1983; Mims, 1983). Mims validated a list of forty-two competencies using judges that first rated the competencies as to acceptability and subsequently as to importance. These competencies were arbitrarily divided into six broad categories, for example, (1) literacy, (2) programming, (3) applications, (4) software/hardware, (5) resources, and (6) educational computing. Thirty-eight of the items had a mean rating of at least medium importance. The five items that ranked highest were (1) justifying and funding computer purchases, (2) meeting instructor training needs, (3) identifying tasks and needs for computers, (4) being aware of the social issues related to computing, and (5) seeking a knowledge of future trends. The major finding of the study was that more emphasis seemed to be placed on knowledge and awareness-type competencies than on competencies related to being able to plan and use the computer for administrative applications.

Computer-literacy components noted by Noonan (1983) are reflected in Figure 1.8. Specifically, he states that the administrator must be aware of the administrative uses of computers and barriers to instructional uses of computers, and be able to develop a computer policy that includes the training of teachers, the computer education of students, and the acquisition of computer materials.

Administrative competencies can also be grouped in the following areas: (1) computer terms and definitions, (2) computer systems, (3) computer information systems, (4) types of computer configurations, (5) hardware evaluation and selection, (6) software evaluation and selection, (7) educational uses of computers, and (8) administrative uses of computers. Specific competencies in these areas are defined below:

1. *Computer Terms and Definitions*
   1.1 Explain the meaning of common names and terms used in computer literature.
2. *Computer Systems*
   2.1 Realize that *hardware* in a computer system refers to the physical components of the system, such as disk drive, display monitor, central processor, and printer.
   2.2 Explain the functions of the different components in a system and their relationship to each other.
   2.3 Know that the central processing unit or CPU, which contains the memory, control, and arithmetic units of a computer, is that part of the computer that carries out the essential and controlling tasks.
   2.4 Realize that keyboards, a mouse, tapes, and punch cards serve as input devices.

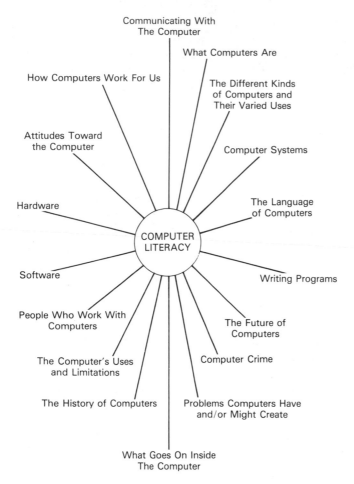

FIGURE 1.8 Computer-Literacy Requirement for Administrators. From Noonan, L. (1983). *Computer Literacy for Administrators.* AEDS Monitor, 22 *(1, 2), 6*

2.5   Realize that display monitors, printers, tapes, and punch cards serve as output devices.

2.6   Realize that the term *mainframe* refers to a large computer or the CPU and its enclosure.

2.7   Realize that microcomputers are small or personal computers which may function as stand-alone machines or be linked to a mainframe computer.

2.8   Realize that minicomputers are smaller than mainframes but larger than microcomputers.

2.9   Realize that *software* pertains to computer programs and includes compilers, operating systems, and user or application programs. The program may be stored on a disk or tape but may also be printed out on computer paper.

2.10 Realize that *documentation* applies to support materials for software programs, which includes operating instructions and the program listing.

3. *Computer Information Systems*
   3.1 Explain the meaning of operational, direction and control, and planning information for administrators, their relationship with each other, and the types of computer information systems.
   3.2 Recognize that the basic elements of an information system are inputting information; processing information by classifying, sorting, calculating, summarizing, and comparing; and obtaining output data or information that has been given meaning.
   3.3 Explain the purpose of a data-processing system, including its applications.
   3.4 Explain the purpose of a management information system, including its applications.
   3.5 Know that data-based management systems (DBMS) are software programs designed to provide output reports such as on students, personnel, and equipment inventories.
   3.6 Explain the purpose of a data support system and its applications.
   3.7 Explain what regulatory procedures may be employed to keep computer systems secure and protect the privacy of individual data files.

4. *Types of Computer Configurations*
   4.1 Explain and analyze a hardware configuration that employs (a) communications software and hardware including modems and protocols, (b) a networking system, or (c) a variety of peripheral devices.
   4.2 Explain the purposes of and differences between centralized, decentralized, and distributed or shared computer configurations.

5. *Hardware Evaluation and Selection*
   5.1 Evaluate hardware systems, applying the following criteria: (a) user information needs, (b) purchase and maintenance costs, (c) memory requirements, (d) software compatibility, (e) printing needs, and (f) external storage needs.
   5.2 Select hardware that meets school or school district bid specifications.

6. *Software Evaluation and Selection*
   6.1 Evaluate microcomputer software, applying the following criteria: (a) user requirements met, (b) documentation clear and understandable, (c) training requirements specified, (d) adequate data storage, (e) custom reports development possible, (f) help menus provided, and (g) damaged disks able to be traded or replaced.
   6.2 Realize that there are various sources available to educators to assist them in evaluating and selecting software.

7. *Educational Uses of Computers*
   7.1 Explain the uses and limitations of computer-managed instruction, computer-assisted instruction, and computer-assisted testing.

8. *Administrative Uses of Computers*
   8.1 Explain the uses and limitations of employing computers to manage student, personnel, financial, facilities, equipment and supply, and transportation record keeping.

School administrators who are in the forefront in having successful computing programs in their schools are those who have expended the time and energy needed to become computer literate. The competencies identified above should help aspiring administrators identify what they must do to attain this goal.

SUMMARY

The microcomputer has had a profound impact on schools, both instructionally and administratively. In the classroom it has given rise to the computer-literacy movement whereby 1 million microcomputers are being used by 15 million students throughout the United States. Computer-assisted instruction has been enhanced as well as the management of instruction through the use of electronic grade books and software to monitor the academic progress of students. School administrators have found that computer technology has facilitated the management of business affairs, expedited student scheduling and grade reporting, and provided information for decision making.

The establishment of a computer information system is the key to the effective use of computers. A hierarchical system, it is composed of three levels: data-processing systems (DPS), the management information system (MIS), and a decision support system (DSS). Data-processing systems provide information on the current operations of the schools which form the basis of the management information system. The MIS focuses on the relationships among the student and financial data collected to help support organizational management control functions and highlight exception conditions requiring attention or corrective action. The data support system utilizes the output generated from the data-processing systems and the management information system to assist top management formulate policies and plans by projecting the likely consequences of decisions.

School administrators, as the educational leaders in the schools, need to be computer literate to promote the establishment and use of a computer information system. Specifically, they need to be aware of the administrative uses of computers, barriers to the instructional uses of computers, and should be able to develop policies respecting the training of teachers, the computer education of students, and the acquisition of computer hardware and software.

2

ORGANIZATIONAL CONSIDERATIONS

School administrators should evaluate periodically the impact computers in their school districts have had on organizational structure, management control, funding, personnel, and applications. Doing so will identify important areas of organizational concern. It has been found in business companies that data-processing services go through stages of growth in their development. By recognizing that computer expansion goes through a sequence of stages, superintendents and principals will have a useful framework to help them place their school or school district's problems in perspective and to help them understand the problems they will face as they move forward.

STAGES OF COMPUTER GROWTH

The stages and the types of growth that must be dealt with as maturity occurs with a computer system that uses a mainframe computer and/or microcomputers are depicted in Figure 2.1. Specifically, according to Gibson and Nolan (1974), computer growth goes through four distinct stages or sequential "cans of worms": initiation, expansion, formalization, and maturity. These stages reflect growth in computer applications, growth in specialization of data-processing personnel, and growth in formal management techniques and organization. Though their pioneering work centered on business firms, the study findings are directly applicable to school districts using computers to process information and prepare reports. Similarities exist in the problems encountered both in organizations and the management techniques applied in solving them at any given stage. Gibson and Nolan note that:

> Associated with each stage is a distinctive informal organizational process. Each of these seems to play an important role in giving rise to the issues which need to be resolved if the stage is to be passed through without a crisis and if the growth of the resource (computer) is to be managed to yield maximum benefit to the company (p. 77).

A major finding by Gibson and Nolan was that the data-processing budget formed an S-shaped curve when plotted over the four stages. The proliferation of applications in Stage 2 caused the budget to increase dramatically. The degree of management control imposed by administrators in Stage 3 to curb this increase also took the form of an S-growth curve, as shown in Figure 2.1. The importance of this curve is that its turnings correspond to the main events—often crises—in the data-processing functions that signal important shifts in the way the computer resource is used and managed.

By describing the problems and issues characteristic of each stage, school administrators should be able to evaluate how computer growth has been managed in their districts.

The Initiation Stage

The initiation stage is characterized by lax management, a loose budget, and little or no control being exercised over the direction data-processing services should take. This stage in educational settings is typically launched when the top administrator is convinced by a staff member that savings can be obtained by computerizing the fiscal records or that a computer is more cost effective in processing information. Special concerns that administrators should address in this stage are (1) What department should be responsible for the computer? and (2) How can the fear of the computer be minimized among employees who will be affected by its introduction into the schools?

Organizational Structure. Critical to the success of a computer information system to support the educational program of a school district is the organizational structure adopted. Since the early 1960s, many school districts have had established computerized systems to manage business operations. This resulted because the business applications of a school·district—such as payroll, budget, and accounts payable—were comparable to

	STAGE 1 INITIATION	STAGE 2 EXPANSION	STAGE 3 FORMALIZATION	STAGE 4 MATURITY
MANAGEMENT TECHNIQUES	Lax Management • loose budget • controls notably lacking • DP organized under office of 1st jurisdiction	User-oriented Management • loose budget • lax controls • user applications promoted • DP manager moved up in organization	Control oriented Management • controls instituted to contain runaway costs, budget justification • programming controls instituted on documentation and standards • Quality control policies introduced for computer system, programming operations, system design • DP office controlled through centralization with steering committee set up to establish project priorities • Senior management officials monitor and evaluate DP services • Management reporting system introduced	Resource-oriented Planning and Control Management • Budgetary planning for hardware, facilities, personnel and new application over 3-5 year time periods • Refinement of management control systems. Introduction of data base policies and standards • DP offices set up as separate functional area • Relationships between computer personnel and users strengthened
PERSONNEL	Specialization for Computer Efficiency • personnel limited to operators, a programmer and analyst	Specialization on Developing a Variety of Applications • expansion of personnel hired to do specific applications	Specialization on control of effectiveness of computer applications • Stabilization on number of personnel	Specialization for data-base technology and teleprocessing • upgrading of personnel to develop and implement data base technology
APPLICATIONS	Applications delimited to those identified by office of first jurisdiction	Applications proliferate in all functional areas	Moratorium placed on new applications • emphasis placed on control	Data base applications introduced • simulation models • planning models

Degree
of
Mgt.
Control

FIGURE 2.1 The Stages of Computer-processing (DP) Growth—The S Growth Curve. Reprinted by permission of the *Harvard Business Review*. An exhibit from "Managing the Four Stages of EDP Growth" by Cyrus F. Gibson and Richard Nolan (January/February 1974). Copyright © 1974 by the President and Fellows of Harvard College; all rights reserved.

27

those handled by computer in the business sector. Computer support, though, for instructional and school-level administrative applications was slow in developing and is just now coming into its own with the advent of the microcomputer. Figure 2.2 shows the general breakdown of data-processing services that may be found in school districts. The fiscal services reflect applications of the "business side of the house" while the student-related services represent the "educational side of the house" computer applications. The extent of these services varies considerably from district to district due to reasons of size, funding, philosophy, and availability of personnel with computer expertise. The services provided are not necessarily exclusive to the district level or school level. A combination of levels occurs at times. An example would be budgeting, which occurs both at the district and school building levels. Computerized payroll typically is a district-level function, while computer-assisted instruction is associated with classrooms within the local school. In the case of a student information system, a state educational agency, school districts, and local schools may be involved. Usually, when several levels of data processing occur, the district has a network that allows the computer capability at the respective levels to be interactive.

A matter of central concern to superintendents and principals is "Which side of the house shall have direct responsibility for administering the computer resource of the district?" Since business management personnel were initially responsible for the development of district computer services, they tended to control the priorities in computer-use applications. What this meant was that when all fiscal-related computer runs were completed, then the student-related runs could be done. There are many school districts today whose priorities of computer usage are controlled by the business management "side of the house." This organizational structure can create a dilemma when a student-related computer run is needed at the same time as a fiscal run. An example is the case of the business manager trying to meet a payroll deadline at the same time the building principals need to have their student report cards run so they'll be available for the scheduled parent-teacher conferences. As realized, both the business manager and the principals have valid, pressing needs for top priority in using the computer. Which run is to be processed first? Which should be processed first? If it's the business manager's decision, it is rather certain the payroll will be run first. The principals, of course, will not be pleased knowing their report cards will be run late. They know that the payroll must be out on time, but they also know their school public relations program stands to suffer by having the report cards come out after the parent-teacher conferences. Is there a solution to the dilemma? Prescheduling of the computer by job priority as a result of communication between the business manager and the principals might have done much to alleviate the problem.

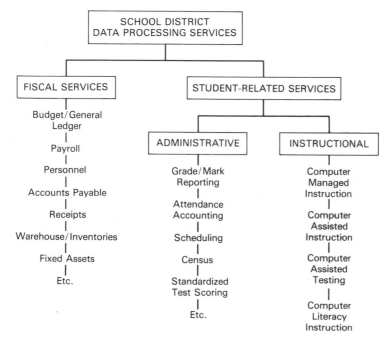

FIGURE 2.2   The Division of School District Data-processing Services

The problems related to computer usage have tended to increase as school administrators and teachers have sought to implement administrative and instructional support applications. When the educational-related uses of the computer seem to be shortchanged, building principals in frustration may purchase a computer for their own schools and assign a teacher to be responsible for managing the implemented system. The result, unfortunately, is the costly expenditure for equipment and personnel to support the proposed computer operation. This typifies how loose budgeting and lax management control can create problems in the initiation stage. Realizing the possible conflict that may occur between the business and educational sides of the house with respect to who should be responsible for administering the computer resource, Candoli et al. (1978) have stated that the school business manager should resist being responsible. Their recommendation was that the data-processing facility should be housed where the computer can serve all areas of the district's programs. They advocated two organizational patterns (Figures 2.3 and 2.4) to provide the flexibility necessary to serve all aspects of the district's fiscal and student-related services with a minimum of conflict among the various departments concerned with control and fund allocation. Both patterns make the data-processing director directly responsible to the district superintendent.

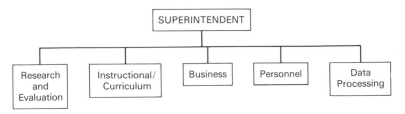

FIGURE 2.3 Organizational Structure of the Computer Resource: Option 1

Computer Anxiety.   Fear of the computer is a real issue faced by many individuals when confronted with the prospect of having to use one or being concerned about being displaced by it. In response to a survey question on major obstacles to increased computer use, 46 percent of the private school respondents cited computer "phobia" (Snider, 1986). School administrators must recognize the effects computer anxiety may have on employees in the form of uncreative and unresponsive work behavior. Workshops that stress anxiety-management and self-control techniques as well as practice in the use of computers may need to be sponsored. What should be communicated to anxious staff is that they do not need to understand electronic technology to use a computer. It should be reinforced that terrible things won't happen to them if they make a mistake.

The Expansion Stage

The expansion stage is characterized by the proliferation of broader and more advanced applications and the increased number of personnel becoming more specialized in the use and programming of the computer. Expenditures for hardware, software, and personnel reflect a steady and steep rise. Clear management guidelines for project priorities are lacking,

FIGURE 2.4 Organizational Structure of the Computer Resource: Option 2.   Adapted from Candoli, J. C., Hack, W. G., Ray, J. R., & Stollar, D. H. (1978). *School Business Administration: A Planning Approach,* Second Edition. Boston, MA: Allyn & Bacon, p. 125.

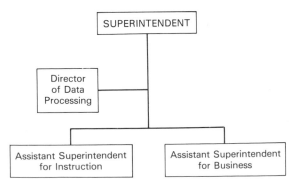

with informal relationships existing among computer personnel and between computer personnel and users. As Gibson and Nolan state:

> It is a period of contagious, unplanned growth, characterized by growing responsibilities for the EDP (electronic data processing) director, loose (usually decentralized) organization of the EDP facility and few explicit means of setting project priorities or crystallizing plans (p. 81).

The effect on top management seems to be one of being attracted to and carried along with the mystique of computer data processing. Once administrators become aware of the explosive effects of uncontrolled growth and a runaway budget, organization controls are initiated which may cause this stage to end in crisis. To alleviate the problems that can arise near the end of Stage 2, management techniques ordinarily used in Stage 3 would be introduced no later than at the onset of Stage 2.

The characteristics noted by Gibson and Nolan as occurring in Stage 2 pertain to the expanding use of a mainframe or minicomputer. The same findings, though, apply equally well to the burgeoning use of microcomputers in the schools. In the beginning, no systematic planning seems to have occurred in school districts with respect to the acquisition and use of these machines. Perceived as the wave of the future, parents, school board members, and manufacturers pressured schools to procure microcomputers. Gross inefficiencies sometimes occurred due to premature actions. Assessment of acquisition and training costs to use the microcomputers frequently was overlooked. Inequities occurred with "have" and "have-not" schools due to the financial ability or inability of districts to purchase machines. Management controls were lax since building principals initially were not heavily involved in making decisions on the introduction and use of microcomputers in their schools. Interested and enthusiastic teachers took up this slack by lobbying for microcomputers to be used in the classroom for computer-assisted and computer-managed instruction. Currently, principals have become more active in this process and are exploring ways the microcomputer may be used to handle administrative tasks (Becker, 1984a). This is heartening since a 1981 study (Corbett, et al., 1982) conducted in California among principals found that few were using microcomputers for administrative purposes for reasons of being too expensive, not having the human resources (teachers or support staff with sufficient expertise), and insufficient time to get started on such a detailed program.

Microcomputer use seems to be in the expansion stage, since the emphases continue to be on hardware acquisition and the writing or buying of software programs to meet instructional and instructional support applications. Instructional applications (Figure 2.5) include computer-literacy instruction, computer-assisted testing, computer-assisted instruction, and

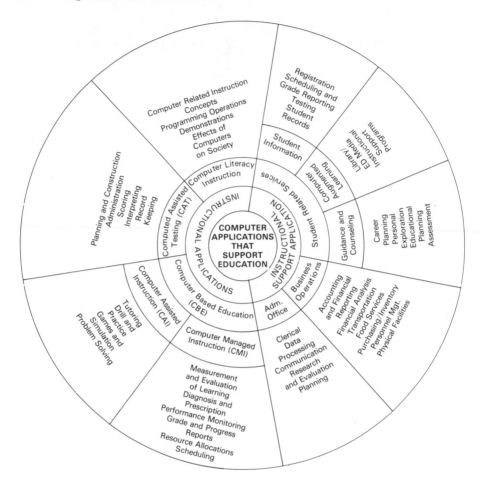

FIGURE 2.5 A Graphic Presentation of Computer Applications that Support Education. Adapted from Salisbury, A. R. (1971). Computers and education: Toward agreement on terminology. *Educational Technology*, 11, 35–40.

computer-managed instruction. Instructional support applications encompass computer programs designed to facilitate office management functions and generate student data for counseling, scheduling, record keeping, and the organizing of learning resources for individual and group instruction.

The Formalization Stage

Stages 1 and 2, as we have seen, were characterized by lax management. Growth in data-processing services was permitted to run its course without much direct attention from top management. As soon as chief administrators became aware of the runaway computer budget and initiated steps to find out what had been happening, the formalization stage began. Typical questions asked were, "Can we afford this data processing effort?" and "Are our needs being met?" In the process of getting answers to these questions, information would be compiled on costs, operating procedures, types of computer programs available, project priorities, personnel assignments, reporting procedures, relationships with others, and so on. The result of these efforts was the institution of control measures. Events most likely to occur were the reorganization of the data-processing department; justification of the computer services budget; the organization of a steering committee to set priorities and to confront and resolve political problems relating to the computer's impact on managers, users, organizational structure, and resource management; implementation of a management reporting system; and assignment to senior managers of responsibility for monitoring and evaluating data-processing services. Formal planning procedures now replaced informal planning. The focus was now on managing data resources and not on the computer.

Controlling the Computer Resource.   Management control of an organization's computer resources can be fraught with crises, as reflected in Stages 1 and 2 of computer data-processing growth. Although their primary function is to educate students, school districts function as a business. Like business firms, they are not immune to having runaway computer costs. To avoid potential crises in computer growth, they too can initiate quality-control procedures, preferably before the onset of the expansion stage.

In seeking to improve management control over the use of computers in a school or school district, school administrators first need to determine or reassess what their informational goals are. This can be done by conducting a needs analysis which would address these concerns: What informational needs are now met? What informational needs are unmet? How do we obtain the information? Who is responsible for what reports? How do we use the information currently available? What resources are available to prepare informational requests? To what agencies are we required to submit informational reports?

Once the goals have been determined or redefined, the school administrator should then seek answers to these questions: Which applications will receive priority? Who will assume responsibility for what operations? How can the computer's full potential be realized? Are adequate resources, budgetary and personnel, available to ensure implementation of a computer system? When and what types of evaluation shall prevail?

The computer resource should be planned and coordinated to satisfy the defined informational needs. Assurances must be obtained that the computer information system provides timely, accurate, and relevant data for prudent decision making by superintendents and building principals.

Evaluating the Computer Resource.   The framework for establishing management control and evaluation of the computer resource (Figure 2.6) consists of asking key questions regarding inputs to the data-processing department, the procedures used to program and process the data, the nature of the relationship between data-processing personnel and users of the data and the output reports that are produced. The main monitoring points are inputs, processing, and outputs. The control points, though, are delimited to input and processing only since outputs are controlled by altering inputs and processing (Dearden & Nolan, 1973). Evaluation devices are suggested to help answer the questions cited. To assist school administrators to monitor and evaluate more thoroughly the computer services of their school district, the following specific questions to which they need answers are presented:

- Are the computers being used to best advantage? What computer technology best meets our needs? Are the data-processing services subservient to us or dictating to us what should or shouldn't be?

FIGURE 2.6 Framework for District Management Control and Evaluation of Computer Resources. Adapted from Dearden, J., & Nolan, R. L. (1973). "How to control the computer resource." *Harvard Business Review*, 51 (6), 77.

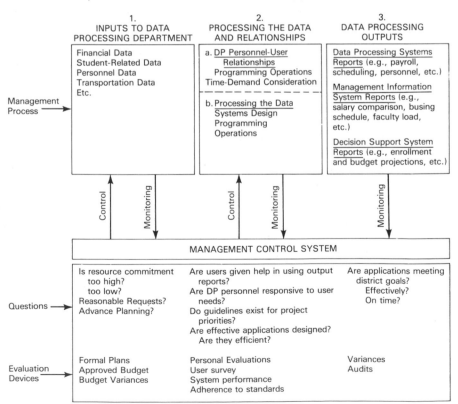

- What has been the long-term impact of data-processing services in the school district? Has having access to processed data resulted in better decision making? Have administrators been freed from routine clerical tasks by having their offices computerized? Has staff productivity increased?

- How many personnel are involved in operating, programming, and servicing the computers used for administrative and instructional purposes? Are they adequately trained? Do job descriptions exist for them? Does effective coordination exist between computer personnel and users in the schools? Do computer personnel routinely keep their users informed about problems, developments, and trends? Are users satisfied with the speed and quality of services?

- Do policy guidelines (Chapter 12) exist relative to the acquisition, use, security, and maintenance of the district computer hardware and software? Has the board of education been briefed and involved in formalizing policy? Does a district steering committee exist to assess procedure and to establish priorities?

- Are the instructional microcomputers strategically located to facilitate optimum use? What computer configuration is best suited to meet our informational and management needs: centralized? decentralized? shared or distributed? Does a networking exist between microcomputers and the mainframe or minicomputer to facilitate interactive communication? Are the microcomputers acquired for instruction purposes compatible with existing computers in the district to permit networking?

- Is the present data-processing system functional? Are the financial, personnel, student, and instructional information needs fully addressed? What is the status of the management information system as an aid in monitoring and directing the schools? What steps have been taken to implement a decision support system?

For school districts seeking to determine if there is a need for data-processing services and for school administrators wishing to assess the adequacy of their existing programs, a checklist (Figure 2.7) has been developed by the Jefferson City, Missouri, Department of Elementary and Secondary Education. Areas evaluated in the checklist pertaining to an existing data-processing program are: data-processing goals and objectives; staff; administration of the data-processing facility; privacy, security, and confidentiality; systems and programming; computer operations; and data input/output.

Budgeting the Computer Resource.   A fully functioning and operating computer resource requires a considerable investment of funds to sustain it. The outlay can run into thousands of dollars. Hardware and software expenditures are heaviest during the initiation and expansion stages. Concern has recently been expressed that the feverish attempts to acquire microcomputers for school use has caused a distortion of school budgets. Funds budgeted for other school programs have been taken to buy microcomputers and needed software. In San Francisco an association of school people opposed to microcomputers was organized because of their

FIGURE 2.7   Checklist to Determine the Need for and the Adequacy of a School District's Data-Processing Program. Department of Elementary and Secondary Education (1980). *Checklist to Determine the Need for and the Adequacy of a School District's Data Processing Program.* Jefferson City, MO: The Department.

Indicate the degree to which the district conforms to the standards, as follows: na = not applicable; 1 = unsatisfactory; 2 = fair; 3 = satisfactory; 4 = exceptional.

PART I—NEED FOR D.P. SERVICES FOR DISTRICTS CURRENTLY WITHOUT D.P. SERVICES

1. The district has sufficient and timely accounting information.   na   1   2   3   4
2. The district has sufficient and timely payroll/ personnel information.   na   1   2   3   4
3. Scheduling of students is accomplished using efficient and effective procedures.   na   1   2   3   4
4. Progress reporting of students is accomplished using efficient and effective procedures.   na   1   2   3   4
5. The district has sufficient and timely pupil information.   na   1   2   3   4
6. The district has adequate procedures available for meeting other informational needs.   na   1   2   3   4
7. The district has given consideration for the utilization of data-processing services.   na   1   2   3   4

PART II—DESCRIPTORS FOR DISTRICTS CURRENTLY UTILIZING D.P. SERVICES

Indicate the Source(s) of D.P. Services:

(Check One)   In-House Installation _____
                     Service Bureau/Cooperative Approach _____

Data-processing Goals and Objectives

8. Goals and objectives are formulated by the total administrative staff.   na   1   2   3   4
9. Objectives are prioritized by the administrative staff.   na   1   2   3   4

Staff

10. The district has a written organizational chart for data processing.   na   1   2   3   4

11. The district has a written job description for   na   1   2   3   4
    each D.P. employee based on written
    performance standards.
12. The district has a formal education program that
    meets the needs of the D.P. staff.   na   1   2   3   4

Administration of D.P. Facilities

13. The district has a written multiyear D.P. plan   na   1   2   3   4
    consistent with both short- and long-range
    objectives.
14. The D.P. plan is evaluated and revised annually   na   1   2   3   4
    or more frequently.

Privacy, Security, and Confidentiality

15. The district has written procedures governing the   na   1   2   3   4
    privacy and confidentiality of data.
16. The district has written procedures providing for   na   1   2   3   4
    the security of software and data files.
17. The district has written procedures providing for   na   1   2   3   4
    the security of the computer facility.

Systems and Programming

18. The district has developed written procedures for   na   1   2   3   4
    requesting and developing D.P. services.
19. The district has developed procedures for   na   1   2   3   4
    monitoring applications during the
    developmental process.
20. The district has written systems and   na   1   2   3   4
    programming standards that are followed in all
    cases.
21. User manuals and/or instructions are provided   na   1   2   3   4
    for each application.
22. The district has developed written procedures for   na   1   2   3   4
    monitoring the effectiveness of existing
    applications.

Computer Operations

23. The district maintains a daily and weekly   na   1   2   3   4
    machine processing schedule.
24. The district has job accounting procedures   na   1   2   3   4
    relative to computer usage.
25. The district maintains operator manuals   na   1   2   3   4
    adequate to schedule and process applications.
26. The district has a written procedure to monitor   na   1   2   3   4
    D.P. supplies.

27.	The district has procedures which control and secure the processing of all incoming data.	na	1	2	3	4
28.	The district maintains a daily and weekly data preparation schedule.	na	1	2	3	4
29.	The data entry section has complete instructions for preparing all input data.	na	1	2	3	4
30.	The district has procedures whereby new and revised forms are reviewed and developed jointly by the users and the D.P. department.	na	1	2	3	4
31.	The district has procedures for proper distribution of all output.	na	1	2	3	4
32.	The district has procedures for proper disposition of test runs or other exceptional output.	na	1	2	3	4
33.	The district has procedures for the verification and accuracy of all output.	na	1	2	3	4

fear of this budget distortion (Rogers, 1984). Frequently, school administrators are unaware of the hidden costs of computerization. Hoover and Gould (1982) have identified a number of such costs principals should be aware of as they acquire and implement microcomputers in their schools. Summarized, they are:

- *TRAINING.* Costs should be assessed in terms of the dollar value equated to the time invested to train principals, faculty, and staff to use the computer.
- *CONSULTANTS.* Funds may be expended if it is necessary to hire a consultant to assist with the needs assessment and determination of what is the appropriate hardware and software to be purchased. If the consultant is retained to give further assistance with technical concerns and writing software, additional funds will be needed.
- *MAINTENANCE.* Once the warranty expires on hardware, is a service contract signed? Also, is a backup microcomputer needed in the event the main microcomputer fails and is in repair for over a week?
- *INSURANCE.* Equipment should be insured against vandalism and theft; insurance is also needed to cover while transporting the microcomputer if it is taken home by the principal to work with during evenings and weekends.
- *WIRING.* Will special outlets be needed for the computer equipment?
- *SPECIAL FURNITURE.* Should a special desk be purchased to house all hardware and documentation? Should a special cart be bought to transport the equipment?

Another cost that sometimes is overlooked when microcomputers are used in schools is the support system required to field technical questions posed by faculty and staff and to do special programming requests. Generally, a teacher with interest and computer technology skills is invited by the principal to handle these functions. Because the time demand can be heavy, he/she may be given release time from teaching. A problem principals have encountered in using a competent teacher to run the school's system is the loss of that person to business or industry because an attractive salary offer has been made to them.

To monitor and control the computer resource budget, on either the district or school level, school administrators should have answers to the following questions:

- What is the total cost of administering, operating, and maintaining the computer resource?
- What proportion of the total budget is allocated to the computer resource? Is it reasonable? Justifiable?
- How much money is tied up in hardware and software? Does an inventory exist of hardware and software that is periodically updated? How efficiently is the inventory being used?
- What costs are incurred to underwrite the fiscal and student-related computer applications? Are they disproportionate? What are the instructional computer costs and how do they compare to the administratively related computer costs?

A scheme for budgeting and prioritizing the computer resource on the district level is shown in Figure 2.8. Superintendents and their administrative staffs would seek budget requests from the data-processing director, district supervisors, and building principals who need special runs or reports. Hardware/software acquisition requests for administrative and instructional purposes would also be submitted, as well as funds to support the computer resource. For districts that have, or intend to implement, a microcomputer administrative system, Kiser (1984) suggests that 35% of the annual budget be allocated for computer support. This would be partitioned as follows: 10% for evolving the starter system to acquire new peripherals, new programs, and program updates; 10% for maintenance, assuming no service contracts; and 15% for supplies, for example, printer ribbons, diskettes, and computer publications.

If school administrators wish to control fully the computer resource, the computer instructional program should not be overlooked in the budgetary process. Though school districts have been making a concerted drive to acquire microcomputers and instructional software for classroom use, it has become increasingly difficult to obtain the needed funds. Administrators, in seeking to supplement district funds, have resorted to obtaining money from local, state, and federal sources; from PTA fund-raising drives; and from corporations. One of the nation's twelve largest school districts, with an enrollment of 126,000 students, spent 90% of its $5.6 million 1983–84 budget on hardware and 10% on software. A total of $2.2 million came from the state and the remaining $3.4 million from local sources and taxes for capital projects, including school microcomputers (EL Survey, 1984). Interestingly, not all school districts in the country seem to

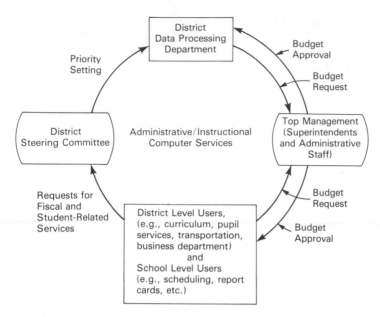

FIGURE 2.8   An Organizational Scheme for Budgeting and Prioritizing the Computer Resource.   Reprinted by permission of the *Harvard Business Review*. An exhibit from "How to Control the Computer Resource" by John Dearden & Richard L. Nolan (November/December 1973). Copyright © 1973 by the President and Fellows of Harvard College; all rights reserved.

have an instructional computer budget, based on the responses of school board members to a survey on the use of instructional computers in their districts. In response to the question, "Does your system have a computer budget?" 49.4% said, "Yes." Virtually all of the respondents (97%) said "Yes" to the question, "Would you vote for future budgets that include computer programs?" (Sixth Annual Survey of School Board Members, 1984). Once all of the administrative/instructional requests have been received, the superintendent and his/her administrative staff need to determine if these requests are compatible with the informational goals of the district. Further, an assessment needs to be made as to what proportion of the total budget can be allocated to the computer resource. In the budgetary process, consideration should also be given as to what outside source of funds can be obtained to supplement local moneys. The net result of all these efforts would be a justified budget.

A District Steering Committee.   Consideration should be given the organizing of a district steering committee, composed of district and school-level people, which would have responsibility for setting priorities in requests for fiscal and student-related services. Their task would not be to determine the day-to-day operations of the computer resource but to make priority recommendations. By having priorities so determined, the dilemma cited earlier about the conflict of running the payroll and school report cards on the same day can be avoided. One way to do this would be to allocate to the business and educational side of the house a given percent of computer usage during prime shift time. Only priority projects that need a quick turnaround would be run during these hours. Doing this would require the business manager and the district's designated instructional administrator to rank their jobs as to which have high priority by time of year. Scheduling done in this manner should optimize use of the computer during prime shift time. Care, however, should be exercised to determine if the overall capacity of the computer can actually meet the expected level of service.

The Maturity Stage

Gibson and Nolan (1974) state that "when the dust has settled over the changes of Stage 3, the computer resource will have reached maturity in the organization, and it will have the potential to return continuing economic benefits" (p. 86). As noted in the initiation stage, when the first computer was introduced into an organization, the move was justified in terms of cost savings. This justification will still be accented in Stage 4, with computer applications being directly devoted to the critical concerns of the organization. Stage 4 also reflects an established management information system and the elements of a decision support system. The computer's role has moved from that of merely providing operational data to that of supporting the manager responsible for making and implementing decisions (Alter, 1976).

It is only in large school districts that have had a history of computer services that the maturity stage will have been reached. Generally, district data-processing departments have lagged behind businesses in using computer resources for management purposes. Though most districts have utilized a computer system to handle business operations, computer support for instructional and school-level administrative tasks has been slow in developing. One reason is that systems analysts and computer systems programmers have focused their efforts on business applications. With the initial introduction of computers in the schools, no serious attempt was made to address student-related needs until some time later. Secondly, since fiscal management personnel were first responsible for the development of computer services, they tended to control the priorities in the use and applications of the computer services rendered. Thirdly, in the beginning school-level administrators and teachers were slow to implement computer technology in the learning environment. With the advent of microcomputers this posture is changing. Finally, the complexity of the instructional setting has made these computer applications difficult to program in contrast to fiscal applications, which have been relatively easy to computerize. This limitation underscores why educational software still has shortcomings for computer-managed instruction and computer-assisted instruction.

The Data-processing Director.   Also inherent in a computer system that has reached maturity is the presence of a highly qualified, competent data-processing director. It has been found that the highest use of computer services with resultant benefits in a number of school districts surveyed appeared to be directly related to the time and money invested in the director's role. District size, though, has a bearing on the hiring of a director, with smaller districts less likely to invest in the position (Hansen, Klassen & Lindsay, 1978). Some differences exist as to what characteristics are most desirable in the director's background. Herzlinger (1977) questions the use of professionals such as educators turned data managers, saying they may be long on professional training and experience but short on technical skills and experience. Hansen et al. (1978), though, feel the most important qualities are inquisitiveness, interest, ability to learn quickly, willingness to work hard, and a desire to meet the needs of users. It is hoped that the director would possess human relationship skills, technical skills, and conceptual skills as he/she works with users to further the data-processing goals of the district.

The data-processing director would be responsible for all administrative and instructional applications and would report directly to top management. Assisting him/her might be a person assigned to coordinate the district's instructional computer program, which is dependent upon the microcomputers housed in the schools. Grossnickle and Laird (1982) have provided a list of responsibilities an appointed coordinator might perform to facilitate computer-assisted instruction and computer-managed instruction. Among other things, the coordinator would be expected to (1) identify the needs of the instructional computer program, making appropriate recommendations; (2) disseminate information to staff with respect to the applications of instructional computers; (3) work with school department chairpersons on plans to integrate microcomputers into the curriculum; (4) provide needed in-service training; (5) be a resource person; and (6) organize and chair a committee of building computer coordinators. Telem (1985) makes a strong case for the building coordinator, calling this person the school computer administrator or SCA. The functions outlined for the SCA are numerous and varied, with the most important dealing with planning, development, implementation, and operation.

The Computer Coordinator.   Computer coordinators are functioning at both the school and district levels according to the first annual survey conducted by *Electronic Learning* (Barbour, 1986). It appears that the district coordinator has responsibility for instructional microcomputers only and not for a mainframe or minicomputer that might be used for administrative purposes. If this is so, the district organization might include both a data-processing director and a microcomputer coordinator. Responses from the district computer coordinators give insight into their characteristics and responsibilities. The typical respondent was forty-three years old, male, with eighteen years teaching experience and four years of computer experience, and considered the role to be part-time (20%) or an additional responsibility (57%). They had an average budget of over $8000 a year and supervised 81–100 microcomputers. Their primary responsibilities were evaluating and purchasing software and hardware (71%); training teachers about computers (71%); supervising computer budgets (65%); writing grant proposals (58%); and maintaining computer hardware (58%).

The job of the microcomputer coordinator, according to Moursund (1985), is "unreasonable." He contends that they have "innumerable responsibilities" "with far too little time to do them." Crucial to defining what the coordinator should do is the drafting of a written job description. Having such, permits a check to be made between what the defined responsibilities are and what the coordinator is actually doing. Moursund also has suggestions on the amount of time coordinators should have to perform their duties at the elementary, secondary, and district levels. At the elementary level, the position ought not to be a permanent one since, after a few years, faculty will become computer literate. If future help is needed the district coordinator would serve as the resource. Secondary coordinators, Moursund feels, won't work themselves out of a job. In fact, for schools having thirty or more microcomputers, the position could become full time. At the district level, for districts of average or larger size, he advocates a full time coordinator. The position, he argues, should not be held by a person who also performs other duties assigned by the district. The danger that too readily exists in secondary and district level posititons, he reminds us, is that the coordinator gets sidetracked into doing routine chores or unrelated tasks.

The Role of Top Management.   Though a school district may have a skilled data-processing director, this person will be hampered in establishing and maintaining an effective and efficient computer information system *if top management is not behind the endeavor*. The same holds true for a district coordinator for instructional computing. Many factors, Herzlinger (1977) states may inhibit success of the system, but one factor accounts for most of the failures: "It lies directly within control of the organization: the characteristics and attitudes of top management" (p. 84). Superintendents, their administrative staff, and building principals, therefore, set the tone on how computer services for administrative and instructional purposes will be received and used in the schools. Their attitudes, interest, support, and enthusiasm are vital. As Hansen, Klassen, and Lindsay state, "Priorities that are developed at high levels (top management) determine what a district is willing to invest in time and money, and the level of use and the subsequent value of the services are directly proportional to this willingness to make the necessary commitment" (p. 8).

SUMMARY

Computer growth in any organization goes through four distinct stages: initiation, expansion, formalization, and maturity. By understanding these stages, administrators are in a better position both to manage and evaluate the effectiveness of the computer resource. Characteristic of the initiation stage is a loose budget, lax management, and minimal control over the direction the computer resource takes. Special concerns relate to organizing the resource and alleviating the fears of employees who feel threatened by the new technology.

Acceptance of the resource prompts administrators and enthusiastic employees to lobby for the acquisition of additional hardware and software so that more individuals will be able to use the resource. Schools having one or two microcomputers, for example, enter the expansion stage by continuing to buy new machines and the array of instructional and administrative software touted for their use. This growth will be uncontrolled if management guidelines are not established which set priorities and invest responsibility in someone to coordinate the enterprise. When this occurs, the formalization stage begins. The maturity stage is characterized by the organization having established policies on computer acquisition and use, with responsible leadership provided by a well-trained director or coordinator. Critical to the overall success of the computer resource, however, is the degree of positive support it receives from the organization's top administrators. In the schools this means the building principals and the superintendent.

3

MANAGING
THE ADMINISTRATIVE
OFFICE

School and school district administrative offices serve as nerve centers, providing a variety of services and performing vital functions for their publics. It is at the school level, where interactions occur with students, parents, and the community, that these services become critical. What exists in these relationships is an informational environment as shown in Figure 3.1. Within the internal environment information exchanges occur among students, teachers, clerical and custodial workers, administrators, and pupil personnel specialists. Within the external environment such groups as the school board, teacher-training educators, accrediting agencies, parents, and the central office administration/supervisory staff make requests and expect services from the school.

The managerial and secretarial services performed by school principals and their office staffs to accommodate internal and external informational needs have been presented by Anderson and Van Dyke (1972) as follows:

1. *Communicating*—exchanging information by such means as intercom systems, bulletins, telephone, correspondence, and face-to-face conferences.
2. *Processing materials*—typing, duplicating, etc.
3. *Handling correspondence and mail*—preparing and filing letters for professional staff and processing staff mail.

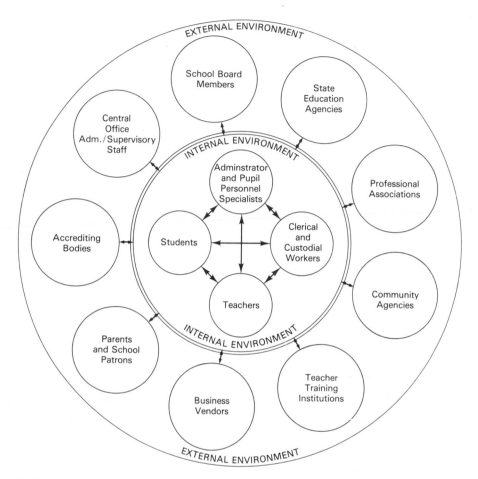

FIGURE 3.1   The Informational Environment of a Local School.   Adapted from Gorton, R. A. (1980). *School Administration and Supervision: Important Issues, Concepts, and Case Studies, 2nd ed.* Dubuque, Iowa: William C. Brown Co., Publishers, p. 351.

4. *Procuring supplies and equipment*—for both the professional and nonprofessional staffs.

5. *Administering attendance*—checking, recording, and clearing student attendance.

6. *Directing the daily program*—control and necessary adjustments in the daily schedule and movement of students.

7. *Administering records*—maintaining, storing, summarizing, and supplying information.

8. *Preparing reports*—the principal's annual report, reports to the state, reports to accrediting agencies, financial summaries, and the like.

9. *Serving as control center for the operation of the physical plant*—making certain that heat, ventilation, lights, cleaning, and other services are functioning.

10. *Implementing relations with the public*—conducting business with lay visitors and providing information.
11. *Troubleshooting*—meeting emergency situations that call for on-the-spot action (p. 477).

Wiles and Bondi (1983), in their interpretation of the functions performed by the school office, speak of centers. Specifically, the office functions as a:

- *Command Center* where directions originate or are passed through to the faculty and staff.
- *Center for Messages* where communication within the school is coordinated and messages from outside are screened and routed.
- *Record Center* where both personnel and property records are stored and retrieved.
- *Service Center* that provides assistance to teachers in class preparation and to students in various health and guidance services.
- *Financial Center* where money is handled and fiscal records maintained (p. 308).

THE PAPER EXPLOSION

To facilitate these functions, the school office serves as an information-processing center staffed with individuals doing paperwork of one kind or another and keeping files and records. The ideal role of the office, according to Jarrett (1982), is to guarantee that the right information is available in the right form, at the right time, in the right place, to assist the right people to make the right decision.

To accomplish the ideal use of information, it must be astutely managed. The complaint frequently voiced today is that government, business, and education offices are inundated by paperwork. Indeed, for many offices paperwork has become a major product. Some have developed acute cases of "record leukemia" resulting from the multitudinous creation and filing of correspondence, forms, reports, memos, and so on. The American Management Association has estimated that American businesses create records at the rate of 100 million cubic feet per year. The federal government alone creates over 4 million cubic feet annually. This amount, if placed in standard four-drawer filing cabinets, would cover eighty football fields (Harding, 1982). A 1975 survey report estimated the annual cost to produce such information at over $35 billion per year (Zaiden, 1975). The rate of generating office paper, per information worker, still continues. Strassmann (1985) reports it has been growing steadily since 1946 at a rate about double that of the growth in our GNP. This surge in information production has largely resulted from the technology revolution in office machinery and methods.

Time and personnel costs to produce and disseminate information in educational institutions is also high. For school administrators a question of concern is how to tame the paper tiger so as not to be a "paper shuffler." Gorton (1980) has illustrated this dilemma in the following case study:

> Ed Brooks, principal at LaFollette School, had returned from a Friday afternoon meeting at the district office and was working late trying to catch up on his office correspondence and reports. He hated paper work, and it seemed that in the last few years there was more and more of it.
>
> As the principal went through the stack of materials on his desk, he noticed several requests from the district office for budget and attendance reports, a request from a university professor for approval for a doctoral student to do research on student discipline at LaFollette School, and a questionnaire from the federal government dealing with the civil rights of students and teachers, particularly minorities and females. The principal had mixed feelings about all of these requests, particularly the questionnaire from the government. He wasn't against minorities or women, although he felt that some of them were certainly pushy, but as he looked again at the questionnaire, which was long and complicated, he started to feel angry.
>
> He had been receiving a lot of questionnaires lately, and requests from different people for reports on various aspects of his school. He thought to himself, "Why don't people leave me alone and let me be the educational leader that I want to be? All I am getting to be is a report writer and a paper shuffler!" (pp. 195–196)

Justification for Ed Brook's complaint is attested to by studies conducted on the school principalship. Pharis and Zakariya (1979), in their study of the elementary principal's role, found that respondents felt they spent too much time doing the clerical work of filing routine reports and record keeping. A comprehensive detailed record of how one principal of a large high school spent his day revealed he handled forty pieces of paper and spent ninety-eight minutes of his day with written communications. Twenty-eight minutes were used giving dictation or instructions to his secretary (Weldy, 1979). Gorton and McIntyre (1978) compared high school principals' rankings of how they planned to spend their time over a two-week period to the actual time rankings. They found principals planned to spend most of their time, first, in program development (curriculum/instruction), followed by personnel (evaluation, advising, recruiting) and management (routines, calendar, finance, plant). The actual time spent over the two-week period in rank order was, first, personnel, followed by school management and then program development.

School superintendents, too, are affected by excessive paper demands. Pitner (1979) observed three different superintendents over a one-week period and accounted for 438 combined activities. These activities were subsequently categorized to show the percentage of total hours superintendents devoted to such activities as scheduled meetings (59%), desk work

(22%), unscheduled meetings (10%), phone calls (6%), and school visits (3%). Pitner noted that routine activities took 91% of the superintendent's time and that each superintendent processed an average of twenty-two pieces of mail, took ten phone calls, visited one school, and attended nine meetings every day.

THE MANAGING OF ADMINISTRATIVE PAPERWORK

The use of the computer, particularly the microcomputer, has been touted as the answer for school administrators on how they might cope with the paper demands placed upon them and their school offices. Pogrow, an authority on using computers in school administration, contends that computerization, if done properly, can reduce paperwork by at least 50 percent (Want to Cut Paperwork, 1986). Though the computer has this potential, it can also be part of the problem and not a solution. Its capability to process information can prove a temptation to users to collect data and generate reports that are not critical to the ongoing operations of the schools. Katzan (1982), in recognizing this concern, formulated the following law: "The increased productivity associated with office automation will increase the proliferation of information—that is, more paper in a system already saturated with loaded file cabinets" (p. 6).

Criteria for Determining the Computerization of Administrative Paperwork

To help principals assess whether a microcomputer can be an asset in helping manage administrative paperwork, the following criteria (adapted from Patterson & Patterson, 1983) may be of assistance.

(1) *Can the tasks be handled better manually?* A microcomputer would be profitable only if it saves money, saves time, assists in decision making, yields more accurate data, and frees human energy for more productive activity. To answer this question, a time management study should be conducted. Experience has shown that all administrative tasks need not be computerized. The scope of the task may be such that it takes less time to locate the information manually than to go through the steps necessary to process and print out the information electronically. The size of the school may also be a factor, for the informational demands of small schools, particularly at the elementary level, may not be as acute as on the high school level. Simplicity of data needs may, as a consequence, be more efficiently handled manually.

(2) *Is the service already available centrally?* If the school district office has a mainframe or minicomputer, fiscal and student-related information may already be available. If so, the risk of duplication exists if each

local school were to buy computer hardware/software to generate similar outputs. If special information runs are needed, principals should communicate these desires to have them incorporated in the overall data-processing/informational goals of the district, as indicated in Chapter 2. Assurances, though, should be obtained that the application is cost effective.

Word processing, using a microcomputer to improve clerical efficiency, is one service that typically is not available centrally, nor is it generally cost effective on a central system using a minicomputer or mainframe. It is in this arena that school administrators and office secretaries may better be able to manage heavy paper demands. It has been claimed that a microcomputer, so used, can increase office secretarial staff's productivity by 20–35% and that a principal's effectiveness can not only be extended by taking over "paper-information retrieval" activities, but will actually give him/her one extra day per week (Corbett, et al., 1982).

(3) *Will the computer improve efficiency without expanding activity?* As noted previously, computer capability may mean producing more reports than are needed. Office activity, it has been found in the business sector, has frequently increased at the expense of efficiency. It remains to be determined if office efficiency can be increased at a school using a microcomputer-assisted word processor. A pilot study would better enable this question to be answered. The contention has been made (Joiner, et al., 1982) that experienced users of large computers have not been supportive in testing out the creative applications of the microcomputer. Consequently, the probability exists that if principals sought their advice, they would not be encouraged to experiment. School administrators, though, after careful preplanning, may have ample justification to pilot the creative use of a microcomputer to assess whether it improves efficiency without expanding activity.

(4) *Which administrative applications receive the highest priority?* If administrative microcomputer resources in a school are limited, competition may be keen as to who has priority to use them. Should it be for the secretary to do word processing? What about the librarian who wishes to use it to manage the library? And how about the principal who wishes to use it for scheduling and grade reporting?

To determine which administrative applications receive highest priority it becomes necessary for the school officials first to identify and list all applications that can be done by computer. Second, those applications that already are being processed adequately by other means should be identified and eliminated. Third, the remaining applications would be prioritized using the following criteria: (1) Will computerization result in cost and time savings? (2) How important is the application to running an efficient school? and (3) Do financial and personnel support services exist to support the applications? (Coogan, 1983). As this analysis is made, school officials should consider the use of existing minicomputer or mainframe resources. It may be that school microcomputers will expedite priority applications by being used as a terminal input to the mini or mainframe through a telecommunications link.

(5) *Can you justify computer technology in the office when it could be used in the classroom?* With limited budgets it may be difficult to justify the acquisition of microcomputers for both instructional and administrative purposes, especially if a central data-processing facility exists. The school budget, though, is not earmarked entirely for instructional purposes. If it can be demonstrated that computerization will free the principal and secretary to spend more time on instructional concerns, the expenditure of funds for this purpose becomes more palatable.

Another criterion to consider with respect to using computers to manage paperwork is:

(6) *Will the computers be fully utilized?* Without proper planning, training, and a functioning support system, microcomputers acquired for management purposes may see limited use. A key factor in determining computer use is the human element. Some individuals are intrigued by a computer and its capabilities, while others feel frightened and threatened. A school business administrator, in commenting on office efficiency, observed that the human factor would determine if the school business office introducing new office automation technology would succeed or fail. School administrators seeking to introduce an electronic office are working with staff personnel who have become competent and efficient using office machines and equipment that they know and understand. Now they are confronted with an unknown element that creates uncertainty and anxiety.

School administrators themselves are not exempt from these same feelings of inadequacy. Unless these attitudes and perceptions are overcome, the goal of an automated office becomes less likely. Mitchell (1982) suggests some guidelines that administrators should consider as they seek to use high technology in school offices. They are:

- Proceed gradually; phase in new automated systems and services gradually rather than introducing them all in one indigestible lump.
- Provide comprehensive and continual training in the use of the new systems both during and after the introductory phase.
- Introduce office automation technology only in those areas where benefits are immediately needed and will be immediately evident.
- Integrate the new system into the existing school structure.
- Combine the new technology as part of the trappings of executive power. Managers will want an executive work station more if it is a benefit regarded as a symbol of success.
- Allow people to adjust to the new system at their own pace without being forced. But let them realize that their refusal places them at a disadvantage. (p. 35).

Simplifying Paperwork

Office paperwork involves staff using communication equipment, employing specified procedures to fill out forms and produce reports that typically are filed in cabinets that occupy space. The purposes of paperwork are to inform, to facilitate decision making, and to meet informational needs of the school and district offices and governmental agencies. Too much paperwork can interfere in the performance of one's job, as observed in the case of Principal Ed Brooks. Though computerization is offered as one alternative to managing and limiting the output of paperwork, school administrators and their office staffs should continually seek to simplify paperwork. The fundamental objectives of paperwork simplification are to: (1) simplify; (2) eliminate part or whole of what isn't needed, or combine if elimination is impossible; and (3) improve one's time and stimulate staff to better work. In striving to simplify paperwork, school officials need to ask these questions (Zaiden, 1975) about reports and materials currently being produced: Does the information serve a valid or logical purpose? Are given needs being met? Is the information currently useful? Is it still required? How is the information used? Does it help to meet the goals of the district and individual schools? Is the value of the information worth the cost to produce it?

Once information is produced, it has to be stored. This is particularly true of student records that by law are to be retained. The storage of these and other records can become a problem. Harding (1982), in addressing this problem, has advocated an integrated archival/records management approach. He contends it can save administrators money by reducing the amount of paperwork produced and the quantity of records kept. This would be done by using cheaper storage space for little-used records and increasing the efficiency of administering office files. Administrators who are serious about taming the paper tiger will want to give serious heed to the eight points Harding advocates as the basis of a successful program.

1. Take a complete physical inventory of the records in all offices and storage spaces to determine what records series there are, where they are, how old they are, who created them, what they deal with, what condition they are in, how they are housed, in what quantity they exist, and how much space is being used.

2. Use this record inventory to create a retention and disposition schedule that tells how long all records and their copies should be kept, what protective conditions should be provided, whether or not the record is of archival value, and if it should or should not be microfilmed.

3. Adopt a "birth control" system that will halt the creation of unnecessary paperwork and help prevent a recurrence of the records storage problem.

4. Institute a forms management program that will decrease the cost and increase the efficiency of the paperwork produced.

5. Use the office machines and related equipment that will reduce the amount of paperwork needed, will store it in less space, and/or make it more readily available. Examples: microforms and data-processing equipment.

6. Adopt the concept of a central records storage center to house and serve those records of noncurrent nature that require retention for several years for legal or other reasons.

7. Select and preserve, under the proper temperature, humidity, dust, and fire protection conditions, those records of all physical types which are of permanent legal, fiscal, and research value.

8. Maintain an archives/records management staff to give advice and aid to the operating offices and help keep the program active and able to adjust to the necessary changes. (pp. 108–109).

The suggestions offered by Harding primarily pertain to the storage of hard copy information. The computerization of paperwork presents a different procedure for filing, archiving, and retrieving information. Various computer storage media can be used such as tapes, magnetic disks, and floppy disks. This means physical storage space requirements can be dramatically reduced. The procedure for accessing the information, however, is different from the manual system of looking up documents by time period and physical location. Computerized information, in contrast, is organized and filed in an abstract structure that is defined by the kind of hardware and software employed. Office personnel, as a result, will need a new set of skills to retrieve electronic stored records (Hebenstreit, 1983).

The sophistication needed to handle a records retrieval system that is effectively automated may be beyond the resources and expertise of school level personnel. They may exist, however, at the district level. If so, the data-processing department should be involved in the planning and implementation of such an undertaking.

THE AUTOMATED OFFICE

Office automation, the electronic office, and the office of the future have become the buzzwords of the 1980s. These terms abound in books and periodicals and are frequently the topic of conferences and seminars sponsored by business and government groups. Office automation has as its purpose the facilitation of the basic functions of an office as an information-processing center. These functions, to which office personnel devote a good percentage of their time, are:

- *Information Gathering*. This entails collecting information from individuals in person, by telephone, from letters or written instructions, or from a dictaphone or recorder.

- *Information Processing.* This function is the heart of most office activities. It may involve typing letters or reports or accounting for funds. Information must be processed to make it useful in serving its purposes.
- *Information Storage.* Information may be stored in file cabinets and desk drawers, on computer tapes or disks, or in one's own memory. The suggestions made above by Harding respecting the storage of records have application here.
- *Information Retrieval.* Information should be readily retrievable to answer questions raised. Various filing systems have been developed to enable records to be readily accessed. Information needed may also be retrieved from resource books, from people's memory banks, and from electronic communication networks.

What technology comprises the automated office? As depicted in Figure 3.2, the automated office may consist of various applications such as word processing, electronic mail, electronic networking, electronic calendars, and electronic filing. It is not meant that every school office adopt and implement all of these technologies. Barcomb (1981) implies they must be tailored and coordinated. If not, office automation can degrade information systems, cause turmoil, and add to expenses.

Bahniuk (1983) recommends that school administrators conduct a feasibility study to justify investing in equipment to automate their offices. Objectives, she feels, that automated technology should fulfill are to: (1)

FIGURE 3.2 Types of Office Technology Applications. This includes both national (regional) and local networks. The electronic network should include the data-base link to the district-level computer (mini or mainframe) where they exist.

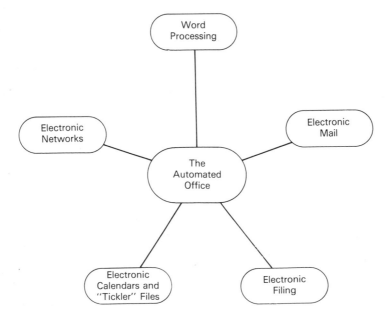

increase efficiency and effectiveness of decision making, (2) increase productivity or performance of staff, (3) promote effective use of human resources, and (4) improve quality and maintenance of consistency.

As internal staff consultants or equipment vendors, separately or in combination, assist in analyzing the school office system, they should provide for top management recommendations that would indicate whether additional equipment can be justified, what would be the best organizational structure, what would be the best layout for a given area, and the suggested performance level for given positions within the office.

Critical questions (Bahniuk, 1983) administrators should answer as they consider office automation are: (1) What kinds of information do we gather and process? (2) What are our patterns of information flow? (3) Can we do the work better, faster, and at less cost with existing resources? and (4) How can we improve performance?

Office automation includes but is more than data processing. The processing of data to give it meaning has been a part of the office scene since the 1950s. Office automation can be perceived as a new way of using old practices, principles, and equipment to help people manage information. The selection of office automation tools, consequently, should fit the goals of an organization. Their use should benefit the entire organization in terms of efficiency. A description of each of the tools that may have implications for use in district and school offices follows.

Word Processing

Word processing, because it has been so widely adopted, has been perceived as the cornerstone or the driving force of the automated office. Wider text and information processing can evolve from a microcomputer used as a word processor. For example, it can be linked to an electronic network permitting documents to be shared within and between school offices or, by using specialized software, it can carry out complex data-processing and informational-retrieval tasks. By acquiring a spelling checker, documents can be checked for typing and spelling errors. With the use of a mail merge program, personalized letters can be prepared for mass mailings such as to the student body concerning school opening or to parents of graduating seniors informing them about commencement activities. Integrated software combining word processing and a data-base program permits the direct transfer of data from the data base to the word-processing program.

Deciding Whether to Use a Word Processor.   In seeking to determine whether a word processor should be introduced into the school office, school administrators and their secretarial/clerical staff should ask such questions (adapted from Chirlian, 1982) as:

- Do we have to deal with large blocks of text such as the school newsletter, minutes of meetings, annual reports, etc.?
- Will that text require revision, corrections, additions, deletions? If so, what percentage will be changed? A rule of thumb used by professional typists is that if the changes total more than 20 percent of the file, then it is less time-consuming to retype the file than to edit it and incorporate the changes.
- Do we use standard information forms that change only in minor ways, such as the date, names, and addresses?
- Do we need to send out form letters to students and parents?
- Can we use an efficient method for storage of text such as manuscripts, proposals, forms, etc.? By using computer disks, these documents can be stored in a very small space. To illustrate, the contents of several five-drawer file cabinets can be stored on disks that take up only several inches on a desktop.

If the answer to any of these questions is yes, serious consideration should be given to acquiring a word processor. If a microcomputer is already owned, then a word-processing software package can be purchased. The ability of a word processor to simplify the production of documents by eliminating repetitive typing and facilitating extensive text editing makes it amenable to performing any of the tasks outlined above.

Some documents can be produced more efficiently by typewriter than by word processor, for example, one-time interoffice letters, memos, or other documents that require no more than one revision and are less than one page long; envelopes or labels for seldom-used addresses; statistical tables or charts requiring no revision; and the responding to infrequently used or single copies of preprinted forms. Only documents that require more than one revision, irrespective of their length, should be considered for word processing (Barcomb, 1981).

Types of Word-processing Systems. Word processing may be performed by one of two types of systems: stand-alone (Figure 3.3) or single-terminal systems and shared-logic or multiterminal systems (Figure 3.4). Stand-alone word processors are typically general purpose microcomputers consisting of a keyboard, display screen, central processing unit, and one or two disk drives. As a peripheral, a printer is attached to provide hard copy of documents produced. Individual schools, especially those in small districts or in remote areas, are more apt to adopt the stand-alone system.

Shared-logic word processors have multiple terminals attached to a central computer. Each terminal shares the word-processing power, storage, and peripherals of the central computer. This type of system provides more processing power and storage capability than stand-alone processors. Other advantages are the users are able to share documents without physically moving disks from one terminal to another, and the cost per work station is generally more cost effective. One school district that has employed the shared-logic system is the Montgomery County Public School District.

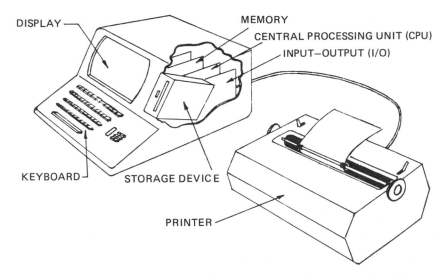

FIGURE 3.3   A Stand-Alone Word-processing System.   From Stultz, R. A. (1982). *The Word Processing Handbook.* Englewood Cliffs, NJ: Prentice-Hall, Inc., p. 45.

Following a competitive bid procedure, they installed the IBM 8100 shared-logic word-processing system. The five IBM 8100s support 90 terminals and 20 printers in the central and remote offices of the district, which operates 155 schools enrolling 91,000 students over a 500-square-mile geographic area (Raucher, 1984).

FIGURE 3.4   A Shared-Logic Word-processing system.   From Stultz, R. A. (1982). *The Word Processing Handbook*. Englewood Cliffs, NJ: Prentice-Hall, Inc., p. 45.

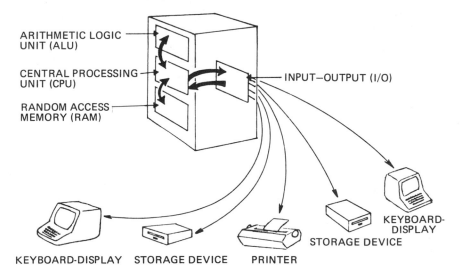

Of special concern to users of word processors is the quality of the documents printed. Software word-processing programs, combined with microprocessor controlled printing, enables a user to print textual and graphic material quickly and easily. The types of printers marketed for use with word processors are dot matrix printers, daisy wheel printers, ink jet printers, and laser printers. Dot matrix printers are designed to produce print material that is referred to as correspondence quality, meaning that it is generally acceptable but not of letter quality. The process involves reproducing on paper, by impact via a carbon ribbon, an output consisting of various patterns of dots configured to form the shape of the alphabet, numeric, punctuation, and other characters required. The advantage of dot matrix printers is their speed, from 80 to 300 characters per second (cps), and their low cost. Disadvantages are the quality of print, which is not acceptable for business correspondence, and that the printed material does not reproduce well on photographic copiers.

Daisy wheel printers produce quality output. The daisy wheel, which does the printing, resembles a daisy. Embossed on its "petals" are individual characters which are positioned electromechanically. When printing, the characters are struck from behind with a hammer, causing them to impact on paper through the print ribbon. These printers have proved to be very popular because high quality can be attained at a reasonable speed of 50–80 cps.

Ink jet printers, which have a matrix of ink jets that squirt characters onto paper, are fairly new on the market. They operate quietly at high speeds (up to 210 cps) and produce high-quality material. A limitation is that multiple copies cannot be produced because no hard physical contact occurs in the printing process.

Laser printers combine high speed with high quality, producing one copy at a time. With proper software, multiple copies of the same page can be produced. With collating ability, the laser printer can produce and collate multiple copies or run several sets in a sequence. The current high cost of the laser printer makes it prohibitive for school use unless it is used on a network of word processors. Prices, however, are dropping rapidly.

Careful consideration must be given by school administrators implementing word processing in their offices as to which type of printer would best serve their printing needs. The decision will be dependent upon speed of printing, quality of output, cost, availability of multiple copies, and the reliability of the printer.

Basic Functions of Word Processors.   The basic functions word processors perform are text editing, screen formatting, print formatting, and the compact storage and flexible retrieval of documents. The editing capability is the most powerful function of the word processor. It is this feature that makes it so attractive to school and business offices which require the revision of textual materials. Word processors can alter or manipulate text with ease.

To edit effectively, the user must be able to jump around in the document at will to make the needed alterations. This can be accomplished by the scrolling function, which enables the text on the display screen to be moved horizontally or vertically. The cursor, a mobile symbol on the screen, is the key to making the actual changes. The cursor can be positioned by moving it across any entered characters as well as up and down the screen. Examples of changes a user can request at the cursor position are insert, delete, replace, and move blocks of text. To illustrate the procedure, a secretary or principal would use the cursor as a pointer to search through the text and then type in an editing command, such as INSERT or DELETE, when the cursor is pointing to the appropriate character, word, line, paragraph, or block of text to be altered. When material is deleted from the document the system typically readjusts (closes up) the remaining text automatically. For material that is inserted or moved (relocated) from one place in the document to another, the system would adjust the text to accommodate the added text.

Some automatic features in a word processor which facilitate the editing function are automatic carrier return, called wraparound; the centering of text between the margins or over a fixed point or points on a line; underscoring lines; the automatic right justifying of a line to a hyphen; column editing of tabular material whereby columns of text in a table can be inserted, deleted, moved, or exchanged; form entry, which enables users to fill out preprinted forms by allowing the form to be displayed and a mask created; and global replace, which automatically allows, for example, a word to be changed throughout an entire document. An effective word processor will have simplified the keyboard work to eliminate having to make complex sequences of keystrokes when making editing changes. Suggestions on selecting a workable word-processing software program are presented in Chapter 8.

Formatting pertains to how text is positioned on the screen or on printed paper in terms of line spacing, print size, and so on. Format can be determined when the text is displayed on the computer screen or when the document is to be printed. An embedded format pertains to commands about the print format keyed in by the user at the time text is displayed on the screen. This approach has the advantage of allowing the user to make margin, spacing, and other decisions at the time of entering or composing the text. Print menu commands, in contrast, occur just before printing the final document. This approach is not as flexible, since it sometimes requires the user to go to the menu (a list of alternatives presented on the screen, from which one chooses) each time a change is wanted in the format, such as changing italics to boldface type.

Many word-processing programs today permit what is seen on the screen to be printed onto paper. Formatting instructions for both screen and print can thus be similar. Some examples of formating features found in word-processing programs, with sample illustrations, are:

- margins (top, bottom, left, and right set at specified widths)
- spacing (single, double, $1\text{-}\frac{1}{2}$)
- columns (the number a page is to include and how many lines per column)
- headings (centered, left, or right)
- justification (having uniform margins on both left and right sides)
- type (underline, boldface)
- page width (set to meet requirements of different printers and for different widths of stationery)
- headers and footers (running heads and feet, standard text used at the top and bottom of each page in a document) printed at proper locations during printout
- page numbering (documents that contain several pages can have these pages numbered sequentially)

Benefits of Word Processing.   Users and advocates of word-processing systems believe that the investment pays dividends. Early studies indicated a 20 percent productivity improvement was possible in creating and editing documents (Prouty, 1983). Radin and Greensburg (1983) drew a similar conclusion respecting the preparation and revision of school documents using an electronic processor. Patterson and Patterson's (1983) survey of several business journals found that word processing was reputed to: (1) save two minutes per page on original documents and eight minutes on revisions; (2) reduce the preparation of lengthy complicated legal documents from six hours to one hour; (3) enable a secretary in a medical office to handle the work of five physicians instead of two; and (4) reduce the time of typing reports by 50%.

The Montgomery County School District (Raucher, 1984) found that their shared-logic word-processing system not only reduced costs but brought to participating departments such benefits as increased productivity, reduction in paper handling, the ability to create and update office information data bases, better-quality documents, and the obtaining of multiple input to a document from office personnel and professionals.

More likely than not, these benefits resulted only after the word-processing system had been fully implemented and the secretaries and other users had become thoroughly familiar with the functions of the software package employed. At the outset, though, problems can be encountered which work against office efficiency and productivity.

Factors Affecting the Use of Word Processors.   A number of factors have been identified that have a direct effect on the use of word processors.

They are power line disturbances, human errors, ergonomic factors, and inadequate or nonexistent training programs.

Power line disturbances can be responsible for computer errors, with impulses, sags, or surges being accountable for the majority of these types of errors. Provision can be made to offset these disturbances by using line-surge protector cords. Outright power failure, even though brief, is a real bugaboo because it can cause one to lose everything on the storage disk. Damage to the disks in the disk drives may also occur. To prevent this occurrence, backup copies of the disk should be made. Also, a power-pack backup system can be installed.

Human errors can result in the loss of textual material due to weariness, worry about doing the task successfully, and unfamiliarity with procedures. Chirlian (1982) calls errors such as failing to make a backup disk of text being processed; entering wrong commands, which causes the machine to go berserk; and putting the disk upside down when storing the file so the filename does not get listed in the disk's directory *fatal errors*. These so-called fatal errors are human errors and can cause one to lose hours of work. Routinely, operators learn that they must make backup copies of all work being produced.

Ergonomic factors pertain to the design of automated equipment to the requirement of the operator. Armbruster (1983) states that ergonomics serves to optimize the interactions between people and technology in the working environment.

Of special concern to operators of word processors are visual and physical problems that can result due to improper furniture and lighting. Figure 3.5 illustrates important aspects in the design of the word-processor workplace. With the introduction of computer technology into offices, complaints have begun to surface. Cohen and Cohen (1983) reported that 89% of the operators surveyed using visual display terminals complained of headaches; 90% reported they have experienced pain or stiffness in the neck or shoulders at one time or another; 88% had back pain; and 83% experienced periods of severe fatigue and exhaustion. Visual problems included eyestrain (93%), tearing or itching (79%), blurring (78%), and burning (77%). Though not conclusive, the suspicion exists that radiation emanating from the CRT contributes to cataracts and birth defects. Caution should be exercised to obtain a proper screen contrast and to eliminate light glare and reflection. To avoid posture problems the chairs should be well designed, desks at the proper height, a footrest installed, and a document holder used. Regular work breaks should also be given the operator. A fifteen-minute coffee break after two hours of continuous work at the word processor under a moderate workload is suggested by Cohen and Cohen (1983). If problems viewing the screen exist, they recommend a fifteen-minute break after an hour's work. School administrators need to

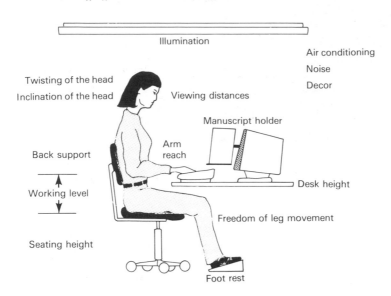

FIGURE 3.5 Important Aspects Affecting the Users of Word Processors.   Adapted from Armbruster, A. (1983). Ergonomic requirements. In H. J. Otway & M. Pelu (eds.), *New Office Technology, Human and Organizational Aspects* (p. 173). London: Ablex Publishing.

take ergonomic factors into account to ensure safeguarding the health of their office personnel and themselves should they opt to use a word processor.

Inadequately trained staff has been cited by school districts using computer technology as the major problem relating to the use of computers. The next major factor was misunderstanding about the capabilities of computers (Educational Research Services, 1982). This finding was verified by the executive director of a state organization for school employees who reported that the training of secretaries to use word processors was limited. To remedy the situation, a series of workshops for its members was being planned.

Although documentation accompanying the adopted word-processing program is available to help ease training, assuming it's written in clear and understandable language, formalized training is necessary. It may be offered by the school district, a consultant, or the vendor selling the program. Training sessions should involve the learner actively in performing work-related tasks. Distributed practice rather than a mass practice approach should characterize the sessions. Once the training is completed, an on-the-job follow-up should be implemented to ensure that the skills taught are used effectively. When updates occur in the program new training should be developed.

The School Administrator and Word Processing.   School administrators have been encouraged by proponents of the microcomputer to use it first as a word processor. Administrators may want to answer the following questions to help them assess whether a word processor is the most efficient way to expedite their paper tasks:

- Do I possess the typing skills needed to use a word processor? If not, am I willing to invest the time to develop such skills?
- How comfortable am I in composing at a typewriter? Can I make the transition from composing by hand to using a word processor?
- How many letters do I generally write out or dictate per day, per week, or per month? Are they of sufficient quantity to suggest the use of a word processor?
- How involved am I in preparing reports—little? heavily? Would a word processor relieve the pressure of being heavily involved?
- Is the time taken for writing, reviewing, and distributing letters and reports reasonable? Might it be reduced with a word processor?
- Would form paragraphs or form letters reduce the need for individually drafted letters? If so, is word processing the answer?

Chirlian (1982) contends that a person's typing ability is one of the most important factors determining whether to use a word processor. For individuals who use the hunt-and-peck approach to typing or have always done their writing by hand, a word processor may not be the answer. She provides this caution: If it takes a person three times as long to produce the typical input and then even longer to edit it, using the keyboard and screen, it may be best to leave things as they are or to get a word processor for one's secretary.

Habit, too, can prevent administrators from using a word processor. We do what seems comfortable, and composing by hand is just that for many individuals. At least this seems true among business executives whose companies had computers. According to a poll of 218 bosses, the preference of most business executives when composing correspondence was the traditional way: 89% used the paper-and-pencil method, 10% dictated to their secretaries, and 1% used the computer (*The Wall Street Journal*, 1984).

With more and more school districts acquiring microcomputers for administrative use, it seems inevitable that school administrators will be involved increasingly in word processing. With the accent in the schools on computer-literacy instruction, the new generation of administrators and teachers will have these skills. With proper training and personal commitment, many school administrators today are using the microcomputer as a word processor. Working independently and with their office staff, they have used word processors to send "personalized" letters to parents, keep an accounting of notes made on school suspensions, develop standardized forms for individual educational plans (IEPs), draft speeches and meeting agendas, and facilitate teacher evaluation reporting. Pennington (1984) used word processing to merge memos to individual teachers with a list of predetermined commendations and recommendations. The benefit of the procedure was to give teachers immediate feedback that was specific and unambiguous.

The possibilities on how the word processor can be used in the schools are great and will expand as administrators and their staffs become familiar with its capabilities. This will occur especially if school administrators recognize word processors as a valuable tool and commit themselves to using them.

Electronic Mail

Another innovation of the automated office is the use of electronic mail systems. Electronic mail refers to the procedure of sending messages from one person to another person by transmitting them over hard wires or telephone lines. Computerized electronic mail systems include teletypewriters, communicating word processors, and computer-based message systems (CBMS).

A computer-based message system can be added to an existing computer system to permit messages to be sent and received electronically. The user is assigned a computer storage area called an electronic mailbox, which is identified by a location code. The sender merely types in a message at his/her terminal keyboard and directs the message to the receiver's electronic mailbox. There it is filed until the receiver makes an inquiry of the system. At a similar terminal the receiver indicates his/her name and password. The message can then be read on the video screen or printed out if desired. The CBMS can be viewed as an electronic desk having an In box, an Out box, an electronic wastebasket, files, forms, and a repository of current work. The electronic wastebasket serves to remove any unnecessary documents. Any mail that requires urgent attention can receive a high priority to permit it to be sent automatically to the top of the pile when the user takes action to work through the In box. The Out box permits the receiver to respond to the sender or to route the message with instructions to a secretary or other professional for follow-up action. Large school districts that install or have a local area network (LAN) of interconnected terminals are in a strategic position to implement an electronic mail system.

Some advantages of electronic mail systems such as the CBMS are: (1) speed, resulting in instantaneous delivery; (2) the asynchronous concept, which means the sender and receiver do not have to be in simultaneous communication; (3) freedom of access, which permits users to send and receive messages as they wish; and (4) increased productivity obtained by decreasing the number of times a sender wishes to contact a receiver (Hallard, Smith, & Reese, 1983).

The asynchronous concept facilitates the transactions of business without losing time through wasted phone calls. Studies have shown that the caller fails to reach a party being called on the first attempt in 28 percent of all business telephone calls (Potter, 1977). The following school scenario illustrates this point and demonstrates how an electronic mail system can alleviate the problem: Principal A needs to discuss a problem with Superintendent B to get some guidance. A places a call to B, but B is tied up in a meeting. When B returns A's call, A is out of the office. When A gets back he/she immediately calls the superintendent, but by this time the superintendent is tied up in another meeting, and so the delay goes on into the day. The computer-based message system can rectify this problem. It permits Principal A's message to be stored in the superintendent's In box until he/she gets out of the meeting. Once the meeting is over the superintendent can read the message and immediately transmit the reply by computer. Principal A, by having a quick turnaround on the needed guidance, is thus able to resolve the problem earlier and not later in the day.

Some of the problems associated with electronic mail are: (1) expensive setup cost, which means dollar savings are not seen immediately, nor will increased productivity and time saving be evident for some time; (2) the fear that the undelivered messages may be lost; (3) rejection of the system because participants see no need to communicate; (4) junk mail can proliferate, with copies of electronic messages sent to innumerable people; (5) good speakers are at a disadvantage because they lose out to fast typists and good writers; (6) the system may become too much a part of a person's life, so that he/she becomes a slave to the machine; (7) weaknesses a person has in grammar and spelling are exposed, which may affect how their supervisor evaluates them; and (8) fear that management will review personal messages, thus intruding on one's privacy (Hallard, Smith & Reese, 1983; Galitz, 1980).

Electronic Filing

Electronic filing of information is an important aspect of the automated office. Instead of filing handwritten, typed, or printed material (hard copy), electronic systems such as word processors, data-based management systems, and computer-based message systems permit data to be stored on floppy disks or hard disks. Some benefits of electronic filing, as identified by Barcomb (1981), are: reduction in storage space, faster access to information, reduction in misfiling, portability of files, and limited dependence on filing systems developed by office personnel. The savings in physical storage space can be considerable. On a double-sided microcomputer diskette, 360KB of information, or over 180 double-spaced pages, can be stored. It has been determined that the contents of a complete filing cabinet could be reduced to a hard disk of less volume than a single cabinet drawer. In contrast to the time expended trying to locate material from a filing cabinet that might be misplaced, the electronic filing system enables data on disks to be retrieved readily in a few seconds. If hard copy is needed, it's a matter of simply having the stored document printed out. A study conducted by Tym Share, Inc., found that 35 percent of all filed papers are never retrieved, and that after a year in filing cabinets, 95 percent of the material is never again accessed. Schools that are obligated to maintain records of their students are confronted with this situation. If an electronic filing system were implemented, the storage of these records would become more manageable. Space requirements would be reduced and information, when requested, could be accessed readily and accurately.

Electronic Calendars and Tickler Files

Appointment calendars and "things to do" or reminder lists (called *ticklers*) help busy administrators manage their time. Meetings in particular account for a major proportion of a principal or superintendent's day. Pitner (1979) found that scheduled and unscheduled meetings accounted for 31 percent of all activities engaged in over a week's period by three superintendents. These meetings summed to 69% of total hours expended by these administrators in performing their duties. Missed meetings waste the time of all participants. If too many people miss the meeting it may have to be rescheduled; if only one or two persons are missing they'll have to be sought out and given a special briefing.

Electronic calendars and tickler files employed with stand-alone or interactive terminals have been touted as useful time-management tools for administrator/managers (Barcomb, 1981; Prouty, 1983). The electronic calendar has the capability, as does the desk calendar, to set up an appointment schedule containing dates, times, expected participants, and space for comments. If an automatic scheduler is obtained with the calendar, meetings involving individuals on the computer network can be scheduled. For example, if Superintendent A wanted to arrange a meeting with Principals B, C, and D, on a Tuesday afternoon at 3 P.M. two weeks away, A or his/her secretary would proceed to access the calendars of these principals to check their availability. If no conflict exists, a notation would be made on B, C, and D's calendars scheduling them for the meeting. The electronic process is considerably faster than scheduling by phone. Prouty, though, reminds us that this method can intrude on one's privacy. Typically, schedulers restrict users to the available blocks of time. Thus, the superintendent would not be able specifically to view the principals' actual appointments and activities.

Electronic calendars are not delimited to scheduling appointments and meetings for the individual. They may also be used to schedule rooms, vehicles, and media equipment. A school electronic calendar can also be created which would record the dates and times of plays, athletic events, field trips, guest speakers, social events, and reporting periods (Joiner et al., 1982).

Tickler files serve as electronic reminders of meetings, deadlines, and personnel and organizational activities that affect the administrator. A given file would remain in the computer's memory until a predetermined advance date, when it would automatically be displayed on the screen for viewing. Once the date had passed, the file would be deleted. An example of how the tickler file works is the case of the principal who, after arriving at his office at 7:15 A.M., accesses his calendar. At the bottom of the screen, just below 5:00 P.M., are the reminders: 1. SUBMIT BUDGET TO BUSINESS DIRECTOR. 2. ELAINE'S BIRTHDAY PRESENT. 3. CALL HAROLD RE: BUS PROBLEM. The attractiveness of the electronic calendar and tickler files is that when displayed on the computer screen they become a more prominent visual reminder than the paper desk calendar and reminder lists.

Electronic Networks

Electronic networks offer users of computer terminals the ability to communicate and share information through the medium of electric wire or telephone lines. Basically, there are two types of electronic networks (Figure 3.6): national/state communication networks and local area networks or LANs. Local area networks, as the name implies, are limited to a local area. Typically, they may be found in large school districts, institutions of higher education, and businesses which have installed for personnel use a fairly large number of computers. Chapter 12 discusses local area networking for a school district.

National/state communication networks have been established by profit and nonprofit organizations to permit subscribers to have access to information stored on data bases or electronic bulletin boards and to communicate with each other using the electronic mail capability previously

FIGURE 3.6 Types of Electronic Networks

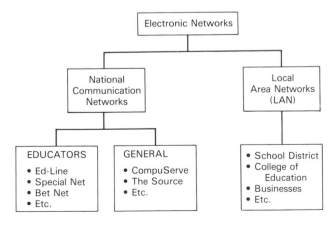

discussed. Figure 3.7 illustrates the important features of communication networks. Besides electronic mail, electronic bulletin boards, and access to on-line data bases, computer conferencing can be conducted.

Electronic bulletin boards store information subscribers wish to share. Communication networks developed for educators in a given field permit accessing information on job openings, calendars of events, announcements, legislative updates, and so on. To keep subscribers informed about the latest developments, the bulletin board generally is updated monthly. Computer conferencing allows individuals with common interests to plan and conduct a workshop/seminar/conference. These conferences may be of short or longer duration depending upon the participants or the sponsor. Information is exchanged among the participants, who may respond by submitting observations, asking questions, or critiquing the material. As

FIGURE 3.7   Features of Electronic Networks

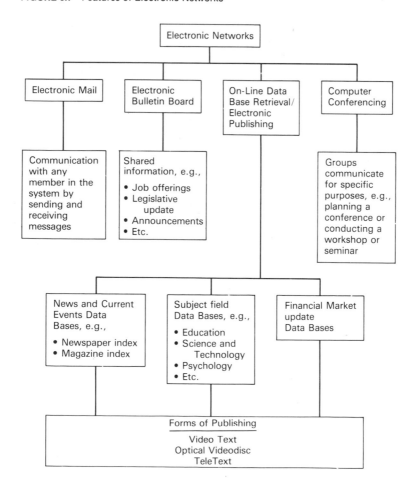

with electronic mail, the information submitted is held in storage until the participant is ready to access it.

On-line data bases may be specialized to a discipline or field such as education, or may contain information that appeals to a general audience such as stock market reports and current news events. Data bases may be accessed by directly dialing the telephone number of the network computer, using the password provided by the vendor. The computer, which has the stored information, is programmed to respond to the search commands that are sent by the user. The modes by which data bases may be searched and accessed are: teletext, video text, and optical video disks. The last two systems are interactive, meaning the subscriber requests information at a remote computer terminal using the keyboard or an adapted TV set or a printing terminal. Teletext is a pseudo-interactive system which transmits text and graphics to users through a broadcast television channel. Texts and graphics in the interactive video text system are transmitted using telephone lines, two-way TV channels, and microcomputers. The optical video disk has the size and shape of a long-play phonograph record. It can store text, motion sequences, color graphics, and even sound. To access the stored information, instructions may be contained on the disk, or the user can employ a microcomputer to control the playback (Emdad, 1984).

Administrators in schools and school districts wishing to subscribe to a national communication network will need a computer terminal, a telephone line, a modem (which stands for *modulator/dem*odulator), and a communication interface card which permits the computer to send and receive data. The modem acts as the bridge between the local computer terminal and the remote network computer by converting computer language into telephone signals and vice versa.

Raimondi (1984), in identifying eight networks targeted for educators and two networks having broad appeal, notes that subscription rates, connect charges, the number of subscribers, and features of the network (data bases, bulletin boards, electronic mail, computer conferencing) are important characteristics to consider when choosing a network. Another important variable to weigh is how the system is managed and maintained.

To maximize the use of national electronic networks users should: (1) obtain hard copies of material to facilitate sharing; (2) regularly check their mailbox and bulletin boards of interest; (3) share in the information exchange; and (4) strategically place the terminal to optimize its use by school personnel (*SPG Electronic Networking,* 1984).

National, state, and school district electronic networks can bring to building principals information from a variety of sources that can be of material help in planning, programming, and decision making. Though the technology exists, it may not be practical for all situations. District size, budget, return on investment, and commitment to use are all variables that affect a decision to set up or participate in an electronic communications network. If an administrator subscribes to a national electronic network, the benefits should outweigh the disadvantages.

SUMMARY

Administrative offices serve as the information-processing center of school systems, providing needed information on students, employees, finances, transportation, facilities, food services, and instructional programs. The result has been the creating of a paper monster in terms of the volume of records produced and stored. Office automation, particularly through the use of microcomputers, has been advanced as a solution to taming the created paper tiger. Savings in physical storage space are touted if an electronic filing system were to be instituted. The computer, though, may intensify the problem because its ability to amass data and generate reports can result in an increased proliferation of information. As a consequence, care should be exercised in determining to what extent administrative paperwork should be computerized.

Various options besides electronic filing are available to school officials who may wish to automate their administrative offices: word processing, electronic mail, electronic networking, and the use of electronic calendars. Word processing is perceived as the cornerstone of the automated office due to the benefits it provides users in terms of increased productivity, reduction in paper handling, the ability to create and update office information data bases, and the production of quality documents.

School administrators contemplating automation of their offices should recognize that all the technologies available to them are germane to their circumstances. Their current operating procedures may be degraded, with resultant turmoil and added expense, if unneeded technologies are improperly selected and implemented. Before purchasing any office automation tool, school administrators should ask these questions: Does the technology fit the goals of our school or district? and Will its use benefit the entire system in terms of efficiency?

4

MANAGING
BUSINESS OPERATIONS

School districts, among other things, are business enterprises. The current budget for educating the nation's approximately 60 million students has approached $100 billion, almost one-ninth of the gross national product (Candoli et al. 1984). School superintendents are responsible for administering the enterprise. In small districts the superintendent is also the business manager. In larger districts this function is generally delegated to an individual who may hold the title of assistant superintendent for business. Building principals are responsible for managing the school-level business operations.

The computer information system (Chapter 1) is indispensable to managing the school business enterprise. A hierarchical system, it feeds operational data to middle managers (principals) and top administrators (superintendents). At the foundation level is the data-processing system (DPS), which generates periodic output documents on the current student/educational/financial operations of the district. The day-to-day and historical reports produced comprise the data base for the management information system (MIS). At the school level, principals may use the MIS to analyze information to identify areas of concern that need attention. The data generated from these two systems may be used by top administrators in the data support system (DSS) to make planning decisions based on projections and simulations.

The purpose of this chapter is to examine business data-processing systems relevant to school districts and to present decision support systems forecasting approaches.

SCHOOL BUSINESS DATA-PROCESSING SYSTEMS

To be effective, a data-processing system should provide school administrators with the data they need, in the form desired, and at a minimum of cost. By using automatic and/or electronic equipment, data from the various transactions of districts can be processed and accumulated. From the accumulated data the reports produced may be used in the management of a district to meet local, state, and federal reporting requirements. Though school districts vary extensively in the degree of automated business applications, activities amenable to computer data processing are: budget/general ledger, accounts payable, purchasing, receipts, payroll, personnel, property (fixed assets) management, and warehouse inventory.

Computerized business data processing has been found to be more cost effective than manual processing. In New Jersey, schools using a manual system were reported as paying twice as much to do accounting functions as schools that used an in-house computer (Data processing, 1979). The Pontiac, Michigan district estimates it has been saving $200,000 per year by using a computerized accounting and student terminal system (Case history workbook, 1983). State-subsidized computerized accounting, which reduced costs by two-thirds, caused thirty-five (87.5 percent) of Utah's forty school districts to contract for financial data-processing services (payroll, accounts payable, and building receipts) from the state educational agency. Regional data-processing centers in other states also offer functional and cost-effective services to school districts.

The school business data-processing system should meet a number of accounting criteria (adapted from Rebore, 1984), for example:

1. Having a reasonable degree of internal controls to ensure the accuracy of recording transactions.
2. Being consistent with generally accepted government accounting principles, incorporating uniformity of procedures, and the use of standard terminology and definitions. More than thirty eight states have adopted the standard classifications of fund accounting specified in the 1973 U.S.O.E. revised *Handbook II, Financial Accounting Classifications and Standard Terminology for Local and State School Systems.* This program cost accounting tool provides the necessary information and feedback to operate such modern management systems as management by objectives and program and performance budgeting.
3. Being simple and flexible to accommodate new programs with minimal disruption.
4. Using a double-entry accrual and encumbrance system.

5. Recording transactions to assure answering these key questions: (a) What was purchased (the object)? (b) From what financial source (the fund)? (c) For what purpose (the function)? (d) For which school (the operational unit)? and (e) To provide what specific service (the program)?

Tasks capable of being performed by a data-processing system in relation to the conceptual basis for operation are shown in Figure 4.1.

The Budget/General Ledger System

Each fiscal year school districts adopt budgets with specified appropriations for transactions that need to be recorded. Estimated budget

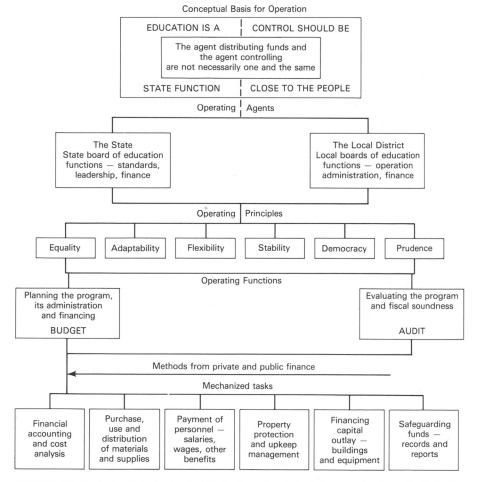

FIGURE 4.1 Business Data-Processing Tasks in a Conceptual Framework *From Mort, P. R., Reusser, W. C., & Polley, J. W. (1960). Public School Finance (3rd ed.). New York: McGraw-Hill, p. 332.*

revenues and expenditures are entered in the operating or current expense fund of the general journal and general ledger. The account title "Estimated Revenue" would show a debit amount, while the title "Fund Balance" would reflect the equal credit amount. These two recordings occur only once each year to prepare for the entry of normal daily transactions (Candoli et al., 1984).

The budget/general ledger system is central to the overall fiscal efforts of a school district. The general ledger (G/L) is the master file from which all accounting statements are prepared. It consists of a group of individual accounts reflecting the account number, designation (accounts receivable, cash, etc.), date of transaction, explanation, posting reference, and whether the transaction was a credit or debit. In short, the general ledger consists of all asset, expenditure, revenue, liability, and fund balance accounts.

The computerized system should have an account coding structure (year, type, program, fund, function, object, etc.) that is flexible to meet reporting needs. The larger and more complex the district becomes, the more sophisticated must be the coding structure. Input into the budget/general ledger application generally comes from purchase orders, receiving reports/invoices, payroll documents, inventory requisitions, checks, budget requests, receivables/adjusting entries, and deposits.

The reporting capabilities of a budget/general ledger software program is critical to school administrators who must submit certain state and federal reports. Reports that are needed but not included in a commercial program must either be programmed locally or handled by some auxiliary means. If the software has a report-generating capability, a user may be able to create some reports (within limits) without having to program them. Software that typically would meet the needs of most school districts should include the following report capabilities: budget program report by object and by location, file recap reports, revenue and expenditure year-to-date report capabilities that will meet state or regional reporting requirements, transaction summaries in various formats and sorts, balance sheets, audit reports, general journal reports, and budget file worksheets.

The Accounts Payable System

Accounts payable refers to obligations, debts, or liabilities of a school district on an open account owed to private persons, firms, or corporations for goods and services rendered. It excludes amounts due from other funds or from other governmental units (Tidwell, 1974). In simple terms, an account that is payable is the same as a bill owed to someone. An effective accounts payable system should enable a district to process routinely checks to pay validated vendor billings on time and once only. Inherent in this function is an orderly handling of vendor account numbers and the ability to keep a current, active vendor file. The system should provide master listings, activity reports, and purge routines plus associated reports.

Checks to be issued are usually handled twice per month. Similar to the payroll function, input to the accounts payable system needs to be user-oriented so the accounts payable department is not caught up in awkward and time-consuming update procedures. Check payment summaries must also be availabe. A typical accounts payable cycle is shown in Figure 4.2.

The purchase order subsystem needs to be complete so that input of data is orderly and straightforward. Credit memo procedures must be in

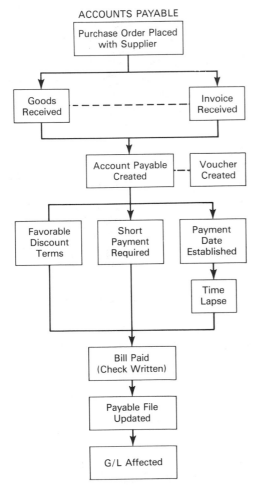

FIGURE 4.2 Flow of an Accounts Payable System *From The Small Computer in Small Business by Brian R. Smith. Copyright © 1981 by Brian R. Smith. Reprinted by permission of the Stephen Green Press, a wholly owned subsidiary of Viking Penguin, Inc.*

place. Outstanding purchase order reports, by vendor, location, and program, are important. Listings of prior payments need to be readily accessible tᴜ the computer user, and accounts payable void-check procedures need to allow for check lists, edits, and validation reports. Problems that can arise are full or partial payments of a purchase order and the incorrect handling or confusion surrounding a particular credit memo. The data-processing system should have routines that handle partial use of credit memos in a concise, clearly understandable manner for both the school district and the vendor. Also, the system should be designed to keep track of purchase orders that have been paid previously. As a result, these orders can be edited effectively.

The Purchasing System

The purchasing system is indelibly linked with the accounts payable and supplies/equipment inventory system in terms of assuring that vendors are properly paid and that there is control on all newly requisitioned or replenished supplies and equipment. The administrative goal of the system should be to purchase the right product at the right price, making it available in the right place at the right time (Jordan, 1969). The instructional goal of the system should be the securing of needed resources for teachers, to ensure a quality education for the students of the district. Figure 4.3 illustrates the flow of a purchase requisition from a teacher-user to the completion of the transaction.

District purchasing policies include competitive bidding. This process involves the drafting of written bid specifications and the soliciting, evaluating, and awarding of bids. A computerized (mainframe, minicomputer, or microcomputer) purchasing system (Temkin & Shapiro, 1983; Candoli, et al., 1984) should be capable of:

- Retaining supply and equipment specifications in permanent files.
- Producing requisition forms based on the specification files.
- Storing quantities of items requisitioned by district teachers and staff.
- Compiling, totaling, and printing formal invitations to bid, which are sent out to vendors.
- Filing for vendors to be awarded bids, the bidder's name, brand and price of items.
- Matching school orders with vendor information.
- Producing vendor bid awards and delivery schedules. One output would be the bid award summary, which is a rundown by vendor of bid awards and total prices.
- Generating a school-by-school listing to permit comparing expenditures against budgets. Schools in danger of exceeding their budgets can thus be flagged.
- Issuing purchase orders to vendors awarded a bid or to those vendors who appear to be the most logical suppliers.

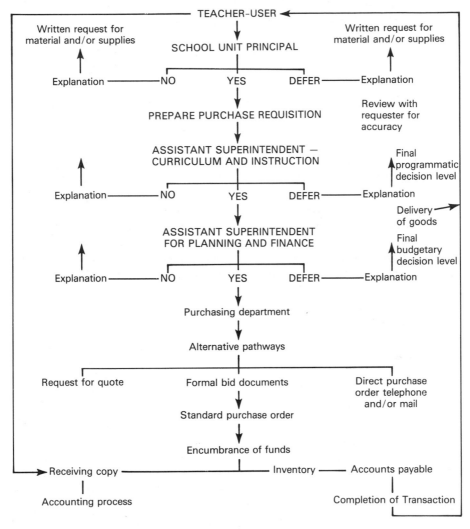

FIGURE 4.3 Flow of a Purchase Requisition *From Hughes, L. W., & Ubben, G. C. (1984). The Elementary Principal's Handbook, 2nd ed. Boston, MA: Allyn & Bacon, p. 303.*

- Tracking purchase orders and reporting on overdue orders.
- Logging in deliveries.
- Automatically reordering for stock replenishment, including the writing of purchase orders.
- Following up all open stock orders, including not only "machine" orders for stock items, but also manually written orders for nonstock, nonrepetitive, custom-made items.
- Checking invoices and payments of invoices by the automatic writing of checks.

- Distributing charges to the correct account code.
- Generating statistical data, including the direct interpretation of such data by machine, for quality control, vendor rating, and similar purposes. Vendor analysis reports can help district officials make decisions about which vendors to drop, for example.

The Receipts System

In public education, a sophisticated system to handle accounts receivable is not necessary since most moneys to be expended by school districts come from few sources. Usually tax revenues are received in large sums at rather infrequent intervals, compared with the ongoing receipt of smaller amounts in the private business setting. Reporting capabilities of a receipts data-processing system should include a receipt register, showing receipt and account number; a revenue distribution report, identifying year/fund/function/object/location/program/receipt number; a summary of general journal entries reflecting year/fund/location/program/object/receipt number; file recap report by fund; cash receipt update; and edit/validation reports.

The Payroll System

Payroll was the first computerized system introduced by business managers in school districts. This made good sense since over 75% of the operating budget in most districts is used in meeting school payrolls. The generation of payroll reports and checks seems to be the business application performed most often using computers, according to a recent survey. Of districts responding to the survey, nine out of ten with enrollments between 300 to 25,000 (or more) pupils had such a system (Educational Research Services, Inc., 1982). Even though payroll is the oldest and most frequently employed processing system, it is subject to a multitude of parameters which change frequently as withholding schedules change. It also must accommodate the variety of ways in which employees are paid. Today, the procedure of producing a written paper check is being replaced by electronic transfers from one account to another; the regular paycheck is being replaced by an earnings statement. The electronic transfer procedure is basically cost effective and usually less hampered by the delays associated with the distribution of payroll checks. School districts are leaders in the trend toward electronic pay due to the size of public school payrolls. For such a system to become operative, computer-to-computer communication between the school district and the participating bank(s) is essential. In some districts this is handled by submitting a magnetic tape to the bank(s) in sufficient time to allow the bank(s) time to process the tape and make the necessary transfers; in others the transfer is done via direct line.

The objectives a payroll system must meet are: (1) paying employees for work performed, (2) accounting for total earnings and for all deductions from total earnings, and (3) producing reports required internally and by governmental agencies. To meet these objectives, the system must be able to compute regular, overtime, or piecework pay and figure appropriate deductions for taxes, Social Security, and other deductions. Current personnel information and year-to-date totals of gross pay, taxes withheld, deductions, and net pay must be maintained on all employees. Checks should be printed automatically and expenses distributed to the general ledger system. Further, the system should be flexible enough to allow the school district to (1) generate payrolls more than once a month, such as bimonthly, weekly, or at special processing times, and (2) handle several payroll schedules simultaneously without creating serious or difficult problems for the payroll department. Figure 4.4 depicts the flow of a payroll system.

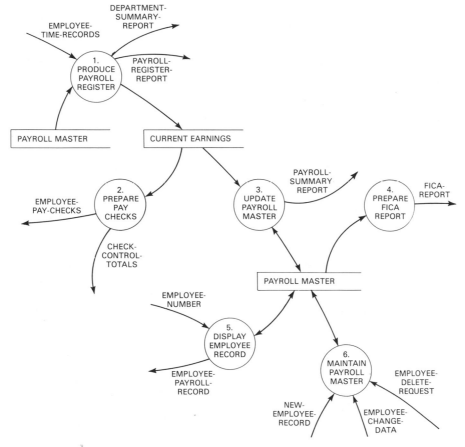

FIGURE 4.4 Data Flow of a Payroll System *From Adams, D. R., Wagner, G. E., & Boyer, T. J. (1983). Computer Information Systems: An Introduction. Cincinnati, Ohio: South Western Publishing Co., p. 130.*

Typical reports produced by payroll systems are:

- Check registers by check number
- Earnings statement register, earnings statement number and location
- Retirement monthly report
- Payroll totals by several different sorts (e.g., location, program, etc.)
- Payroll deduction reports
- Cross-reference lookup listings or terminal capability
- Account distribution reports by several different sorts (e.g., budget/general ledger account number, program/function/object, employee name, and others)
- Tax reports for state and federal agencies
- Quarterly Social Security report
- W-2 forms
- Time and attendance listing
- Payroll input register and payroll register
- Check printing

The Personnel System

Needs associated with personnel records are closely tied to the payroll system. Depending on the particular school district and also the relative size of the district, the payroll and personnel responsibilities may or may not be handled in the same department. Should a school district see a need to have these two functions operate as separate departments, care must be exercised to ensure that the software selected will in fact allow these two areas to be handled in an acceptably autonomous manner. This does not imply the need for separate computer files. Responsibility, however, for particular data elements in the common file must be updatable by the responsible department. With multiple terminals, respective departments usually are able to retrieve only the data elements they need to perform their duties. This requires the system to have security routines that can select flexibly between add, change, and delete transactions. An example of a personnel/payroll data-processing system is shown in Figure 4.5.

School districts vary considerably as to the extent of personnel data they maintain in their computer files. The differences are a function of district size, available computer capability and capacity, district commitment to particular data needs, and potential reporting needs. Some personnel data, for example, may be kept in order to meet state/regional reporting requirements, or to meet a mandate from the local board of education.

Items typically included in a personnel system are:

- Name
- Address
- Telephone number

- Location within the school district
- Birth date
- Current contract salary
- Special contract arrangements
- Vacation, sick leave, and other leave
- Salary schedule information (lane, step)
- Health data
- Ethnic background and gender
- Fringe benefits
- Certification (if applicable)
- Current assignment (teaching or classified)
- Evaluation data
- Special information, such as special talents (plays piano, etc.)

If a school district maintains salary information on lane and step, salary forecasting by account number and by salary schedule becomes possible. Personnel data combined with payroll data provide a data base to generate useful information needed for decision making by district administrators and board of education members.

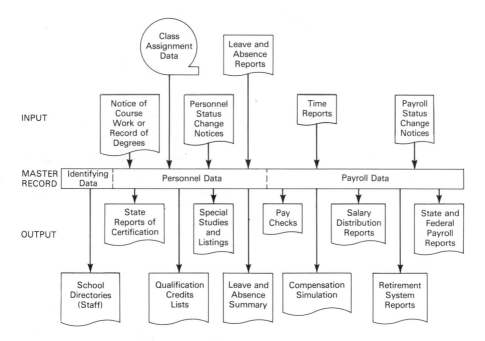

FIGURE 4.5 A Personnel/Payroll Data-processing System *From Candoli, I. C., Hack, W. G., Ray, J. R. & Stollar, D. H. (1978). School Business Administration: A Planning Approach, 2nd ed.* Boston, MA: Allyn & Bacon, p. 99.

Reports capable of being produced by the personnel system include:

- Employee demographic reports of various combinations
- Contract status
- Adjustments and allowance reports
- Salary reports of many types
- Salary forecasting algorithm and associated reports
- Evaluations
- Continuous service
- Personnel directory
- Leave status summaries
- Employees by assignment
- Location reports
- Health reports

In establishing a personnel system, district officials should view it as a vital resource in decision making. By having an adequate data base, relevant information can be analyzed to assess productivity, evaluate performance, and identify the right person for the right job at the right time. (Hasledalen 1978).

Supplies/Warehousing and Fixed Assets Inventory Systems

School districts are required to maintain an inventory of all supplies and equipment. The physical inventory should be taken annually, with accounts and records agreeing. The inventory list should identify each item by date of purchase, cost, location (building and room number), property control number, and date of last inventory. The inventory system should facilitate adding new equipment and furniture to the master list, removing old or obsolete equipment, and recording property transfers. By having an effective inventory system, school districts can (1) enhance the educational program, (2) aid cost accounting and development of a program budgeting system, (3) prevent duplication in ordering, (4) facilitate the exchange of equipment and materials throughout the district, (5) promote buying economies, (6) aid in cost comparisons between and among programs and departments, and (7) reduce insurance costs by providing data for perpetual inventories (Candoli et al., 1984).

School warehousing pertains to such activities as receiving, storing, and distributing supplies, equipment, materials, and mail (United States Office of Education, 1973). The objectives of warehousing are to (1) maintain appropriate inventory levels, (2) provide effective shipping of items to desired locations, and (3) keep unexplained inventory losses to a minimum. To be effective, warehousing information must be updated continually. Unless the system responds on the spot to changes (items coming into inventory or out of inventory), unexplained shortages in inventories develop.

A number of inventory control software programs for microcomputers have been marketed (Chapter 11) which are designed for businesses that store and ship their products. School districts interested in any of these programs would have to make modifications to meet local needs. Many large districts having a high volume of warehousing transactions have developed their own software. Features of such programs include:

- Calculation of on-hand, on-order, and allocated quantities
- Calculation of efficient reorder points-of-order quantities that would be most economic
- Production of receipts and shipping orders
- Updating of transfer files
- Development of item wage histories
- Generation of an annual physical inventory report
- Forecasting of orders based upon past demands and delivery dates

Some states mandate that school districts maintain fixed assets inventories. General fixed assets include such physical items as equipment, furniture, machinery, buildings, and land. To be classified as a fixed asset, items of property should possess three attributes: (1) a tangible nature, (2) a life longer than the current fiscal year, and (3) a significant value. Many individual assets may be tangible and long-lived but have values so small that the time and expense of maintaining detailed accounting and inventory records on them are not justified. Suggested bases for placing a valuation upon fixed assets are (1) original cost of the asset as determined by invoice or other document and (2) estimated historical cost. Fixed assets are costly, and to preserve their useful life constant expenditures are made by districts for their maintenance, repair, and renovation. To safeguard assets of a fixed nature districts typically establish a separate group of self-balanced accounts supported by a detailed cost of the assets represented (Utah School District Guide, 1983). The maintenance of the general fixed assets group of accounts serves to keep taxpayers and school board members aware that all assets acquired through taxation are accounted for until disposed of by proper authority or retired. A good fixed asset record can do more than meet accounting requirements. It should also address the question of when an asset should be repaired or replaced. By conducting regular inspections of fixed assets, items needing attention can be identified, maintenance verified, and costs accumulated. Using this information, administrators can forecast when repairs or replacement are necessary and budget the funds needed to do the task (Golz, 1984).

Fixed asset accounting can be computerized. Usually the file size requirements for such an effort can be extensive. Not only must the school district know where the respective equipment/properties are, but they must keep track of costs and depreciation. Adequate software capabilities should include appropriate depreciation schedule algorithms. Initializing the fixed assets system in a school district can be an extensive task, particularly if the school district is large. After the file is once established, ongoing resources are required to keep the file current.

The number of reports a system can produce depends on the computer software employed. Examples of reports that can be generated by a fixed assets software system are (1) property accounting summaries; (2) property site recap; (3) maintenance audit list; (4) trend and depreciation control; (5) retirement, additions, adjustments, and transfer reports; (6) insurance and property control; (7) insurance master recap; (8) insurance site recap; (9) back trend original cost reports; and (10) report generator audit.

OTHER COMPUTERIZED APPLICATIONS

Computer technology has also been employed by school districts to conserve energy; manage the custodial, food services, and transportation programs; and develop program budgets.

Energy Management

Energy crises, inflation, and budget erosions have caused school districts to turn to computer technology to conserve energy. Energy management has as its purpose the conservation of energy while maintaining a comfortable environment in each building. Many districts have been able to accomplish this by using either a large, floor standing computer or microcomputer to (1) schedule the optimum time to start and stop equipment, (2) cycle equipment operation to each building's needs, such as directing heat only to needed areas, (3) control the right mix of outside and air-conditioned air, (4) determine how many chillers should be running at any given time for maximum efficiency and energy savings, and (5) limit electrical demand to cut excess use charges (Cecilia, 1983).

Using appropriate software, a microcomputer with graphics capability can plot cumulative energy usage curves for each school in a district for several years on the same chart, giving simple visual depiction of yearly, quarterly, or monthly usage. The graphs serve as a tool to help administrators spot problems that need correction.

Custodial Services

The computerization of custodial services is still in the infancy stage. Some minicomputer and microcomputer software programs have been developed, but it remains for school administrators to specify their needs. Rather than just jumping on the bandwagon by purchasing a computer, directors of custodial departments should first assure they can answer in the affirmative such questions (Kantglehner, 1983) as: Do we (1) maintain accurate weekly or monthly beginning and ending inventory data? (2) know the individual cost and pack for each item which is consumed? (3) maintain detailed usage and reorder data? (4) have established material and labor costs for each area involved? and (5) have personnel available in custodial services to operate a computer?

If several "no" answers are recorded, a good manual procedure should be worked out first before implementing a computerized system. Computerized custodial management programs (Kantglehner, 1983) should be able to provide users with the following data or reports:

- An ending, on-hand inventory record that would show the amounts on hand, usage per day, reorder amounts, and cost of items used.
- Costs for monitoring different areas of the school plant in terms of janitorial items used and the total wages paid custodial employees in that area. These costs would then be analyzed to show the (1) cost per square foot or cost per area, (2) cost per student per student day, and (3) costs per working day.
- Inventory items on order and current inventory status.

Determining custodial staffing needs in times of growth and recession is a task confronting school administrators. In lieu of applying the historical rule of thumb based on the number of custodians per number of square feet, or rooms, or students, or staff, multiple linear regression procedures have been developed, using a computer, to predict staffing needs. One such program is CUS/STAFF, written by the Massachusetts Association of School Business Officials Cooperative Corporation or MASBO CO/OP (Keniston, 1983). This program estimates staffing needs based on such variables as: number of professional staff, number of students, total area in square feet, and adjustments unique to a district. The adjustments are: (1) time adjustments (work year, partial year, or school year), (2) custodial activities adjustments (special facilities, non-school-year use of facilities, traffic-related activities, skilled preventive maintenance activities, etc.), (3) building characteristics (floor finishes, size and location, heating plant, building configuration and layout, etc.), and (4) other adjustments (cleaning frequency, methods and equipment, etc.). A value of the program is its ability to answer "What if" questions such as, "How will decreasing enrollments affect custodial staffing? or "What effect would changing from daily cleaning to every-other-day cleaning have on staffing needs?"

Administrators of a district's custodial department would be well advised to examine approaches taken to computerize their services. Microcomputers and minicomputers have proven to be effective tools to plan and monitor custodial work, control inventory, and determine staffing needs.

Food Services

Food services make up an essential support system of a school district. Local, state, and federal policies dictate the operation of the program, which may be centralized or decentralized organizationally. Components of the program include staffing, inventory, purchasing, menu management, the food preparation system, financial accounting and cost analysis, and reporting. Critical to the success of the program is having a clear line of authority established within the organization. Management should be entrusted to a food service director or administrator to avoid splintering responsibility among school principals, business managers, superintendents, lunch monitors, secretaries, and school custodians (Friese, 1981).

Menu management of the program is highly related to cost management and accountability (Friese, 1981; Van Egmond-Pannell, 1981). Menus not only determine the food to be purchased but also affect the amount of labor necessary for preparation and serving, food equipment and facilities selection, and sanitation and custodial costs. To keep a rein on costs, the supervisor of the food services operation should (1) follow well-planned menus, (2) purchase on bid or from wholesale vendors, (3) have sound purchasing practices, (4) purchase food that yields the optimum quantity, (5) check deliveries, (6) account for food purchased and prepared, (7) follow standardized recipes, (8) use portion control, (9) reduce excessive leftovers and waste in preparation, (10) utilize USAD-donated foods, and (11) institute sound storage practices.

Accounting and reporting practices should be able to provide information on the total program and by individual schools to permit conducting comparative cost analyses. Districts that have instituted computer technology are able to monitor operational costs and income, keep accurate cost per unit inventories, provide an audit trail for easy access of information, and provide data for monthly state reimbursement reports. Though computers cannot be used in all areas of food services, they are ideally suited to handle financial management and reporting requirements.

At the onset of the 1980s, few school districts seemed to be using computers to handle functions relating to food service operations. Of those surveyed, less than 10% reported the computerization of free/reduced eligibility lists (8.0%) and menu planning and inventory control (6.1%). Larger districts were the leaders in this use, with programs primarily developed in-house (Educational Research Services, Inc., 1982).

The Food and Nutrition Service (FNS) of the U.S. Department of Agriculture has been in the forefront to promote the use of computers by schools. In cooperation with several states and local school districts, this organization was instrumental in having separate but interrelated software programs developed to help automate school food services. Currently, FNS offers two programs (Chapter 11) that are available to all schools in the country at no cost except a fee to defray the expense of copying the software. The one set of software is designed for small to medium-sized school districts with up to sixty schools and a central warehouse; it runs on an Apple II. The second set of software can work with a larger number of schools; it was developed for the IBM PC and CP/M operating microcomputers.

Another resource provided for school food service administrators by FNS is a directory (United States Department of Agriculture, 1984) which contains information on computer hardware, software, and applications currently being used by 101 reporting schools from twenty-six states. Twenty-six schools used either a microcomputer or mainframe computer for their applications, while twenty-seven schools used a mainframe in combination with microcomputers. A cumulative total of twenty-six different applications were reported by ninety-five of the responding schools. By category, record-keeping applications ranked first (38.5%) followed by financial accounting (30.8%), inventory and purchasing (19.2%), and menu planning, recipes, and nutrient analysis (11.5%). The application reported most frequently by users was payroll (73.7%). Other computerized applications schools seemed to find valuable were: inventory at individual site and/or warehouse (62.1%), participation data (53.7%), profit and loss statement (45.3%), state reporting (44.2%), food and nonfood supplies (42.1%), free and reduced meal applications (38.9%), and personnel records (37.9%). General-purpose software was also being used by a number of the sixty-one schools having microcomputers. Thirty-four (55.7%) reported using electronic spreadsheets, sixteen schools (26.2%) a word processor, and only two schools (3.3%) a data manager to assist in data filing.

The trend among states in food services seems to be the promotion of computer initiatives. Wyoming, in cooperation with the Mountain Plains Regional Office of the U.S. Department of Agriculture's Food and Nutrition Service, has been refining and rewriting a multi-unit service that was first developed in Gaston County, North Carolina. The Mountain Plains Region school districts in Colorado, Kansas, and South Dakota are implementing parts of this system. Utah has developed software called the "School Lunch Network" that is being used by schools in the state. The thrust of these and other states in the fostering of computerization is the development of task-specific micro-computer software. The major concern is that the software be adequately field tested before being marketed. Even then, modification may have to be made in a program to meet local requirements.

Transportation

Transportation is the most visible support system in a school district. In the minds of students, parents, and the community, the yellow bus that transports children to and from school is the most obvious symbol of schools. Buses have also been associated with the movement to desegregate schools as mandated by court orders. Critical to the success of a district-operated transportation program is a functioning routing and schedule system and the systematic inspection and maintenance of the bus fleet. Computers are currently being employed with more frequency to perform these essential tasks.

Computerized student transportation systems began in the early 1970s with the use of large mainframe computers. The use of computer technology, though, had not spread widely. At the onset of the 1980s, less than one in five districts surveyed used computers to generate bus passenger lists (17.5%), develop route/driver schedules (13.5%), and maintain vehicle performance and maintenance records (8.1%). District per pupil expenditure seemed to be related to computer use. For example, although one-fourth (25.9%) of the districts that spent $2600 or more per pupil used computers to generate passenger lists, none of the districts spending less than $1300 did so. By size of district, the corresponding percentages were 34.7% for large (25,000 or more pupils) districts and 5.6% for very small (300 to 2499 pupils) districts (Educational Research Services, Inc. 1982). The use of microcomputers, which now have adequate storage capability (more than one million bytes of RAM storage and hard-disk storage of one hundred million bytes) has opened the door for small and medium-sized districts to computerize their transportation programs.

Specific applications for which task-specific software have been written are: routing and scheduling, vehicle or fleet maintenance, geographic analysis, and inventory control. General-purpose software has also been used to advantage to forecast enrollments, manage personnel information, perform cost analyses of salary schedules, and do textual work.

Routing and Scheduling. The purposes of determining individual bus schedules are to (1) reach the optimum level of the most trips per bus in the least amount of time and mileage and (2) maximize safety by eliminating overcrowding to assure that students who live in congested areas are not dropped off during rush hour traffic. A number of factors impinge on determining schedules, for example, population sparseness or density, traffic conditions, road quality and conditions, school schedules, distances children must walk to the pickup point, handicapped needs, geography of the route, and weather (Candoli et al., 1984). Specific scheduling tasks that are performed by a transportation software program (Dembowski, 1984c; Bensen, 1983) are:

- Calculating route times. An opening/dismissal time analysis helps determine which buses are to be assigned to particular schools and how many trips each bus would make.
- Calculating route capacities.
- Recalculating stop times.
- Retrieving and displaying routes. Retrieval options might be by specific route number, by bus number in order of start time, or by school. Other information that might be retrieved for use by building principals is student census data combined with routing information in terms of a specific stop on a route or for the entire bus route.
- Route indexing by student name and address. The index facilitates assigning new students to routes and provides them and their parents with answers to questions about transportation concerns.
- Generating reports. Sample reports might be the number of miles traveled by bus; the names, addresses, and phone numbers of students transported; a listing of students by ethnicity; bus route listings; and time/mileage exception listings that report deviations from a driver's regular route.

Vehicle Maintenance. The purposes of fleet maintenance are to (1) avoid cost overruns, (2) assure that buses are in good operating order, (3) generate alerts for overdue maintenance checks, and (4) determine when parts and supplies are to be ordered. The computerized system would seek to maintain on each vehicle in the school fleet information on gas/oil usage, repair costs, scheduled maintenance, vandalism costs, and the individuals assigned to work on the bus. Much specific information about each vehicle can be kept on the computer using a code number (adapted from Levin, 1984):

- The vehicle's make, year, registration number, capacity, and weight
- The year-to-date dollar totals of all gas, oil, and antifreeze used and all maintenance performed
- The times when each vehicle is due for having its brakes checked, engine tuned, transmission checked, and serviced for parts and regular maintenance
- The miles-per-gallon ratio the vehicle achieved since its last fill-up to determine if it gets the expected ratio
- The dates maintenance work was performed; parts replaced, reflecting price; and the mechanic's identification number and number of hours worked

Having access to this computerized information, a transportation supervisor would be equipped to answer such management questions as: (1) Are we living within our budget? (2) Are we obtaining a satisfactory level of vehicle performance? (3) Can we reduce the amount of time spent on brake lining or tune-ups per job or per man? and (4) Are excessive costs incurred to replace certain parts? (Levin 1984).

Geographic Analysis. Geographic analysis is a technique used for school redistricting (Rust & Judd, 1984), the designing of attendance areas, and school district consolidation. Census files combined with geographic residential information enable an analysis to be made of a district's enrollment areas. A detailed analysis (Bensen, 1983; Dembowski, 1984c) would show student housing patterns by street, community, attendance area, grade level, or school. School administrators would be able to use the information to study the effects of redistricting, grade promotions, and population shifts on transportation routes.

Inventory Control.   Replacement parts for the district's fleet must be kept in stock. Though a district may have a general inventory control system, the transportation program may not be directly tied into it. Provision, though, must be made for the stocking of parts, tires, tools, and equipment. Benefits can accrue to a district if the inventory maintained is determined in conformity with the predicted need. Management questions that can be answered from an effective inventory control system (adapted from Dembowski 1984c) are (1) What parts are in stock and what needs to be reordered? (2) What parts have been replaced on what buses and what do they cost? (3) Are parts missing from inventory, which may indicate pilferage? (4) Are too many parts being replaced in some buses, indicating that those buses should be replaced? (5) What are the vandalism costs on each bus? Is each part needed? (6) Are certain drivers harder on buses than others?

Planning/Forecasting/Simulations

When top administrators in a school are involved in making planning decisions based on projections and simulations, a data support system (DSS) is in the making (Chapter 1). A functioning DSS utilizes (1) day-to-day operational information derived from the established student/educational/financial data-processing systems, and (2) control information, which stems from the management information system (MIS). Control information reflects the degree of discrepancies found between what is and what is expected when comparing actual occurrences and district/school goals.

Central to the data support system is the ability of top administrators to forecast future enrollments. Concrete data on enrollments affect decisions made about facilities, teacher/staff employment, budgeting, bus routes/stops, and so on. Predicting a district's financial future regarding anticipated revenues and projected expenditures is also important. Computer technology has been employed by a number of districts to do forecasting and simulations. Among 1000 districts responding to the use of computers, approximately one-third (32.1%) stated they used computer technology to do budget projection/simulations, over one-fourth (27%) maintained school boundary and census data, and 26.5% indicated they could do computerized enrollment projections (Educational Research Services, Inc., 1982).

Enrollment Forecasting.   Assumptions underlying enrollment forecasting (adapted from Candoli, et al., 1984) are:

- The mortality rate for any age group will be constant or the rate of change will be predictable.
- The change in birth rate will not be dramatic; any change will be predictable.
- Boundary changes will be permanent; changes would be included in the analysis.
- Local economic conditions will be stable or will change at a predictable rate.
- Administrative policy will be constant during the time period or change will be predictable.
- A major catastrophe will not occur.

Enrollment forecasting methods employed that provide accurate estimates are: cohort-survival, percentage-survival, and graphic technique. Survival ratios that reflect all of the individual factors influencing enrollments are generated in the cohort-survival method. The series of produced survival rates permit the administrator to have an indication of the fraction of students in any given grade who will "survive" to the next grade the next year. Overall, this method has proven to be fairly reliable for short-range projections. The percentage-survival method is similar to the cohort method except in the process of calculating kindergarten enrollment from birth data. The percentage method bases past kindergarten changes from year to year or some base period that covers a time period ranging from three to ten years. The graphic technique method is also called the time-trend technique or the law of growth principle. It is usable for either long- or short-term projections. The method employs a formula to calculate simple linear regression, with one variable being a year code and the other representing enrollment figures. The produced results can then be charted in graphic form showing enrollment curves for a selected period of time.

The method used by a district may be dependent upon its philosophy. One position is to use all three of the above methods. Doing so would produce a pattern of estimated enrollments that school administrators could use to make, from the analyzed results, the best subjective prediction (Shoa, 1984). Another position is that two separate methods should be used, one for district projections and the other for the individual schools. The cohort-survival method is advocated for district forecasting since it takes into account such variables as historical enrollment trends, family mobility, local and state birth rates, and other community variables (Candoli et al., 1984).

Financial Forecasting.   Financial forecasting has as its goal the inclusion of as many relevant factors as possible in the planning process. To predict a district's financial outlook, three steps have been advocated for use by school administrators (Sloan & Yudewitz, 1983). They are: (1) deciding what counts in the district's finances, (2) evaluating each of the identified variables to predict how they might affect the finances, and (3) organizing all this data into a complete package that can effectively be communicated to school board members and the district's "publics."

The first step, *deciding what counts,* entails conducting an analysis of the district's current financial status. Information would be gathered both from within and outside the district. Data sources from within would include staffing and retirement projections, audit information, student enrollments, salary schedules, investments, and recent spending patterns. Outside data would be that compiled on the assessed value history of real estate in the community, state, and federal aid moneys, and national and state financial and educational trends. Specific areas administrators should examine to assess fully the current picture (adapted from Sloan & Yudewitz, 1983) are:

- Pending litigation and its potential impact on the district
- Pending or new legislation respecting educational programming, property taxation, and educational funding
- The growth and stability of the business/industrial community. Within the district are any new businesses closing down? What about new construction and/or residential construction?
- The value of school supplies and equipment
- Major equipment maintenance, repair, and replacement cost estimates
- Unmet needs or new problems of the district, such as declining enrollments
- Salary increases offered teachers and support staff in neighboring districts
- Methods neighboring districts are using to cope with similar problems
- Cost figures on insurance, energy, borrowing, and items unique to the district

The second step, *determining how much it counts,* involves sorting the data and assessing the impact of each variable. An example would be determining the percentage increase expected in expenditures over the next five years. Once the trend has been established, using data from past and current years, other factors that might affect expenditures would be considered. Using this strategy, an administrator is better equipped to project what the probable increase would be. Once all the variables and factors affecting them have been analyzed, they would be rank ordered as to potential impact. Next, possible scenarios, ranging from worst possible to best possible situations, would be created. These scenarios, with alternative approaches, would be presented to the public for their response and input.

The final step in the process of developing the financial forecast is *organizing the information.* This entails organizing the data in a packaged, readable form that would best present the district's financial forecast to the public. Graphics would be included to communicate maximally the developed budget and supporting documents to the school board and patrons of the community.

Computer technology, as noted above, has been utilized to do enrollment and financial forecasting. One of the problems inherent in writing business software for schools has been computer programmers who did not fully understand the educational system. Besides designing the software to imitate existing manual procedures, these specialists wrote software that was highly task specific and not interrelated, thus lessening its value. With the advent of the microcomputer a new tool, the electronic spreadsheet (see Chapter 11), became available to school administrators to do forecasting and simulations. Available to educators today are integrated software programs that combine word-processing, data management, and graphics features with the spreadsheet.

The Electronic Spreadsheet. The electronic spreadsheet is an all-purpose problem-solving tool having built-in functions for calculating relationships and analyzing information. Similar to an accountant's pad, it consists of a matrix or grid made up of rows and columns with thousands of cells or individual boxes formed by the intersections. The rows are identified by numbers and the columns by letters (Figure 4.6). A number (value), label, brief title, or formula can be entered into a cell. An example of a formula, which is a symbolic expression of a principle or rule or calculation, is $B8=B4+B5$. Interpreted, this means the computer is instructed to "Take the value stored at cell B4 and add it to the value stored at cell B5 and store the results in cell B8." Most spreadsheets provide about 254 rows and 65 columns, to produce 15,000 cells capable of storing data. The power of a spreadsheet lies in its ability to remember and recalculate the math formulas or functions within it. This means that if one number is changed, all related values are recalculated almost instantly.

Electronic spreadsheets perform five major functions: creating, revising, formatting, printing, and file handling (Alberte-Hallam, Hallam, & Hallam, 1985). A file is created when values, labels, and formulas are initially entered into the spreadsheet. Revision occurs when entries in a cell, column, or row are replaced, deleted, or inserted. As one example, a screen display or printout can be simplified by deleting unnecessary rows and columns. The display screen can be formatted or adjusted to present different sections of the spreadsheet. Typical format options are adjusting the column, displaying formulas and label borders, determining the number of decimals shown in a number, rounding to the nearest integer, using dollar and cents, and designating certain cells as label cells using al-

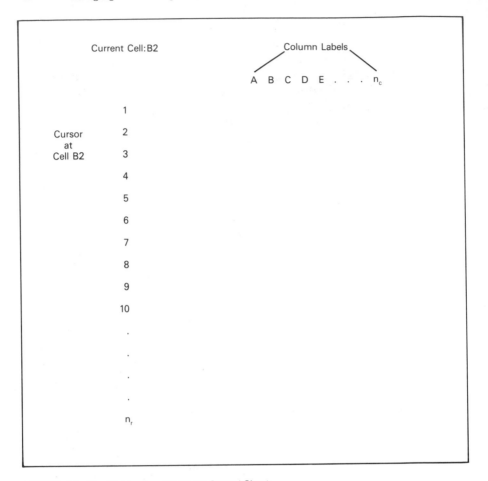

FIGURE 4.6 The Matrix of an Electronic Spread Sheet

phanumerics. A finalized spreadsheet may be stored on a floppy disk or hard disk or sent to a printer to produce a paper copy. Printing options include specifying column widths and determining the outside matrix dimensions. File handling includes the copying, deleting, moving around, or consolidating of files.

The spreadsheet is very useful for modeling problems requiring "what if" questions. To facilitate this type of analysis, the user should consider designating the worksheet with an entry space above and to the left of the main body of the table for entering underlying assumptions. The most common form of "what if" analysis is to change one or more assumptions to assess what would happen under different conditions. This means modifying a worksheet to determine what would happen if one of its elements were examined in more detail (Williams, 1984). Applying this procedure to the projection of future school expenditures, the administrator would change assumptions on such variables as: inflation rate, salary levels, number of students, the student-teacher ratio, the number of students transported by bus, and the number of custodial staff per school building (Dierdorff & Smith, 1984).

Examples of "what if" questions (Dierdorff & Smith, 1984; Craner, 1983) are:

- What will it cost if we add/reduce five teacher aides?
- What changes in the budget will occur if we lose/gain 500 students?
- What change in the property tax rate will occur over two years if a building program is commenced?
- What impact will be had on the district's operating budget if the amount of state aid is decreased/increased?
- What will be the total cost to the district if an 8 percent increase in salary is given to custodial employees?
- What would be the effect on the school's budget if changes occurred in revenue and staffing?
- What changes would occur in the anticipated state-aid revenue if various factors were altered?

In the area of financial planning, electronic spreadsheets have proven to be invaluable tools for modeling financial statements, analyzing and managing budgets, forecasts, and cash flow. With respect to the budget, they permit (adapted from Dierdorff & Smith, 1984):

- Changing specific dollar amounts or deleting certain objects on a "global" basis, such as incrementing salaries across all teaching personnel
- Modifying program budget information at any level to obtain the most desirable educational program and revenue allocation
- Changing the development criteria to simulate different program parameters
- Producing program budgets in different formats for use by building-level and central office administrators

In the area of enrollment forecasting, a spreadsheet can compute automatically cohort-survival ratios for each grade for each school in the district. These statistics can be combined to obtain a district enrollment summary by grade level (Kacanek, 1984). With access to these projections, a district suffering from declining enrollments and eroding operating funds can be in a better position to decide which schools to close, where staff should be reassigned, and how buses should be rescheduled.

In the business community, the primary use of microcomputers in the executive office is for spreadsheet analysis. Reported usage by executives surveyed range from about an hour a week to more than thirty hours (Lechner, 1984). In the educational community administrators are becoming increasingly aware of the potential applications of the spreadsheet.

The expectation is that the electronic spreadsheet will become an indispensable tool to administrators as they refine their decision support system.

SUMMARY

School business affairs were among the first operations computerized in the school system for reasons of cost effectiveness. Applications commonly employed by districts are: payroll, personnel, budget/general ledger, accounts receivable, accounts payable, warehouse inventory, purchasing and property (fixed assets) management. Other computer applications being adopted more widely relate to energy management; custodial services; food services; transportation; and planning, forecasting, and simulations techniques used in decision support systems.

The increased emphasis being given to the establishment of data support systems (DSS) makes it vital that top administrators (superintendents) have information on projected enrollments, revenues, and expenditures to make planning decisions. The electronic spreadsheet has proven to be a useful forecasting tool due to its ability to model problems requiring "what if" questions. A functioning data support system relies on the day-to-day operational information derived from the student and financial data-processing systems and the direction and control information that stems from the management information system.

5

MANAGING THE EDUCATIONAL PROGRAM

School administrators perform various roles in their assignments such as instructional leader, human relations facilitator, evaluator, and conflict mediator. To many onlookers, the role of manager—the one who keeps things running smoothly—is the major role (Gorton, 1983).

The management of the educational program is of primary importance to the school administrator, particularly at the building level. The major component of the educational program (Figure 5.1) is the curriculum that is taught to students enrolled in the school system. Vital to the development and implementation of the curriculum is public support and acceptance, which is fostered through a dynamic and ongoing school-community relations effort. The actual operation of the educational program is dependent upon having qualified and competent personnel; adequate funding, facilities, instructional resources, and support services; an effective pupil personnel program; and an organized student scheduling/records system.

THE COMPUTER AND THE EDUCATIONAL PROGRAM

The computer has been used to facilitate the instructional program through computer-assisted instruction (CAI), computer-managed instruction (CMI),

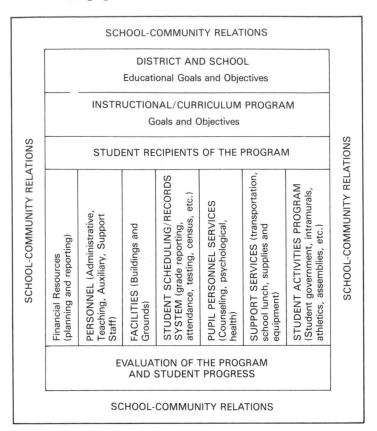

FIGURE 5.1   Components of the Educational Program of a School System

and computer-assisted testing (CAT). Similarly, the computer has proven to be a valuable tool in supporting the instructional program, with software programs written to perform business operations, manage student scheduling/records information, account for library/educational media resources, and assist students in educational and career planning (Chapter 2, Figures 2.2 and 2.5).

The purpose of this chapter is to focus on student-related administrative applications such as student scheduling, grade reporting, attendance accounting, standardized test scoring and reporting, and the use of a student information system to make record keeping more efficient.

Nature and Extent of Administrative Computer Use

Efforts have been made to determine the extent to which computers have been used to manage administrative tasks. A 1977 national survey conducted to identify exemplary data-processing centers obtained responses from 323 computer operations (Ely, 1977). The majority of the centers (44.9%) were using IBM, followed by Burroughs (13.6%) and Honeywell (13.6%) mini/mainframe computers. Over 40% of the centers had operating student scheduling (48.9%), grade reporting (48.9%), attendance accounting (42.7%), and census (28.5%) software programs.

A 1979 study conducted by H.J.B. Enterprises for the National Institute of Education found that 78% of all secondary schools were using computers to perform tasks in student accounting, testing, educational resource management, research, and guidance and counseling applications. The extent of usage in primary and middle schools, while somewhat lower, was termed impressive (Even-Tou, 1984).

During the 1980–81 school year, school districts across the country were sampled by geographic areas to assess their uses of computer technology (Educational Research Services, Inc., 1982). It was found that 91.5% of the 1484 school districts responding used an in-house or contracted computer service. The technology was used for both administrative (88.8%) and instructional (77.4%) purposes. The median date for introducing computers was 1972, with larger districts and those with higher per-pupil expenditures tending toward earlier introduction. Only 59.4% of the reporting districts said they either owned or leased their computer hardware. The remaining districts resorted to purchasing services from an educational regional service agency, commercial agency or college, or they participated in a time-sharing arrangement. Almost two-thirds of the districts that either owned or leased equipment or participated in time sharing reported that they were using at least one microcomputer (Apple or Radio Shack) either alone or with other equipment. Over one-fourth (27.1%) of these districts used microcomputers only. A mainframe or minicomputer, though, was the hardware used by the majority of responding districts. Student administrative applications used by the responding districts were as follows: class scheduling (77.4%), grade reporting (68.8%), attendance (55.4%), and the scoring and analysis of tests (65.8%). Substantially higher proportions of the large districts (25,000 or more enrollment) used computers for scheduling.

The impact of the microcomputer on managing administrative tasks in the schools since the early 1980s has not been fully assessed. The big thrust has been in instructional computer use. The estimate (Computers, 1985) has been made that local administrators spent $390 million on microcomputer hardware during 1984–85. At the end of the 1983–84 school year, 83% of the nation's schools were estimated as having microcomputers, with the percentage increasing to 90% in 1986 (Ingersoll & Smith, 1984). The likelihood is great that many of the nation's schools are using these computers for administrative purposes in response to the concerted efforts of hardware and software vendors and editors of educational computing journals to promote this use.

SCHEDULING FUNCTIONS

It has been said that nothing has more effect on the total school program than the master schedule (Bennett, 1981). Ways in which the schedule impacts administrators, counselors, teachers, students, and parents are: It (1) reflects the nature of the educational philosophy of a school with its goals and objectives; (2) dictates how the human and physical plant resources of the school are used to support the instructional and curriculum program; (3) communicates to parents the means by which they can assess whether their children are attaining educational goals; (4) integrates the various elements of the educational program, that is, students, teachers, curriculum, time, and space; and (5) affects the morale of students and teachers dependent upon their needs being met.

Scheduling has been defined (Hughes & Ubben, 1980) as "the plan to bring together people, materials, and curriculum at a designated time and place for the purposes of instruction. Its basic purpose is to coordinate the requirements laid down by previously reached decisions regarding curriculum, instruction, grouping, and staffing" (p. 173).

In examining student scheduling as a management application, administrators need to be aware of the characteristics of a good schedule, the process of scheduling, the various types of schedules, and how computerization has been used to build the master schedule and prepare student and teacher schedules.

Characteristics of a Good Schedule

Criteria of a good or effective schedule, regardless of type, have been determined by Landers and Myers (1977) and Anderson and VanDyke (1972). Summarized, the criteria are/a good schedule should:

- Provide maximum support for the goals and objectives of the school
- Allow each student to pursue the course of study he/she needs or desires
- Assign teachers to courses for which they are qualified and, when possible, for which they have a preference
- Involve teachers, specialists, administrators, and even parents and students at certain levels in the decision making
- Provide for optimum utilization of all rooms relative to the building capacity and student enrollment
- Meet all minimum standards for time allocations as designated by the state department of education and other accrediting agencies
- Provide planning time for each teacher every day
- Make provisions for special groups to accommodate the need for special education classes, ability groups, and the like
- Plan lunch periods in the most convenient way for student, faculty, and food service personnel

- Provide for a good balance in the distribution of class sections in the schedule, section size, and in the number of students and sections assigned to teachers
- Contain no conflicts between courses for more than a small percentage of students
- Be clear and complete so as to be ready by the first day of school
- Function with a minimum of confusion and change after the first few days of the school year

The Scheduling Process

The scheduling process consists of two phases: planning and implementation. Their roles are highly interrelated and indispensable to a smoothly running school.

The Planning Phase.   Scheduling involves careful planning. In this phase the principal must make decisions with respect to curriculum offerings, assigning teachers to courses, the amount of freedom students should have in choosing class periods and teachers, the times courses are to be offered, which facilities to use, and the particular type of schedule to be employed. Concerns principals should address in these areas are presented as curriculum, faculty, student, and time/space factors, since these elements are basic to the scheduling process.

THE CURRICULUM

Respecting the curriculum, an assessment should be conducted to determine what courses are still to be in the curriculum and which are to be added. It may be that new courses are to be included due to changes in district or state requirements. Further, requests from students and faculty, if judged worthwhile, may also be incorporated in the curriculum. It should be assured that those courses needed by students to progress from grade to grade and for their eventual graduation be offered. In the compilation of course offerings there will be the required courses that must be taught daily and have a set number of instructional hours; special courses such as music, art, and industrial arts; and electives, independent study programs, and minicourses of six- or nine-week duration.

THE FACULTY

Typical concerns teachers have about the scheduling process are: "What classes am I to teach?" "How many students will be in them?" and "How many preparations must I make to institute instruction?" Opportunity should be provided teachers to voice their preference for certain courses and to suggest new offerings. In the scheduling process the principal needs to take into account the experience, certification qualifications, training, course interests, emotional stability, health, and personal needs of each teacher.

STUDENTS

In the desire to expedite the scheduling process and get on with the business of running the school, the concerns and needs of students may become secondary. This prompted Parker (1973) to advocate a student-centered scheduling model to humanize the process. The model would take into account students' interests, needs, learning styles, social and emotional levels of behavior, and so on as the composition of classes in the different courses is considered. The goal would be to provide the best match of teachers with courses and with individuals and groups of students who have special needs. In this context, the schedule would be viewed as a tool to implement educational goals students should attain rather than being inflexible, designed only to dictate the curriculum and staffing patterns of the schools (Shaten, 1982).

TIME/SPACE FACTORS

The time allocations of the master schedule adopted by a school must be in conformity with state regulations and any additional standards imposed by local school boards or accrediting agencies. Examples are: adherence to the minimum length of a normal school day and the minimum number of minutes of supervised instruction stipulated for nonlaboratory and laboratory courses. These regulations have planning implications for the administration with respect to the opening and closing of the school day, the number and length of class periods, the time between classes, and the time allocated for student activities and assembly periods. The schedule that emerges from the planning and implementation phase represents a school's best effort to manage time in an organized, sensible, and feasible fashion.

To ensure that classroom space is optimally used, the principal should use a floor plan of the building which would show for each available room the number of student stations and the type of equipment housed in the room. The desired optimum use of classrooms during each period should approximate 80 percent (Wood, Nicholson, & Findley, 1979).

TYPES OF SCHEDULES

School administrators have a choice of schedules dependent upon what they deem the best possible way to bring together students, teachers, and the curricular program. If the purpose is to schedule students as a group because the academic program is weighted toward required courses with few electives, the *block method* can be employed. Students required to take the same subjects would be scheduled as a group staying together during the day. On the other hand, if a school's philosophy is to permit student selectivity in the choice of courses and the times they can take these courses, a principal could employ the *individualized or mosaic method*. The name *mosaic* stems from the practice of building a mosaic pattern by assembling small stones together. Applied to course construction, this concept means students first register for courses and then the schedule is built that fits all the requirements (Hughes & Ubben, 1980). This method has received wide acceptance in middle and secondary schools.

The increased emphasis placed on individualization of instruction in the late 1960s and early 1970s resulted in the *modular approach* to scheduling. The rationale was that greater variability could be obtained in partitioning the hours of the school day. The result was modules of varying lengths of time to accommodate the requests for labs, large group lectures, small group seminars, work-study programs, studio work, and so on. The modular approach does not seem to be in vogue today largely due to the public's demand for strengthened graduation requirements. Also, difficulties were encountered in handling the blocks of free time in the student's schedule.

Which type of schedule administrators choose for their school is basically dictated by the degree of flexibility desired to rotate the schedule daily and in offering classes that vary in size and frequency of meeting. Once this decision has been made, consistent with meeting student and faculty needs and the defined time/space requirements, the implementation phase of the scheduling process can occur.

The Implementation Phase. The implementation phase includes the preregistering of students, the building of the master schedule, and the actual scheduling of students. Scheduling options are the arena (student self-scheduling) approach, use of the computer, or a combination of these approaches.

PREREGISTRATION

The flow chart in Figure 5.2 illustrates how one school handles the registration process. The first step is that of preregistration, which takes place in the spring. The major task in preregistration is to acquaint students and parents with the curriculum program of the school preparatory to each student selecting courses for the new school year. For students this is typically done in an orientation session under the direction of the counseling staff. Here students would be given a booklet containing

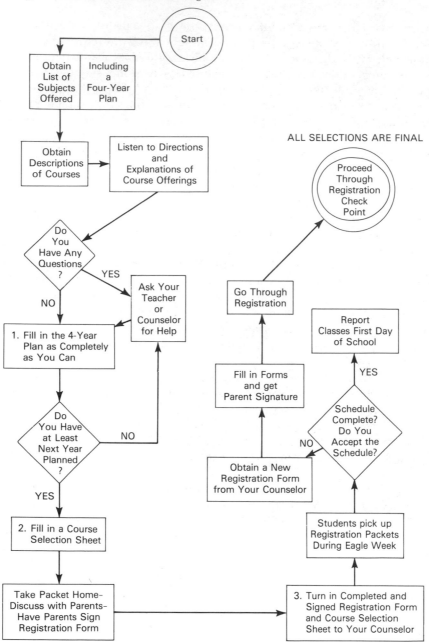

FIGURE 5.2 The Registration Process at Lindberg High School   From Barker, B. H., Penningroth, G., & Rogers, G. F. (1980). Arena vs. computer scheduling. *NASSP Bulletin, 64(434),* 115.

descriptions of all course offerings and graduation requirements. Opportunity would be given to ask questions prior to filling out a tentative planning work sheet. Once the students felt confident that they were ready to declare their course selection, they would fill out a registration form. The last step in preregistration would be for students to obtain parental approval of their course selection as indicated by a signature.

BUILDING THE MASTER SCHEDULE

Once the students' preregistration materials have been received, the task of the school is to determine as accurately as possible the number of students requesting each course in order to determine how many class sections, teachers, and rooms are needed. This is done by tallying the student choices. To enable administrators to assess which classes might cause potential conflict when student programs are placed in the master schedule, a conflict matrix is prepared. By carefully examining the class tallies and conflict matrix, a skilled and experienced administrator can design the best workable master schedule within the constraints imposed on the school. The greatest difficulties encountered in building the master schedule are related to (1) classes that are offered only once or twice during the school day, (2) too many classes that are offered only once during the school day (commonly called "single section classes"), (3) inability to limit the curriculum offering to existing resources, and (4) unrealistic student requests for classes. The key to a successful master schedule is that it should "provide the greatest degree of flexibility while producing the least amount of scheduling conflict" (Stronge & Turner, 1983, p. 56).

SCHEDULING THE STUDENTS

Following the development of the master schedule, students would be individually scheduled. At this point undetected conflicts will emerge and classes identified that are either seriously overloaded or relatively underenrolled. This will necessitate revising the master schedule. Once consensus exists among school personnel that the schedule is as fine-tuned as possible, student schedules and teacher class rolls can be prepared which will be ready for the opening day of school.

Though schools have a choice in scheduling students either manually or by computer, the latter method seems to provide benefits that outweigh the former. Krahn and Hughes (1976) raised the following research questions in their 1974 study to assess computer benefits:

1. Would a computer be able to better satisfy student course requests?
2. Would the computer make it possible to schedule more complex teacher course design requests?

3. Could better balance of students in courses of multiple sections and overall balance of students throughout the schedule cycle be achieved?
4. Could better use be made of rooms and facilities?
5. Will the computer be so limited that it is unable to cope with unique situations?
6. Is a computer necessary for scheduling programs involving team teaching, large and small group instruction, and student independent study?
7. How do factors such as student enrollment, grade levels, number of terms, modular versus traditional, and computer-generated schedule versus manual construction affect the results of computer scheduling? (pp. 106–107).

The study was conducted in 124 of 142 Wisconsin secondary schools that were identified as using computers for scheduling. The findings revealed that the majority of the schools were able to: reduce the time spent by professionals and nonprofessionals in scheduling, enroll students in additional courses without encountering undue course conflicts, improve student balance in courses of multiple sections, obtain better room and facility utilization, enhance the scheduling of special groups like team teaching and large and small group instruction, and meet teacher-re-quested special course designs. Over one-fourth (26.0%) of the schools reported the computer was not helpful in resolving such problems as scheduling certain students, like those having discipline problems, together as a group in all classes and having many classes on one day alternate with few classes on the next. Overall, 116 (93.5%) of the 124 responding schools felt the costs of computer scheduling were justified in terms of the benefits.

The computers used for scheduling in the 1974 survey were mini and mainframe computers. Increasingly in the 1980s, microcomputers are employed to perform administrative applications at the school level. They have been touted as being able to reduce the cost and time school officials spend in scheduling. Stronge and Turner (1983) present documentation to support this claim. For a "typical" school they have computed both time and cost estimates to schedule students manually compared to using a microcomputer. Defined, this school is a comprehensive grades 9–12 high school having an enrollment of 500 students. The time figures (Table 5.1) support computer-assisted scheduling. This method requires only 54 per-cent of the time needed by the manual method if no changes are required in the original master schedule. The percentage, however, declines to 51 percent, or a savings of 115.5 actual working hours, if changes must be made in the master schedule.

Computer-assisted scheduling also emerged as the winner when com-paring costs (Table 5.2) incurred in scheduling. Personnel costs were determined using annual salaries, estimated as follows: principal—$30,000; counselor—$20,000; clerical assistant—$10,000. Six hours constituted the working day. Although software and hardware would have to be acquired by the "typical" school to do computer-assisted scheduling, these start-up

TABLE 5.1 Comparison of Time Requirements for Completion of Traditional and Computer-assisted Scheduling*

SCHEDULING ACTIVITY	TRADITIONAL SCHEDULING	COMPUTER-ASSISTED SCHEDULING
Preparation of preregistration material	15 hours	15 hours
Preregistration orientation	4 hours	4 hours
Student/parent conferences	50 hours	50 hours
Collect and collate student choices	10 hours	10 hours
Type preregistration data	0 hours	10 hours
Tally student choices	15 hours	¼ hour
Build a conflict matrix	10 hours	5 hours
Type/print conflict matrix	4 hours	½ hour
Decide on master schedule	10 hours	10 hours
Enter master schedule data	0 hours	1 hour
Type/print the master schedule	4 hours	¼ hour
Handwrite or print student schedules	50 hours	5 hours
Make changes in master schedule	4 hours	4 hours
Rewrite/reprint student schedules	25 hours	5 hours
Type student schedules	15 hours	0 hours
Type/print class rolls	20 hours	½ hour
Total Working Hours:	236	120.5

*From Stronge, J. H., & Turner, J. H. (1983). Computer scheduling: Is it worth the effort? *Electronics Education*, 3(1):57.

TABLE 5.2 Comparison of Cost Requirements for Completion of Traditional and Computer-assisted Scheduling*

COST FACTORS	TRADITIONAL SCHEDULING	COMPUTER-ASSISTED SCHEDULING
Supplies (paper, printing, etc.)	$ 75	$ 75
Principal's salary	$ 250	$ 250
Guidance counselor's salary	$2179	$1208
Clerical assistant's salary	$ 558	$ 215
Annual costs	$3062	$1912
Start-up costs for software		$ 500
Start-up costs for equipment (48K micro, 2 disk drives, monitor, dotmatrix printer)		$2200

*From Stronge, J. H., & Turner, J. H. (1983). Computer scheduling: Is it worth the effort? *Electronics Education,* 3(1):57.

costs could be recouped within two years. Over a five-year period, as based on the estimated figures, the comprehensive high school would realize an approximate savings of $6250.

Computer scheduling involves use of a partial or complete software package. The partial package uses a computer algorithm to load students in classes on a schedule developed manually by school officials. The complete package uses the computer to develop the master schedule as well as to load students into course sections. The kinds of data entered into the computer for the partial package are student course requirements, expected course offerings, expected master schedule, and alternate course offerings. When a completed package is employed, additional data on the total resources of the school, such as rooms, staffing, and so on, are entered as a prerequisite to developing the master schedule.

In the beginning phase of computer scheduling, such outputs as an alphabetized listing of students by grade, the class tally, and the conflict matrix are generated. The alphabetized list serves to confirm that no student course requests were omitted from the run. The class tally informs the administrator how many students request particular classes, which can be broken down by gender, grade level, and individual name. The conflict matrix is used to resolve potential conflicts when students' programs are entered into the master schedule. A major advantage of computer loading is the ability to run simulations of the master schedule to determine its workability. If the schedule needs modification, the administrator can make adjustments and load the schedule again and again until the optimum plan has been achieved. In the final phase of computer scheduling, various reports are produced such as individual student schedules; rosters of all students scheduled into each class; the number of students scheduled by period, by day, by semester; and lists of all teacher/staff assignments.

Criticisms have been levied against computer scheduling to the effect that it dehumanizes the process (Bennett, 1981) and deprives students of the opportunity to select which classes, teachers, and periods they would like (Wall, 1979; Wall, 1976; Leussler, 1976). This gave rise to the student self-scheduling movement of the 1970s. The process entailed providing students with a master schedule that listed the classes offered by period. Students would then proceed to an arena or open area (similar to that employed on some college campuses) to build their schedules. In the process of selecting their classes by period and teacher they would become aware of any conflicts. Though they would have to make alternate choices, the students would be involved totally in this decision. Wall (1979) contends this process is course selection in contrast to class scheduling. In the former, students decide what courses they want, being actively involved with the school staff to resolve any head-on conflicts. In this way their chances of obtaining a custom-tailored schedule would be enhanced. Class scheduling, by comparison, involves the school staff taking students' course selections and developing them into class schedules using the computer. When a student schedule is rejected due to conflicts, the adminstrator or counselor, rather than the student, assumes major responsibility for resolving the conflict. However, in many cases the administration works with the student and/or parents in a cooperative effort to resolve the conflict.

The proponents of self-scheduling have implied their system (1) reduces the number of class changes after the start of school since more students would receive their first choices, and (2) improves student attendance and classroom behavior because individuals have selected their teachers. These claims have been contested with the charge that self-scheduling sets up an environment that allows a high percentage of students to drop classes they really want in order to enroll in classes in which they are not too interested simply to be in the same classes with their friends. (Tilwick, 1975; Kelly, 1979).

To resolve these limitations, yet allow for direct student involvement in conflict resolution, the strengths of student self-scheduling (arena style) have been combined with the benefits of computer-assisted scheduling (Bennett 1981). The procedure (Figure 5.2) brings students to the school one week prior to opening day. Here they have opportunity to accept or reject their schedule, which has been prepared previously. If the computerized schdule is rejected, students have the opportunity, using arena scheduling, to rework their programs. Counselors and teachers are available to assist them in this task. Information from the arena scheduling is then fed into the computer system to update the student schedules. Students, as a consequence, are involved in making any required final class choices. This process, it is felt, ensures a better-balanced master schedule and realizes the goal of reducing class change requests. This accomplishment enables the first day of class to be for instruction and not for schedule changes.

Which type of scheduling should school administrators implement—computer-assisted scheduling? Student self (arena) scheduling? Or computer scheduling combined with arena scheduling? The choice, it seems, should address the issue of humanizing the process without forfeiting the benefits derived from utilizing computer capability.

GRADE REPORTING

Grade reporting was one of the first computer applications to be introduced successfully into the schools. Virtually every school district that has a data-processing program uses it for this purpose. Its popularity has continued with the adoption of microcomputers in schools to facilitate managing the educational program. Reasons for the success of computerized grade reporting are: It reduces personnel costs to operate and maintain a manual system; accuracy of recorded information is improved; it can speed up the generation of report cards for school personnel, students, and parents; and the auxiliary reports produced serve to assist the school administration and guidance and counseling department to work with students having special needs.

A computer grade reporting system requires the development of student report forms, the compilation of student and teacher information that is to be recorded on the form, the determination of the grading scale, and the types of auxiliary reports that will be produced. Specifically, the following characteristics should be examined when grading software is either developed or evaluated:

1. The types of marks to be given, for example A, B, C, D, E or 1, 2, 3, 4, 5, etc.
2. The option within the program to award "+" or "−" marks and to have them figured in or out of the grade point average (GPA).
3. The program's system of GPA calculation. Are weights for P=Pass, S=Satisfactory, CR=Credit, etc. established that will be compatible with letter grade weights to permit class rankings, GPAs, and honor rolls to be generated?
4. The program's method of GPA calculation.
5. Cumulative GPA capabilities to reflect a student's grade history for the year.
6. The format used to generate the reporting form. Will the form produced be flexible permitting the grading practice of a school to be reflected? Is provision made to record teacher comments?
7. The program is integrated with the student scheduling program. If this capability exists, each student's schedule can be entered into the grade reporting system.
8. The production of mailing labels to facilitate the distribution of the grade report to each student's home.
9. The generation of gummed labels printed with the courses taken and the grades earned that can be affixed to the student's permanent record.

The real benefits of a computerized grade reporting system over a manual system are the reduction of manual errors and the production of a variety of reports for administrative and guidance and counseling purposes. Typical reports produced are: grade distribution summaries, honor rolls, rank-in-class summaries, failure lists, and eligibility lists. Further, once grade information is entered into the computer with other student data, it can facilitate research. For example, studies can be conducted to determine the relationship between student demographic variables and grades, attendance, test performance, and so on.

A perennial problem faced by school administrators is the retrieval of student transcript information requested by former students who may be seeking admission to college, applying for specialized training programs, or entertaining a career in the military. To satisfy these requests, school personnel, on occasion, have had to search frantically through student permanent record cards stored in dusty attics or basements. Recent efforts have been instituted (Chapter 3) to store records systematically for ready retrieval through such means as microfilming. Computerized grade reporting systems that store data on tape are amenable to this process. The procedure is one of preparing the tape with the essential print images. The tape can then be sent to a firm that specializes in this type of conversion. Administrators having or instituting a computerized grade reporting system should formulate guidelines on how they wish the records of former students to be stored for later retrieval.

ATTENDANCE ACCOUNTING

School attendance of students is a matter of concern to administrators, teachers, and counselors. State laws require attendance accounting, often stipulating that excused absences are only for specific "lawful" reasons. This has resulted in the establishment of elaborate attendance systems that have sought to monitor accurately the daily attendance of students. Absenteeism, in the opinion of many principals, is considered their "most perplexing student problem" (National Association of Secondary School Principals, 1975). Administrative procedures have been instituted to deal with nonattendees by suspending them and deducting points from their grades. Chronic absenteeism serves as an indicator to members of the administrative, teaching, and counseling staff that students are experiencing home, personal, and/or school problems.

An attendance accounting program instituted in a school should do more than just monitor attendance for reporting purposes. The information collected should also be used by administrators to meet the needs of students who have a disproportionate number of absences. Specific objectives a program should meet are to:

- Accurately obtain the daily attendance of students. At the secondary level, attendance is typically reported and recorded on an hourly or period-by-period basis.
- Systematically report attendance data to the district office and/or the state board of education.
- Encourage the regular attendance of students to help them progress academically.
- Reduce the clerical time required to check absences from school and classes.
- Place responsibility for attendance where it belongs: on the student.
- Communicate absences to the homes of the absentees.
- Supply attendance data to school administrators, guidance counselors, teachers, and pupil personnel specialists.

- Provide raw data that can be used by school personnel to analyze attendance patterns and the effect attendance procedures have on school organization and the instructional program.
- Enable attendance data to be entered on the grade reporting form.

As compared with a manual attendance program, a computerized version seems better able to meet the above objectives. Most attendance accounting software (Chapter 10) provides the capability to record absences, reasons for absences, period or hour of absence, disposition on the absence (excused or unexcused, etc.), entry and exit dates from school, type of entrance and/or exit, form letters to be sent to the home, summary reports, and telephone call lists. A few programs enable the home to be called routinely, though the phone-calling sequence can be skipped when the student is absent for a known reason. Other provisions some programs offer are the reporting to teachers of students administratively excused from classes and those having medical appointments. Care should be exercised in the use of the automatic phoning feature since it has invoked the horrors of Orwell's *1984* depiction of "big brother" watching over people. Caution should be exercised by administrators not to alienate their patrons.

Entry of attendance data (Figure 5.3) into the computer is typically done with a card reader. Using a form similar to a standardized test answer sheet, teachers would make a heavy black mark in the circles that relate to the period each student is absent. An optical scanner then reads the pencil marks on the absentee forms submitted. By this process student attendance is kept current and school staff are provided absence summary sheets.

The computerized attendance program may be part of a student information system (SIS), a district-administered data-processing program, or a microcomputer software program adopted for use in a specific school. An advantage of the former approaches is their ability to summarize the attendance data submitted over each school's terminal for submission to district administrators and to accounting officials at state board of education offices.

A harbinger of things to come in attendance accounting is an innovation recently introduced into New York City high schools (High Schools Find Use of Electronic Cards by Students Boost Security Attendance, 1984). It involves the use of plastic credit-card ID's by students to get into school and have their attendance recorded by computer. The procedure requires all students entering the school building to insert their card in an attendance terminal to record their being present for the day. The terminals can be programmed to signal when certain cards are inserted. Students having such cards must go to another terminal where their card activates a display that may say they are wanted by the dean or that they can pick up a bus pass or need an immunization record. The security

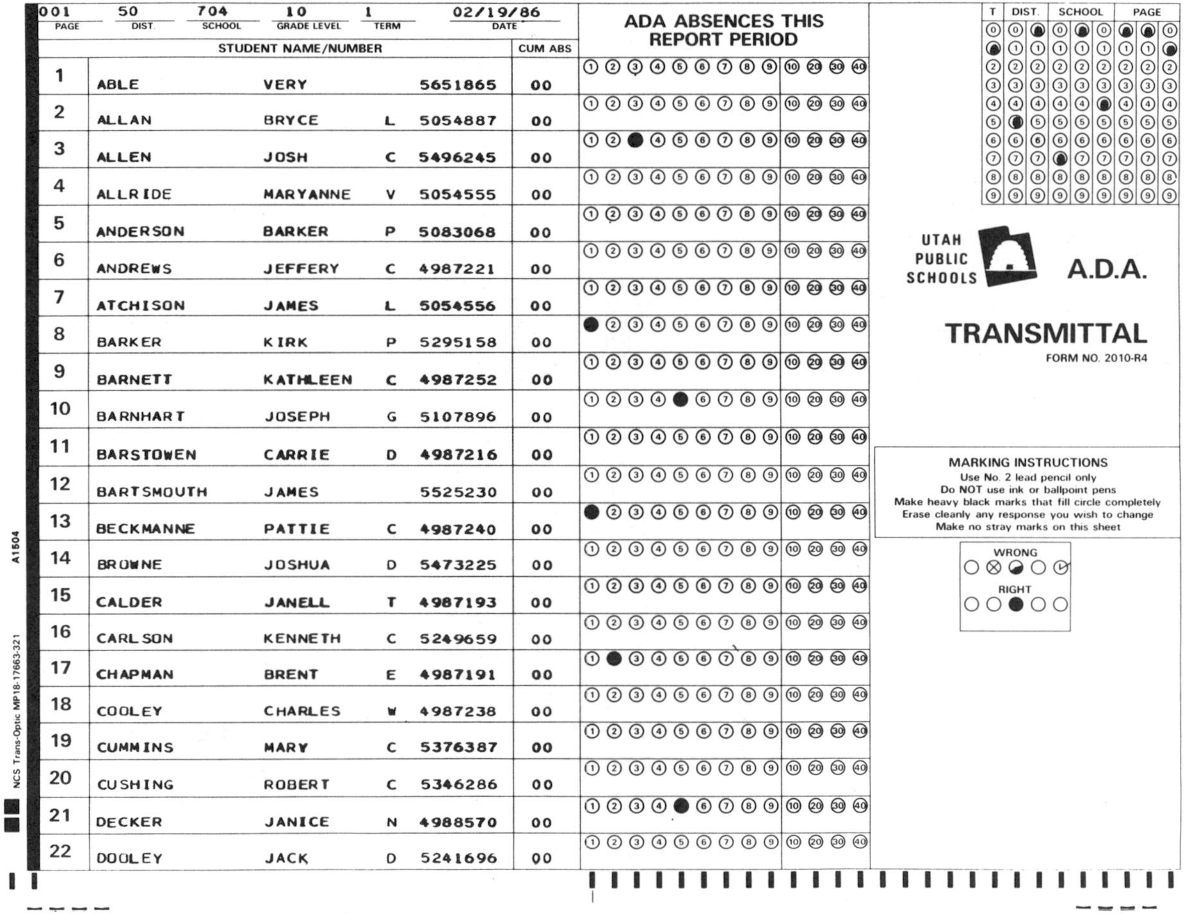

PAGE	DIST.	SCHOOL	GRADE LEVEL	TERM	DATE
001	50	704	10	1	02/19/86

ADA ABSENCES THIS REPORT PERIOD

	STUDENT NAME/NUMBER				CUM ABS
1	ABLE	VERY		5651865	00
2	ALLAN	BRYCE	L	5054887	00
3	ALLEN	JOSH	C	5496245	00
4	ALLRIDE	MARYANNE	V	5054555	00
5	ANDERSON	BARKER	P	5083068	00
6	ANDREWS	JEFFERY	C	4987221	00
7	ATCHISON	JAMES	L	5054556	00
8	BARKER	KIRK	P	5295158	00
9	BARNETT	KATHLEEN	C	4987252	00
10	BARNHART	JOSEPH	G	5107896	00
11	BARSTOWEN	CARRIE	D	4987216	00
12	BARTSMOUTH	JAMES		5525230	00
13	BECKMANNE	PATTIE	C	4987240	00
14	BROWNE	JOSHUA	D	5473225	00
15	CALDER	JANELL	T	4987193	00
16	CARLSON	KENNETH	C	5249659	00
17	CHAPMAN	BRENT	E	4987191	00
18	COOLEY	CHARLES	W	4987238	00
19	CUMMINS	MARY	C	5376387	00
20	CUSHING	ROBERT	C	5346286	00
21	DECKER	JANICE	N	4988570	00
22	DOOLEY	JACK	D	5241696	00

FIGURE 5.3 An Optical Scan Student Attendance Reporting Form *Courtesy of Utah State Office of Education, Salt Lake City, Utah.*

guard stationed at the terminal may be alerted if a student has been suspended or if the card has been reported lost.

Attendance has risen in the schools where this system has been put into operation; this change appears to be due to more accurate reporting rather than fewer absences. The cost of the system seems high, about $70,000 per school, but school officials justify it as a one-shot effort that has served to obtain more state aid and to enable the schools to be run more safely. Though the computer hardware vendor hopes the idea catches on nationwide and abroad, school administrators need to question whether the system is cost effective and would be accepted by their communities. Computerization of attendance accounting has its place, but the question to be answered is how far it should go in regulating the lives of students.

TEST SCORING AND REPORTING

An indicator of how well the educational program of a school is fulfilling its goals is the academic performance of the enrolled students as measured by paper and pencil tests. Two types of tests have been administered by schools—standardized tests and competency tests (see Figure 5.4). Standardized tests are "the most visible and universally used tests in the United States" (Porter, 1983). Every American school system today has a standardized achievement testing program in which an average of five test administrations occur each year. (Sproull & Zubrow, 1981). As an example, one district administers these tests yearly in grades 1–6, 9, and 11.

Standardized achievement tests meet the criteria of having established procedures for both administering and scoring the test. The majority of tests administered are norm-referenced. This means the scores students obtain in a given school are compared to those obtained by similar age and/or grade level students who comprise the standardized norm group. Comparisons can also be made to local or district norms. Examples of norm-referenced scores are percentiles, stanines, and grade equivalents. Using these scores, school administrators are able to determine how well their students are achieving compared to other students in the nation. For concerned school board members, parents, legislators, and community residents, the released scores help answer the question, "How are our schools doing?" It permits them to assess what students know and can do in a subject matter area like reading or natural science. Using the national norms, conclusions can be drawn as to whether the local students are performing at, above, or below the level of achievement of the typical American student of comparable age or grade level.

Competency tests, in contrast to standardized norm-referenced achievement tests, are administered by school districts to assess whether high school seniors have met the minimum competencies defined as necessary to graduate. The minimum competency testing movement began in the 1970s

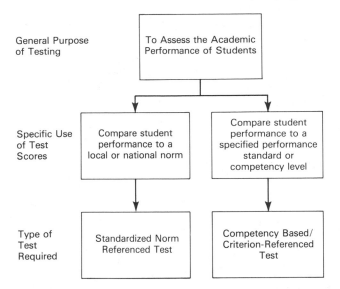

General Purpose of Testing — To Assess the Academic Performance of Students

Specific Use of Test Scores — Compare student performance to a local or national norm / Compare student performance to a specified performance standard or competency level

Type of Test Required — Standardized Norm Referenced Test / Competency Based/ Criterion-Referenced Test

FIGURE 5.4   The Relationship Between Test Purpose, Use, and Type of Tests

when the public began to question the quality of education in the public schools. Their major concern was over high school graduates who did not possess the skills deemed necessary to function in society. This gave rise to the passage of legislation or state board of education adopted rulings which mandated some type of minimum competency testing. The tests to be administered generally emphasized the basics, whereby students intending to graduate could demonstrate they had met or exceeded the minimum performance standards set in reading, writing, and arithmetic. These minimum standards are determined at the local or state level. Students failing to meet the minimum performance standards were to receive remedial work. In the event a student repeatedly failed the test, a certificate of attendance or special diploma might be given in lieu of the regular high school diploma.

Minimum competency testing has raised some serious concerns that district administrators have had to deal with. The following questions (adapted from Cook, 1982) are illustrative:

1. Will minimum competencies be tested?
2. What competencies will be tested?
3. How should they be measured?
4. When should they be measured?
5. How many minimums should be established? Will the special-needs student be recognized? Should there be a single standard for all? A differentiated standard for different departments or areas within a school? Negotiated standards for each student?
6. How high should the minimum be?

7. Where does the district place the minimum?
8. Are the competency tests for the schools or for the students? Should it be left to the student only to worry about meeting minimums?
9. What should be done with students who repeatedly fail? Lower standards? Redesign programs? Remediate? Stop student advancement? Refuse diplomas?

Standardized norm-referenced achievement tests and competency-based tests are readily available from test publishers. In the latter case, some state educational agencies and local school districts have opted to develop their own tests. The practice also exists among some school districts of using standardized achievement tests to assess minimum competencies of students in the basics.

With the preponderance of academic performance tests administered in the schools of the nation, heavy reliance has been placed on the computer to provide scoring and analysis services. For norm-reference standardized tests, the computer can provide summary results of student performance by class, building, and district. Item analyses, which show the number and/or percent of students that answer each item correctly, can also be produced. Other computer-related services that may be obtained are local versus national norm comparisons and narrative reports that summarize the score profiles of individual tests. Similar kinds of computer reporting are available for competency-based tests except the reporting of normative data. Instead, recipients receive a listing of all students who did or did not meet the minimum performance standard.

A decision school administrators have to make regarding their district testing program is who will do the scoring and analysis. Four options exist: using the services of test publishing companies, contracting with a regional cooperative computer center that operates independently of test publishers, utilizing the services of an educational service district (O'Driscoll, 1980), or setting up a district-administered program. Large school districts have been more apt to exercise the latter option. An advantage favoring the use of test publishers is that they have an established program that is constantly being upgraded. Further, when revisions of their tests occur, the costs of revising the software are absorbed by the companies.

Reasons school districts decide to operate independently of test publishers are (1) they wish to generate reports that are better tailored to their needs; (2) the time it takes publishers to score and return the test results is unacceptable; (3) preprinted answer sheets can be obtained to eliminate the cost of buying sheets from publishers; and (4) local autonomy and control over the process is desired. It should be understood that the development of independent scoring services is costly. Not only must the scoring and analysis software be developed, but additional expenditure is incurred in revising the software to accommodate revisions of a test. If the optical-scan score sheets of the publisher are used, royalties must be paid.

School districts that have established centralized standardized test scoring and analysis services generally make them available to their schools to handle competency-based and/or teacher-made tests. Computer-assisted testing software for microcomputers, though, is now available to perform this task at the school level. Regardless of what type of testing services school districts contract or develop, administrators should recognize the benefits derived from computerization. Computer-produced reports provide a wealth of information that could not be produced manually. When properly used, this information can help improve the instructional/curriculum program and enable students, teachers, parents, school board members, and counselors to assess the degree to which the defined eductional goals and objectives of the school and district are being achieved.

A matter of critical concern for administrators is how best to report standardized test scores to avoid misinterpretation and misunderstanding. Dreher and Singer (1984), in a series of studies with superintendents, principals, school board members, teachers, and parents, found that instead of presenting the usual numerical scores (grade equivalents, percentiles, stanines), all these groups preferred reports that included both self- and norm comparisons and samples of what a student can successfully do. The process of self-comparison involves readministering, for example, a fifth grade test in the sixth grade and interpreting it according to the norms at the time the student originally took the test. When repeated testings of this nature occur, recipients of the test results are better able to determine whether students have mastered information they did not grasp at the time of the first administration. A sample of what a student can do successfully would be the reporting of the most difficult item a student passed. In this way interested observers can obtain a much clearer picture of how well the student performed compared to using a numerical score by itself.

An effective way to communicate the results of a district standardized achievement program is to use charts and graphs. Doing so helps recipients of the information to grasp better the implications of the data. Schools and districts having the right microcomputer capability are able to prepare complex multicolored charts by using a graphics program. Graphics programs may be task-specific or part of an integrated package. When selecting a program, consideration should be given to the following concerns (adapted from Williams & LeCesne, 1985):

- Will the program be able to produce pie charts, line graphs, and bar charts?
- Can three sets of data be plotted on the same graph, which can then be saved for later use?
- Can value on the different axes be set automatically as well as manually?
- Can reference points of one's own choosing be labeled on the axes or does the program limit the labeling to the highest and lowest points only?
- Can a variety of lines (dots, dashes, etc.) and shadows be plotted for a graph?

Hardware needed for a computer color graphics system are a microcomputer with a color monitor, a color printer adapter card, a graphics board to produce a high-resolution image on the monitor, and a graphics printer or plotter. Plotters draw continuous lines, compared to the individual characters that are typed by a printer. Plotters permit the creation of more complex shapes. They are available as single- or multi-pen models. Multiple-pen devices are characterized by their ability to change colors automatically. Information on inexpensive plotters and task-specific packages that meet the software selection criteria listed above is provided by Williams and LeCesne (1985).

The Cincinnati Public School District, which comprises eighty-five schools serving 50,000 students, has used a graphics program like VisiTrend or VisiPlot to good advantage. Using microcomputers, they turn districtwide data compiled in the mainframe into customized profiles that highlight for each school census data; achievement test performance; and parental, student, and teacher attitude responses toward schooling. The standardized test data profiles reflect student achievement in grades 3, 6, and 9, the critical transition grades. By examining this profile, a building principal is able to determine, over a five-year period, what percentage of students score above the national norm and the district norm. In this way problem areas that need attention can be spotted. The district director of curriculum and instruction has indicated that the school profiles help them to understand their schools better, predict what may happen to them, and assess what they can do about it (Up front, 1983).

THE STUDENT INFORMATION SYSTEM

Computer information systems (Chapter 1) have been developed to assist school administrators manage the educational program of a school and district. Three types exist: data-processing systems, management information systems, and decision support systems. Data-processing systems are the key to a comprehensive computer information system. Student and financial information-processing systems, for example, provide operational data that are used in a management information system (MIS) and a decision support system (DSS). In the MIS exception or discrepancy conditions (the difference between desired and actual practices) are identified that may require administrative attention or corrective action. Reported information on enrollment and financial trends are used in the DSS to project their impact upon the future status of the district. The purposes, applications, and approaches used to design and implement a student information system are presented in this chapter.

Purpose and Applications

An implemented student information system allows the creation of an integrated data base on students that can be updated and maintained in a coherent, effective, and efficient manner. Stored and analyzed information can be retrieved using the terminal screen or in printed form. The potential also exists to create special reports such as those required by state agencies requesting student attendance data. The benefit of an SIS is that it can offer users accurate, timely, and economical management of student data faster and with better service than can be produced manually. The record-keeping responsibility of schools and districts, as a consequence, is enhanced and improved.

The application potential of an SIS is unlimited, but the integrated data base typically includes demographic information, attendance accounting, grade reporting, scheduling, test services, health information, individual education plans (IEPs), academic progress, and transcripts. Figure 5.5 depicts a representative student information system showing the input sources for the respective applications and the types of outputs that can be generated.

Computerized Student Information System Approaches

Three ways in which a student information system may be designed and used are: computer located in the school building, shared use of a large computer, and use of a commercial service bureau (Delf, 1982). Though interest has been expressed in using the microcomputer housed in the school to implement an SIS, software programs currently available are limited. The integrated data base packages that exist are restricted to two or three applications featuring a combination of scheduling, attendance, and/or grade reporting. For this reason the use of a district or state agency computer that is shared by users or the contracting of services from a commercial bureau are the approaches most commonly found.

Figure 5.6 depicts the use of a shared central computer. A telecommunications link permits microcomputers or minicomputers housed in separate schools to have access to the central computer. This permits distributed processing whereby data may be transferred (uploaded) to the central mainframe for processing and the results returned (downloaded) to the in-school computers.

At this level data may still be manipulated and/or formatted to local specifications. The uploading may be done by batch or on-line interactive. With the batch system, users fill out entry data forms which are then sent to the central computer. In contrast, the on-line interactive method permits schools to update files immediately and have direct access to the student

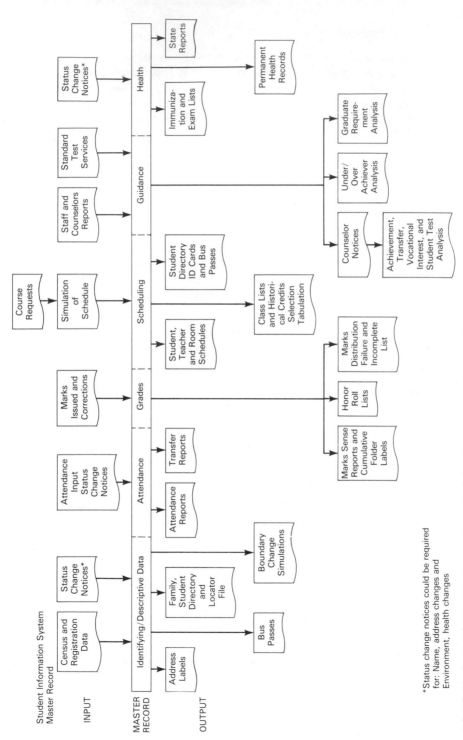

FIGURE 5.5 Student Information Subsystem Input/Output *From Candoli, I. C., Hack W. G., Ray, J. R. & Stollar, D. H. (1978). School Business Administration Second Edition. Boston, MA: Allyn & Bacon, p. 98.*

*Status change notices could be required for: Name, address changes and Environment, health changes

120

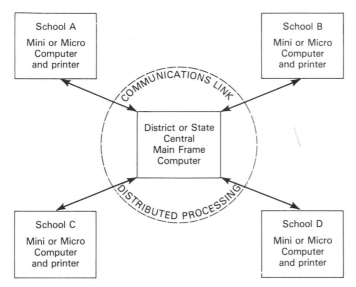

FIGURE 5.6   The Deployment Structure of a State Educational Agency or Large District-shared Student Information System

data base at any time. Hard copies of output reports may be obtained if a printer is attached to the local terminals. In the beginning stages of development the download capability will be limited until local users have time to establish all the subfiles that are part of the overall SIS. Initial entry to a functioning SIS may be obtained using the student's school and district code numbers as well as the student's last name. The use of the surname accesses a list of enrolled students' full names and identification numbers. The retrieval of any information about a given student may be accomplished using this ID number.

Commercial service bureaus offer many of the common integrated applications found in a state- or district-shared student information system. Being in a competitive market, some vendors have delimited their applications to a primary specialty such as a financial information system. This raises the issue of whether these vendors would have the program and interest to meet the local SIS needs of a school or district. Additional concerns (Delf, 1982) school adminstrators should address before contracting with a bureau for an SIS are: (1) What is the total cost of the service? (2) Is it a complete student information system? (3) How good is customer support? (4) How flexible is the system? (5) Is the output well organized? (6) Is the service available on-line? (7) How much development is being done on the system to keep it up-to-date? (8) What is the turnaround time?

Examples of Student Information Systems

An example of a district-operated SIS is that developed by the Management Information Division of the Los Angeles Unified School District (Freeman, 1982). The system is menu driven and runs on a series of minicomputers housed in the district's 124 secondary schools. Each minicomputer may operate as a stand-alone but is also linked to the central office's mainframe. The goals of the system are to provide the schools with (1) an attendance accounting capability to generate daily absence lists, absence mailers, and all mandatory attendance reports; (2) the ability to assign students to classes in an arena environment, produce student and teacher schedules, and facilitate the process of changing schedules; (3) reports of student performance for sending to parents at selected times of the school year; (4) cumulative records and updates; (5) ready retrieval of course marks for individual students; and (6) reports and information needed on students and the academic program. The modular programs have been written in COBOL, which make them transferable to districts using different makes of computers.

The Utah Student Information System is state operated, becoming operational in 1983. Thirty-six (90% of Utah's forty school districts) participate in the system. Linked to the mainframe computer at the Utah State Office of Education are over 500 microcomputers. Though school districts using the system pay user fees, they benefit from state matching funds on a two-to-one basis. As more users sign up, operating costs decrease. Use of the SIS is at the secondary level, with elementary applications planned. Forty-three screens have been designed that cover most school-related

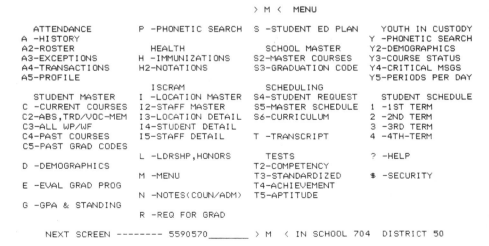

```
                              > M <  MENU

     ATTENDANCE         P -PHONETIC SEARCH  S -STUDENT ED PLAN     YOUTH IN CUSTODY
A -HISTORY                                                    Y -PHONETIC SEARCH
A2-ROSTER                  HEALTH             SCHOOL MASTER   Y2-DEMOGRAPHICS
A3-EXCEPTIONS          H -IMMUNIZATIONS     S2-MASTER COURSES Y3-COURSE STATUS
A4-TRANSACTIONS        H2-NOTATIONS         S3-GRADUATION CODE Y4-CRITICAL MSGS
A5-PROFILE                                                    Y5-PERIODS PER DAY
                          ISCRAM               SCHEDULING
    STUDENT MASTER      I -LOCATION MASTER  S4-STUDENT REQUEST    STUDENT SCHEDULE
C -CURRENT COURSES     I2-STAFF MASTER     S5-MASTER SCHEDULE  1 -1ST TERM
C2-ABS,TRD/VOC-MEM     I3-LOCATION DETAIL  S6-CURRICULUM       2 -2ND TERM
C3-ALL WP/WF           I4-STUDENT DETAIL                       3 -3RD TERM
C4-PAST COURSES        I5-STAFF DETAIL     T -TRANSCRIPT       4 -4TH-TERM
C5-PAST GRAD CODES
                       L -LDRSHP,HONORS       TESTS            ? -HELP
D -DEMOGRAPHICS                             T2-COMPETENCY
                       M -MENU              T3-STANDARDIZED    $ -SECURITY
E -EVAL GRAD PROG                           T4-ACHIEVEMENT
                       N -NOTES(COUN/ADM)   T5-APTITUDE
G -GPA & STANDING
                       R -REQ FOR GRAD

    NEXT SCREEN -------- 5590570_____  > M < IN SCHOOL 704  DISTRICT 50
```

FIGURE 5.7 Screens Comprising the Utah Student Information System *From Information and Instructional Services (1984). SIS Student Information System.* Salt Lake City, UT: Utah State Office of Education.

information, with thirty already in production (Figure 5.7) The major subsystems containing these screens (Cummins, 1984) are:

- *Demographic*. Such information as birth date, gender, ethnic background, previous schools attended, parents or guardians, bus route stop, fluency in a second language, and cumulative credits are profiled for each student.
- *Grade Reporting* (GR). Included in this subsystem are course grades of students, the producing of report cards, honor roll and failure lists, class rolls, grade distribution summaries, cumulative grades, and so on.
- *Student Scheduling System* (SSS). This subsystem produces course tallies, conflict matrices, master schedules, and class schedules.
- *Attendance Accounting Management* (AAM). Attendance of all students showing days enrolled, days present, and days absent are computed by term and by year. From this data statistics on gradewide, schoolwide, and district-wide attendance are produced.
- *Self-Contained and Resource Management (SCRAM) System.* Records are produced by SCRAM that monitor the academic progress of special education students.
- *Competency-Based Testing* (COMBAT). Screens display student results on competency-based (classroom and standardized) tests, standardized achievement and general aptitude tests that are prepared by the test scoring system (TSS).
- *Guidance and Counseling*. Screens developed in this area report student education plans (SEP), career goals, leadership and honor positions, health immunizataions, graduation requirements, completed courses yet to take, and counseling notations. (pp. 411–416)

Figure 5.8 illustrates two integrated screens that report a senior's cumulative credits awarded and those yet pending to meet requirements for graduation in the defined areas.

A third example is the Student Data Base System used in the Oakland Intermediate School District of Pontiac, Michigan. The system, which maintains records for some 200,000 students, facilitates grade reporting, transcripts, period-by-period or half-day attendance, and interfaces to student scheduling. The student record also stores standardized test data that is scored locally; special education IEPs as well as objectives and achievement information; and vocational education data that is maintained for state education agency reporting. In addition, transportation scheduling is accomplished and route information is maintained in the student record (Grisdale, 1985).

A WORD OF CAUTION

In using computer technology to manage the educational program, the danger exists that too much trust may be placed in the results when making decisions. School administrators, consequently, should keep these

```
     JONES, JOHN P.              5590570 > D < DEMOGRAPHICS   HISTORY CONTROL
* CHANGE MODE *
LAST NAME: JONES            FIRST NAME: JOHN      INITIAL: P  BLOCK: ____ SIDE: _
ADDRESS: 7560 SOUTH 6300 WEST      CITY/STATE: SLC UT              ZIP: 84112
HOME PHONE:  531 7172 BIRTH DATE: 07 06 66   SEX: M BUS RTE: ___ PREV DIST: 98
BUS. PHONE: M221 0317 ENTRY DATE: 08 13 82  RACE: _ BUS STP: __  PREV SCHL: 998
BUS. PHONE: F221 2341 WTDRL DATE: __ __ __  GRADE: 12
EMER PHONE:  731 7116 MAINT DATE: 11 06 85  TCHR: ___              PL874: __
CUM HIST POTENTIAL CREDIT: 21.50  CUM HIST GPA: 3.313    FILE 1: _  TRACER: _
                                                        FILE 2: _  FILE 3: _

GUARDIAN LAST NAME: JONES           FIRST: WILLIAM   INITIAL: H RELATIONSHIP: P
                                                SECOND LANGUAGE/LEVEL: BB / 1

ORIGINAL ENROLLMENT: E1 DROPOUT: __ RETENTION: _
FIRST TERM--   DAYS BELONGING: 45  DAYS ABSENT: 02  LAST TRANSACTION: __
SECOND TERM-   DAYS BELONGING: 45  DAYS ABSENT: 02  LAST TRANSACTION: __
THIRD TERM--   DAYS BELONGING: 00  DAYS ABSENT: 00  LAST TRANSACTION: __
FOURTH TERM-   DAYS BELONGING: 00  DAYS ABSENT: 00  LAST TRANSACTION: __

S.E.P. CAREER GOAL: 14 1901
VOC. C/L/T CODE: _ COOP STD: _ CONT. INST: _   INST. SETTING: M  H: _ D: _ L: Y

     NEXT SCREEN -------------- 5590570 > D < IN SCHOOL 704  DISTRICT 50
```

FIGURE 5.8   The Utah SIS 'Requirements for Graduation" Screen   *From Information and Instructional Services (1984). SIS Student Information System.* Salt Lake City, UT: Utah State Office of Education.

points in mind (Adapted from Martin, 1981): First, while the ability of microcomputers to provide easy update and retrieval of information makes them especially suited to management, only certain portions of any management process can be assumed by the computer. Proper planning, programming, data collection, data input, and interpretation of results by human decision makers is still necessary and critical to the success of any computer application (Figure 5.9) Second, computer-generated results are not necessarily more accurate nor more significant than their manually generated counterparts. There is a tendency to give special consideration to computer printouts over handwritten or typed reports; however, neither one is inherently better. They both are the result of human planning, and are only as good as the logic and data with which they were produced.

FIGURE 5.9   The Danger of Misinterpreting Computer-generated Results   *Holbrook, B. (1984, August 18). On the fastrack. The Deseret News, p. C6.*

Finally, the microcomputer should not be considered a panacea for all administrative ills. It will not offset poor decision-making practices, nor replace weak administrative procedures. However, it can become a valuable and effective tool for the decision maker who understands his information needs and goals.

It should also be noted that a microcomputer alone may not meet the complete information-processing needs of a school. More sophisticated hardware and software and the personnel to run and maintain a more elaborate system may be required.

SUMMARY

Building principals are responsible for managing the educational program of their schools. Regarding students, this entails keeping track of their attendance, scheduling them into classes, reporting the grades they earn and the scores they obtain on district-administered competency and standardized tests. The computer, especially since the introduction of the microcomputer, has proven to be a valuable resource in performing these functions.

Compared to manual scheduling, computer-assisted scheduling has been found by many users to be more cost effective, with resultant savings in the amount of time invested by individuals in the process. Regardless of these benefits, criticisms have been levied against computer scheduling on the grounds that it dehumanizes the process and deprives students the freedom of making choices. To address these criticisms, the strengths of student self-scheduling (arena style) combined with computer-assisted scheduling has been advocated.

Computerized grade reporting has proven to be popular among school systems for reasons of reduced personnel costs, improved accuracy of reporting, and the speed at which report cards can be generated. Computerized attendance reporting, too, has proven to be a boon to school officials. Not only does it produce useful reports, but the use of automatic dialers has freed personnel from making home calls to parents about their students' absences.

Four options are available to school administrators regarding how district-administered tests will be scored and analyzed. They are contracting with test publishers, a regional cooperative computer center or educational service district, or they perform these functions independently. Regardless of the method chosen, computerized test scoring has the advantage of being able to produce a wealth of information that could not be produced manually.

The development of a student information system (SIS) is an approach some state and local educational agencies have implemented to integrate the various educational applications described above. Methods have included using integrated software on a school microcomputer; employing distributed processing, using a central mainframe or minicomputer and in-school computers; and the use of a commercial service bureau. Regardless of the approach adopted to manage the eduational program, school administrators should not relinquish responsibility for decision making to the results of a computerized system. The human variable is critical to proper planning, programming, and interpretation of the generated information.

6

MANAGING THE INSTRUCTIONAL PROGRAM

The purpose of the instructional program of a school district is to educate students. The program should reflect the values, beliefs, and desires of the school community as stated in the district/school goals and objectives. These goals/objectives are then translated into a curriculum having organized instructional units. Teachers, using lesson plans, give direction on how the curriculum is taught. Exposed to well-planned instruction, student learning should take place (Rebore, 1984).

Curriculum coordinators, building principals, and classroom teachers all have a vested interest in the development, implementation, and evaluation of the curriculum. When assessing the curriculum, three questions are fundamental: What should be taught? How should it be taught? and How will we know that learning has occurred? Question one pertains to the objectives that are established for each instructional unit. They reflect the ends or outcomes of the teaching-learning process. Question two raises the issue of what instructional methods, techniques, procedures, or activities should be implemented to facilitate the attainment of the defined instructional objectives. Question three entails the collection of quantitative and qualitative descriptions of student behavior to determine the degree to which the behavior specified in the instructional unit has been achieved. Management and evaluation procedures are central to both questions two and three respecting organization, data collection, and record-keeping activities. Management includes such tasks as deciding what instructional strategies and materials to use; keeping track of attendance; the storing, analyzing, and reporting of student records; and keeping class records. Evaluation is the process of providing feedback information to teachers, counselors, and administrators to enable judgments to be formed and decisions made regarding student progress and the success of the curricular programs.

Classroom evaluation embraces three types—summative, formative, and diagnostic evaluation. The teacher who is concerned with student outcome—what the child can do, demonstrate, or produce at the end of an instructional unit or reporting period—will engage in *summative* evaluation, also called *outcome* or *product* evaluation. The monitoring of student progress in an instructional unit or the assessment of the effectiveness of teaching activities designed to help students learn are examples of *formative* or *process* evaluation. *Diagnostic* evaluation has two functions, that of preassessing learning difficulties and identifying causes of learning deficiencies. All three types of evaluation are used by teachers in the teaching-learning process.

> *Summative* evaluation measures student outcomes.
> *Formative* evaluation assesses the effectiveness of teaching-learning activities.
> *Diagnostic* evaluation enables learning difficulties to be identified.

Computers have been used in the classroom to facilitate learning and to manage and evaluate the teaching-learning process through such means as computer-assisted instruction (CAI), computer-managed instruction (CMI), and computer-assisted testing (CAT). Computer-assisted instruction (CAI) is a vehicle to facilitate learning—to make it easier and more likely to occur. By having students interact directly with the computer, CAI serves both as a medium of instruction and an information delivery system. What occurs is the computer engaging students in instructional dialogue while delivering information to them. Computer-managed instruction (CMI) is a management and evaluation tool. The management function is served by monitoring what happens instructionally and by supplying support service in the form of materials appropriate to specific instructional objectives at specific stages of the student's progress. CMI, as an evaluation tool, involves testing, diagnosis and prescription, and performance monitoring. Computer-assisted testing (CAT) serves as a support tool for the instructional program by assisting the teacher in the planning, constructing, scoring, and interpreting of tests (Figure 11.2). Some of these features are included in comprehensive CMI programs that endorse a prescribed curriculum having specified goals and objectives. Software developed by vendors to reflect this emphasis are called curriculum management programs (Chapter 11). Figure 2.5 depicts how CAI, CMI, and CAT, as computer applications, support the instructional program.

The purpose of this chapter is to examine computer-managed instruction in terms of usage, concepts, functions, justification of a CMI system, implementation guidelines, strengths and limitations, and issues.

CMI USAGE

Computer-managed instruction, using mainframe computers, dates back to the early 1960s, with an increasing number of educators recognizing its potential in the mid-1970s. The introduction of the microcomputer enhanced this potential. Extensive usage, however, has yet to be realized. A nationwide survey, conducted by Educational Research Services, Inc. (1982), found that computers were used for computer-assisted instruction in 56.5% of the responding districts. In contrast, only 28.8% used the computer for computer-managed instruction. Special education teachers appear to use CMI programs more frequently than regular teachers, at least in one state. A 1985 survey among Utah's forty school districts found that twenty-six reported 76%-100% of their special education teachers had access to computers. All districts surveyed reported using the computer for instruction, with twenty-five of thirty-nine districts indicating the primary use was for instruction. Seven districts reported that instructional management was their primary use. In response to future use, emphasis was placed by the majority of districts on noninstructional applications, for example, instructional management, administration, and IEP management (The Sector Report 1985).

School board members seem to be supportive of the use of computers for managing instruction. A recent survey conducted among school board members about the use of computer technology in their schools found that 69.5% felt that computer management of classroom paperwork was necessary at all grade levels. Further, 55.9% felt the primary use of computers should be for the individualization of instruction (Sixth Annual Survey of School Board Members, 1984).

Currently, the computer curricular area emphasized least by school districts is computer-assisted instruction. In presenting computer program emphasis trends, Duane (1985) states that computer-assisted instruction receives only 9% emphasis compared to 40% for literacy and 35% for programming. His five-year projection shows CAI increasing to a 25% emphasis, with literacy and programming decreasing from 75% to 15%. Computer-managed instruction, though not specifically identified, is often incorporated in CAI software programs. What seems to be evident from the usage surveys is that CMI, notwithstanding its potential, has yet to receive the complete backing of administrators, curriculum supervisors, and teachers. With respect to teachers, many lack training, making them unsure how the new technology fits into the classroom. Other teachers seem reluctant to change their teaching methodology or, being older, do not wish to invest the energy required to learn the new technology, or they may be alienated or intimidated by the technology (Mind sets, 1985). What must occur before computer instructional applications will make larger inroads in school districts is to change educators' mind sets toward computer use.

CMI CONCEPTS

District and school administrators considering the implementation or evaluation of a computer management program should understand the underlying concepts. The concepts are rooted in mastery learning and the individualization of instruction. Individualized instruction can be defined as an organizational process in the teaching-learning environment which allows students to progress at a rate and level determined by their own unique abilities and interests (Hunter, 1970). Individualization can also be defined in terms of its dimensions (Klausmier, 1977), for example: (1) the assigning of specific learning objectives to individual learners; (2) the use of diagnostic and prescriptive activities; (3) the existence of alternative learning sequences and paths for the individual learner; and (4) the use of small group or individual pacing.

> Individualized instruction enables students to progress at a rate and level consistent with their abilities and interests.

There are two major premises governing the individualization of learning. Students learn at different rates and learning is incremental. Various individualized programs have been developed over the past few decades that seek to incorporate these premises. They include individually prescribed instruction (IPI), individually guided instruction (IGI), process individualized curriculum (PIC), personalized system of instruction (PSI), and precision teaching (PT). Learning activity packages (LAP) have also been developed and used to implement individualized instruction. A LAP contains learning objectives the student is to achieve, a pretest based on these objectives, learning activities designed to teach the skill or knowledge the objective specifies, and a post-test to assess the degree of learning that has taken place. The individualized educational plan (IEP), required by law for all handicapped children, also seeks to have students learn at their own rate consistent with attaining their defined annual goals.

Mastery learning has been referred to (Block & Anderson, 1975) as a philosophy about teaching—a belief that all students can and will learn most of what they are taught under appropriate learning conditions. In other words, mastery learning provides students with multiple opportunities to master goals at their own pace. It is a way to address the issue of individual differences among learners. Mastery learning differs from conventional classroom instruction in (1) its emphasis on mastery of small learning units, (2) the use of criterion-referenced formative and summative tests, (3) providing additional time for students to attain mastery, and (4) its emphasis on corrective procedures for helping students overcome learning difficulties. The mastery learning model, according to Guskey (1985), is a group-based, teacher-paced approach to instruction in which students learn together with their classmates. The model, however, can be adapted to an individual-based, student-paced format, with instructional time and format being less restricted.

> Mastery learning has as its goal the attainment by students of a specified level of performance on instructional units and course objectives.

The methodologies employed in individualized instruction and mastery learning have much in common and are conducive to computerization. The procedures are reflected in the instructional/evaluation model shown in Figure 6.1. The process entails (1) specifying the instructional objectives that students should be able to achieve when they have completed an instructional unit; (2) determining the type of learning asked of a student using a technique such as task analysis; (3) conducting a preassessment to determine if the student (a) possesses the learning skills necessary to complete the task or demonstrate mastery of the concept or skill to be taught, or (b) has already mastered the skill or concept specified in the behavioral objectives; (4) selecting appropriate learning strategies and materials; (5) implementing the corrective strategies and materials; (6) using formative criterion-referenced tests and teacher observation to assess student progress and the effectiveness of the strategies and materials used; (7) instituting remedial or corrective activities as needed; and (8) administering a summative or post-test to evaluate whether the student has mastered the skill or concept being taught. A typical criterion for mastery of an instructional unit is the scoring of 80 percent or better on either the preassessment test, the formative monitoring test, or the post- or summative test.

CMI FUNCTIONS

The early development of CMI systems was to help teachers cope with the tremendous output of detailed information generated by programs of individualized instruction (Baker, 1978). Later, CMI was recognized as a tool that could support the management processes or functions associated with programs of individualized instruction (Bozeman, 1979). Dennis and

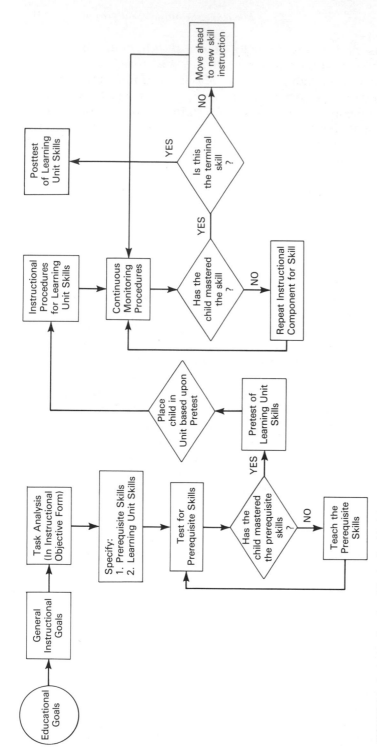

FIGURE 6.1 An Instructional and Evaluation Model

Kansky (1984) have categorized these functions as *supervisory management* and *executive* functions. Supervisory management includes such clerical tasks as assigning, recording, arranging, and reporting. Executive functions, being on a higher level, provide teachers with data that can be used in decision making. These functions involve planning, evaluating, commanding, coordinating, organizing, and controlling instruction. The computer thus becomes an indispensable tool in instructional management, which is defined as "the process that controls the content, context, duration, and pace of instructional events (Smith, R.M., 1981, p. 7).

Computer-managed instructional programs range from simple to sophisticated. At the lowest level, student and class records may be kept by the teacher. The electronic gradebook (Chapter 11) has received wide acceptance in the performance of these tasks, for it provides teachers and students with useful feedback. A sophisticated program includes both supervisory management and executive functions (Figure 6.2), specifically, curriculum organization, diagnosis and prescription, performance monitoring, resource management, reporting, and evaluating program effectiveness. The data collected, recorded, analyzed, and interpreted serve as a valuable resource for teachers, students, administrators, curriculum developers/supervisors, counselors, and evaluators in promoting the goal of effective learning in the classroom. To orient educators to the full potential of a computer-managed instructional system, the functions of a sophisticated program are discussed.

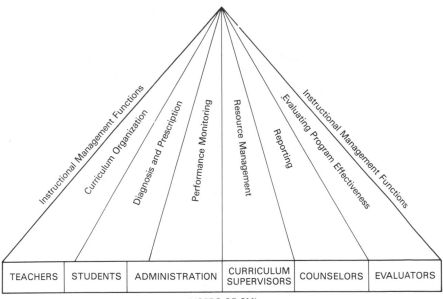

FIGURE 6.2 Instructional Management Functions and Users of CMI

Curriculum Organization

Careful planning is requisite to organizing the curriculum preparatory to implementing any instructional program, but is critical to a computerized program. Planning relates to determining the instructional objectives, the prerequisites for each objective, how each objective is to be assessed, and what teaching-learning strategies and materials will be used to promote student achievement of the objectives. The determined objectives should be specifically stated and arranged in a hierarchy. By sequencing the objectives, skills prerequisite to other skills can be taught in order and the diagnostic and prescriptive functions facilitated. Instructional objectives typically relate to intellectual skills in the cognitive domain, but can also emphasize psychomotor skills and affective behaviors such as attitudes and appreciations.

In a CMI program, standardized instructional objectives are coded and stored in a data bank categorized by subject area, level, and special need area. Objectives can be accessed and printed out, such as for an IEP, when a teacher enters the appropriate code numbers into the computer. One IEP software program has a data bank that contains up to 300 goals and 700 objectives distributed among different content and subcontent areas. An example of a goal and objective in the math content area is, "Improve skills in sorting and classifying—see/sort objects of the same shape (40–60 items per minute)." The ideal organization calls for keying the teaching-learning activities and the criterion-referenced test items to the specific objectives assigned to students individually or to groups of students. Doing so should enhance learning and the evaluation of student mastery of the objectives. An example of this organization is the six-volume data bank of goals, objectives, and resources developed by the Kendall School in Washington, D.C., called the Curriculum Management System and marketed by Learning Tools.

Diagnosis and Prescription

The diagnostic-prescriptive approach in mastery learning means that the results of any assessment should lead to a specific plan or "prescription" for instruction. In an instructional unit, preassessment or pretesting of students is conducted to measure their entry skills, permitting appropriate placement in an instructional sequence. Gerhard (1971) states that this pretesting serves as a "surveyor's" tool, for it enables the teacher to map the territory realistically. Advantages to this procedure as perceived by her are:

> It provides us with information in terms of what pupils know; it identifies their strengths, their weaknesses, their misconceptions. It identifies pupils with similar needs, allowing us to group the pupils for specific purposes; it designates a series of launching points from which individual pupils or

groups of pupils can enter the learning experience. It eliminates the review syndrome which so many children are needlessly subjected to which serves to produce problems which can readily be avoided. It provides us with a series of tentative hypotheses about our pupils. We obtain a sketchy profile of each child which becomes more distinct as we interact and learn together. We have a basis for describing specific sections of the learning unit for each child or groups of children. We are not making blind decisions as to what the "class" requires or what is "good" for all children. (p. 212)

Preassessment may be conducted by the teacher through the administration of pretests or placement tests. Pretests may be standardized, customized, or teacher constructed. Teacher-made or customized instructional unit tests, being criterion referenced, are generally more effective since they are constructed to specifically measure the prerequisite and learning skills the student needs in order to demonstrate mastery of the skill or concept being taught. Preassessing enables the teacher to know where instruction should begin for each student. For some, prerequisite skills must be taught. For others, instruction will begin at the level of their competency. Enrichment experiences may be provided students who demonstrate mastery of the instructional objectives. Students needing corrective aid may be assigned to individual tutoring, text materials, media materials such as slides, films, television, computer-assisted instruction, individual practice, laboratory work, consultation with a teacher, or group work (Figure 6.3). Group-based instruction should be appropriately paced and at an appropriate level of difficulty (Guskey, 1985). The prescribed teaching-learning strategies and materials should provide students the opportunity to practice the behavior called for in the objectives. In a computer-managed instruction program a pretest would be administered to students assigned specific objectives to determine if mastery was achieved. If mastery was not attained, the system would enable prescription lessons to be determined based on user-defined resources. The program would also provide the teacher information on objectives completed by individual students, the grouping of students working on a common objective, and the progress of students in relation to the instructional objectives assigned.

Performance Monitoring

Testing is a vital cog in the development and implementation of a computer-managed instructional program. As just observed, tests may be administered at the beginning of an instructional unit to (1) measure prerequisite skills needed for instruction, (2) determine where a student should be placed in an instructional sequence, and (3) determine what instructional objectives students have already mastered. Tests are also used to monitor student progress through the instructional sequence prescribed a learner. These tests, known as formative tests, serve to give students and teachers feedback information about learning successes and failures. For

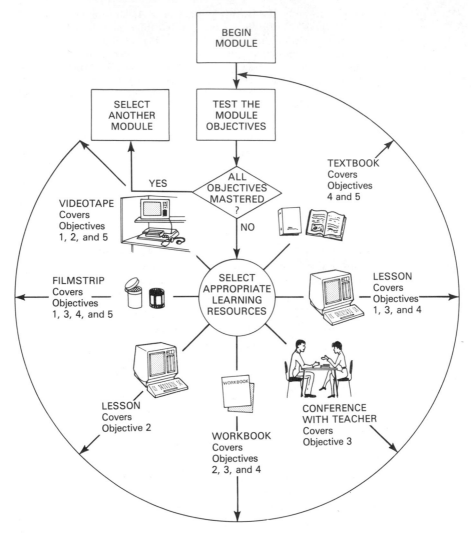

FIGURE 6.3   Sequential Steps in a CMI Module   From Stern, R. A., & Stern, N. (1982). *An Introduction to Computer and Information Processing.* New York: John Wiley & Sons, p. 21.

students the feedback can provide reinforcement of successful learning and identify specific learning errors still needing correction. The feedback for teachers enables them to modify instruction and prescribe alternative teaching-learning activities to help those students still needing to master the objectives of the instructional unit.

Formative tests, since they generally cover a predefined segment of learning such as an instructional unit, have test items that encompass a limited sample of learning tasks. The items may be easy or difficult, depending upon the learning skills or concepts emphasized. The tests are typically criterion-referenced mastery tests constructed in such a way that prescriptions for remedial or alternative instruction are keyed to each item or to each set of items in the test measuring a separate skill (Gronlund, 1981).

The importance of formative testing and the feedback it provides is underscored by Carnine and Silbert (1979). They state:

> The sooner a teacher detects a problem, the easier it will be to remedy that problem. Each day a student's confusion goes undetected, the student is, in essence, receiving practice doing something the wrong way. For each day a student remains confused, a teacher may have to spend several days reteaching that skill to ameliorate the confusion. Thus careful monitoring is a prerequisite for efficient instruction. (pp. 20–21)

Monitoring also entails determining if, at the end of the instructional unit, the student has mastered the assigned objectives. The results will dictate whether the student is ready to go on to the next instructional unit. The tool used in the management program to provide this information is a summative test. Summative tests:

- Are administered at the *end* of an instructional unit, reporting period, or course. In the sequence of mastery learning they are called posttests.
- Are criterion referenced, with the criterion typically being a percent-correct standard such as the student being able to correctly answer 80% or 90% of the test items.
- Provide feedback of a student's overall mastery of all the objectives of an instructional unit. Students successfully meeting the criteria would move on to the next unit, whereas those students who have some yet-unmastered objectives would be channeled back to receive corrective instruction.
- Are designed to be compatible with a unit's overall objectives and the prescribed strategies of instruction.
- Cover concepts most central to an instructional unit.
- Focus on broad ability and total unit outcomes rather than on the specific details of each instructional unit.
- Include more test items than a formative test to ensure having an adequate sampling of the skills and concepts being learned.

A sophisticated computerized instructional management program is well equipped to handle the required testing tasks. Having an established test item data bank, a test can be constructed that seeks to match perfectly the instructional objective(s) and the prescribed instruction. Following student administration the test can be scored, analyzed, and interpreted to permit judgments to be made about mastery attainment.

Resource Management

Resource management requires that the teaching-learning materials needed by students to correct deficiencies are available to them in sufficient quantity at the time needed. A CMI system should be able to facilitate the managing of resources by:

- Cross-referencing the resources to the instructional objectives and the test items of the examinations (pretest, formative, and summative tests) constructed to assess student mastery of these objectives.
- Matching students with the appropriate teaching-learning resources prescribed them.
- Providing a detailed description of the learning resources that would be assigned a student. These resources may pertain to behavior management as well as to the typical academic areas of reading, mathematics, and language arts.
- Enabling the listing of resource strategies and materials by objectives to be revised or updated.
- Supporting the scheduling of limited resources, primarily equipment such as microcomputers, for use by students who may need to use them at the same time. Dennis and Kansky (1984) state the CMI system should take into account the resources needed for any prescription, the quantity of each resource in relation to the number of students that may use it simultaneously, and the amount of time each student is expected to spend with a given resource. Having these variables under control, it becomes possible for a teacher to concentrate the use of resources by as many students as possible.

Reporting and Evaluating Program Effectiveness

Inherent in a computer-managed instruction program is the establishment of a student data base. Examples of student data stored in the computer's memory are: demographic information, current placement, instructional objectives mastered, performance on administered tests, and prescriptive activities recommended to help a student achieve mastery of outstanding learning objectives. A major benefit of a CMI system are the reports that can be generated from this data base. The summarized data may be analyzed by recipients to obtain a "snapshot" of the current status of the curriculum program and to assess program effectiveness. Examples of reports produced are:

- *Student profiles* showing student mastery and nonmastery of all instructional objectives.
- *Grouping report* displaying groupings of students by skill need to show who needs work on skills yet to be mastered.
- *Class report* summarizing the mastery performance of all students involved in an instructional unit.
- *Item analysis report* identifying good or bad test items and reflecting group performance on the tests administered.

- *Parents' report* illustrating the results of their students' performance, with suggestions made about ways they can help their children learn.
- *Prescription report* listing for each student the corrective strategies and materials that may be used to promote attainment of objectives yet to be mastered.

Suggested ways recipients of CMI reports can use them to evaluate the effectiveness of the instructional program and to make decisions are:

- *The Classroom Teacher.* Information derived from the reports may be used by teachers to make decisions on student placement, corrective activities, and grading. A determination can also be made as to which teaching-learning activities seem to be most effective and which instructional objectives appear to be most difficult for students to master. Subject to the analyses, modifications can be made in the curriculum to improve student learning.
- *The Building Principal.* Principals analyzing the results of the school and class reports are in a position to identify the strengths and weaknesses of the curriculum. Steps can then be taken to budget for needed resources and to shore up the weak areas of the curriculum.
- *Curriculum Coordinators/Supervisors.* An important concern for the curriculum coordinator/supervisor is whether the CMI program is more effective than alternative methods of instruction. Further, information is needed on whether the program is cost effective. Answers to these questions may dictate whether the CMI program should be expanded to other schools in the district. Though the reports generated by the CMI system may shed some light on these questions, a comparative study should be conducted to give more definitive information. The curriculum supervisor will want to work closely with district administrators and building principals to explore how such a comparative study should be conducted.

JUSTIFYING THE ADOPTION OF A CMI SYSTEM

School administrators and curriculum supervisors wishing to recommend the development or purchase of a computer-managed instruction (CMI) program should first carefully assess their existing instructional program as to purpose and effectiveness. Five questions have been identified (adapted from Patterson & Patterson, 1983) that administrators should answer as they address this issue. They are:

(1) *Does the philosophy of the district's instructional program match the philosophy underlying CMI?* As noted above, the concepts underlying CMI are rooted in mastery learning and the individualization of instruction. If the district's philosophy is to compare student success in relation to how other students perform (norm-referenced) and a reliance on large group-paced instruction whereby students receive the same instruction simultaneously, the introduction of a CMI system does not seem appropriate.

(2) *Is the instructional cycle of teaching defined sequentially? Instructional cycle of teaching* refers to how students are exposed to a segment of

the curriculum. In the area of mathematics, the instructional cycle of teaching a given objective typically involves preassessing what a student knows, prescribing appropriate teaching-learning activities, and then monitoring the progress made toward attainment of that objective. A CMI program, as noted previously, is equipped to handle data produced in this process. If the instructional cycle used by teachers in the district does not follow a predetermined pattern (Figure 6.4), a CMI program would not be helpful since the computer would be hard pressed to guess what the teacher would want students to do next.

(3) *Does the approach taken to manage the district's instructional program require computer support?* Is the manual system presently used by teachers to collect, analyze, and record data on student learning functioning adequately? Do teachers rely almost exclusively on qualitative data such as personal judgment, observation, and mental notes to diagnose, prescribe, and record student performance? If the answer to these two questions are affirmative a CMI system seems unnecessary. With respect to the latter question, a CMI program seems irrelevant because it is designed to handle quantitative data generated by test scores to assess student performance.

(4) *Can the district or school justify the costs of a CMI system?* The development or purchase of a CMI program adds additional costs to those expended for a conventional curriculum. The real cost of a CMI system lies beyond the required hardware and software (Smith, R.M., 1981). To answer this question a district needs to determine the accumulative costs associated with hardware; software; hardware maintenance; expendables like diskettes and printed paper; facility costs, including space and utilities; staff training; consultant costs for problem solving; and salary and benefits for personnel involved in managing the system. Districts opting to develop their own system will incur greater costs than the district that buys a commercial program. A CMI system can be expensive. Though it may have desirable features, administrators need to ask whether the costs outweigh the benefits.

IMPLEMENTATION GUIDELINES

The implementation of a CMI system requires more than the acquisition of the necessary hardware and software. Planning is requisite if administrators, teachers, and curriculum supervisors are to have an effective system. A key principle in the planning and development phase is to involve those who will use it. As Smith, R.M. (1981) states, "Without ownership, implementation will be difficult" (p. 7). Critical questions that should be addressed by curricular planners are:

(1) *What grade levels and subject areas should receive CMI emphasis?* An examination of available CMI software and the reports of districts

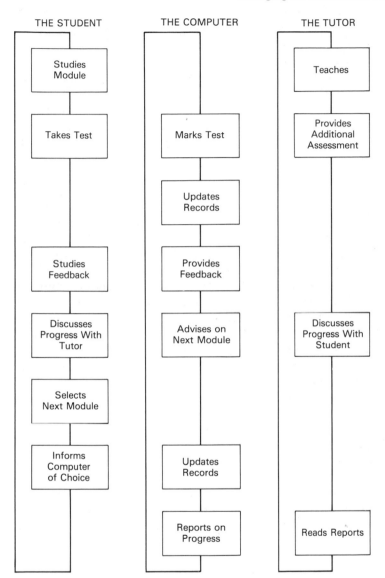

FIGURE 6.4 The Instructional Cycle in a CMI Program *From Leiblum, M.D. (1982). Computer-managed instruction: An explanation and overview. AEDS Journal, 15(3), 137.*

having functioning programs indicate that (1) mathematics, reading, and language arts are the subject areas mostly accented; and (2) the majority of these programs occur at the elementary level (Patterson & Patterson, 1983; Smith, R.M., 1981). One should not infer from these findings that other subject areas and grade levels cannot be considered. In determining these emphases planners should give careful thought to the curricular needs of the district, the projected costs, and the resources available. All things being equal, it may be best to start small and expand when experience has been gained as to what works best.

(2) *Should the program be implemented in just one or two schools only or across the entire district?* Some school districts initially restricted their CMI implementation to just a few schools as part of a pilot project to test out the system. Subject to positive findings, expansion was made to include additional schools. Other districts have implemented more broadly because of prior experience with computers for instructional use, such as the Houston Independent School District, or they sought consultant help to develop a districtwide master plan. Available to districts for adoption are some centrally installed districtwide programs, for example, Program for Learning in Accordance with Needs (PLAN), Individually Prescribed Instruction/Management Information System (IPI/MIS), Instructional Management System (IMS), and the Wisconsin System of Instructional Management (WIS-SIM). Planners should realize CMI, to be cost effective, should not be delimited to just a few classrooms in a school. Doing so negates having continuity and program coordination for students as they move through the grades. Financially, it is more advantageous to have an entire school's curriculum on a CMI system, assuming a computer would be exclusively devoted to this task (Patterson & Patterson, 1983).

(3) *How should the CMI system be organized?* Though a CMI system may be organized across a district, the base of the operation occurs at the building level. Originally, CMI programs were supported by a district mainframe computer or time-sharing computer located elsewhere. The microcomputer has opened the door for virtually all school districts, regardless of size, to implement a CMI system. Cost, user control, access, and convenience are reasons cited by McIsaac and Baker (1981) to justify using CMI on microcomputers. The implementation of CMI on microcomputers seems to be less expensive than on a large mainframe computer. User control implies that the CMI teachers or aides are able to reboot the system should it fail or, if maintenance is needed, school officials would control the maintenance decisions. If a remote computing facility were used by a school, this direct control would be lost. User access is facilitated by menu displays, on-line explanations, and the speed of transmission.

Having a CMI microcomputer system in a school, compared to in a remote facility, gives users complete access to the system. They can work late and generate reports as needed rather than having to face high-cost long runs or have delays due to a business report having higher priority (Chapter 2). Priority decisions, as a consequence, would be made on the basis of instructional need.

Organizationally, microcomputers may be (1) housed in each teacher's classroom to give them more direct control of the system, (2) networked at the school level with a district mainframe computer, or (3) networked with a central computer housed in a school. Advantages and disadvantages exist for each of these options. District planners must take into consideration existing computer practices, budgetary allocations, the computer expertise of staff, and other factors that are part of formulated district policy (Chapter 12) as they seek to determine what would be the best CMI configuration.

(4) *Should the CMI software implemented be custom developed or commercially purchased?* A number of districts, sometimes working in cooperation with university personnel, have developed their own CMI system. An example is the Comprehensive Achievement Monitoring (CAM) system developed by the Hopkins Independent School District in Hopkins, Minnesota. The CAM and a number of other similarly developed programs are now available commercially. The advantage of these programs is that they were developed by educators, thus making them more attractive than programs written by programmers in the employ of a software vendor. Notwithstanding this strength, they may still need to be modified to meet local need. For that matter, commercial programs also may have to be customized. The trend today, dictated by districts acquiring microcomputers, seems to be the buying of commercial programs (Chapter 7). Unanimity, though, does not exist as to their quality. One computer expert states he would like to recommend fully a management system for elementary and secondary schools, but is not impressed with them. He contends the majority are simply record-keeping systems with little provision for feedback (Bork, 1985).

When choosing CMI software, district planners and evaluators must recognize that the program may have to be adapted or modified to make it fully functional. Guidelines for selecting and evaluating CMI software are discussed in Chapter 11. Additional questions of relevance to district officials that should be weighed in the selection process (Barrett & Hannafin, 1982) are: (1) For what subject or curriculum areas will student progress be monitored and for how many students within the selected grade levels will data be kept? (2) How frequently will students be tested at the various grade levels which will require test generation and scoring? (3) How extensive a student achievement history file is needed to meet the criterion of district instructional accountability? (4) What types of reports are needed by (a) teachers to help plan their day-to-day instruction, (b) administrators and curriculum supervisors to better manage and evaluate the instructional program, and (c) parents to better help them understand the progress of their children?

CMI STRENGTHS AND LIMITATIONS

The strengths and limitations of a CMI system should be weighed by school administrators and curriculum supervisors studying the feasibility of implementing a computerized instructional management program. Some of these factors relate to philosophy, the improvement of instruction, and cost effectiveness.

Strengths

Major strengths identified (Riedesel & Clements, 1985; Milner, 1980; Budoff, Thormann, & Gras, 1984; Willis, Johnson, & Dixon, 1983; Patterson & Patterson, 1983; Wagner, 1983) with computer-managed instruction systems are:

The Clerical Tasks of Teachers are Reduced.   A major thrust of a well-developed and -tested CMI system is to reduce the clerical work of the teacher. Some educators have estimated that classroom teachers devote well over 50 percent of their time preparing, keeping records, administering and grading tests, and filling out required forms (Willis, Johnson & Dixon, 1983). In an individualized instructional environment the percentage is even greater. A computerized system, compared to a manual one, is able to handle and process the data faster, storing it for ready access. The benefit for teachers is the increased instructional time that can be used to counsel students about their learning. In one study that compared the time variable in a CMI program to a non-CMI program, CMI instructors were found to have spent less time reviewing records, correcting tests, and providing remediation and a greater proportion of their time instructing and counseling students than non-CMI instructors. Further, it was found that CMI instructors had 7 to 17% more free time than their counterparts teaching in two non-computer-based individualized settings.

The Testing/Instructional Process is Enhanced.   A forte of the computer is its ability to generate, administer, score, and analyze tests uniformly and reliably. The administration can be done either on-line, with the student taking the test at a computer, or off-line, with the individual recording responses on optical scan sheets that subsequently are read, stored, and analyzed. This process assures ready feedback for the teacher on student mastery or the prescription of teaching-learning activities recommended to correct deficiencies. The capability of a comprehensive CMI system to access readily student performance data via testing facilitates the direction of learning activities.

Communication between Teachers, Students, Administrators, Parents, and Curricular Supervisors is Facilitated.   The curriculum/student data base created by the CMI system provides useful, objective information to all parties directly involved or interested in the instructional program. This is possible due to the reporting capability of the CMI system. The reports, which contain the same information for all recipients, help foster an environment for open communication about issues affecting student learning and the quality of the instructional program. To illustrate: Teachers are in a position to share strategies and materials that have proven successful in teaching students specific skills and concepts. Administrators are able to discuss with their teachers ways to better the program. Parents, in meeting with teachers informally or at formal parent-teacher conferences, are able to focus attention on specifics as they relate to the progress of their children. Regarding administrators and curriculum supervisors, they are able to discuss mutually the strengths and limitations of the functioning CMI programs.

Large-Scale Individualization of Instruction is Possible. A manual system is not conducive for managing an individualized curriculum that is schoolwide or districtwide. To collect, process, and store the massive amount of information generated requires the capability of a computer or the hiring of new support personnel to handle the increased volume of data. The machine capability, though, is better equipped to handle the change from a group-paced instructional approach to an individual, self-paced one.

Student Evaluation and Program Evaluation Are Enhanced. The tracking and monitoring of a CMI system provides teachers and administrators with systematic and ongoing information to enable diagnostic, formative, and summative judgments to be made about student performance. The evaluation of each student's progress leads to effective planning for future objectives. Further, the results of this evaluation can be used to redesign and improve each step in the educational process. By charting initial instructional decisions against a student's actual gains should diminish teacher error rates and help them become more precise. By using standardized tests, it is possible to compare student achievement to national norms or to non-CMI students. In short, the evaluation function of a CMI system materially helps a district meet its accountability goal.

Teachers and Students Generally Feel Positive about the Program. Findings from the Sherman Elementary, Madison, Wisconsin, CMI program found that teachers not only supported CMI but felt it was superior; students preferred CMI; and parents misunderstood its functions (Chapin, 1977). Direct benefits of CMI for teachers seem to be: It (1) helps them administer and guide the instruction process, (2) reduces the time spent on clerical tasks such as scoring tests, and (3) enables them to match student needs with appropriate prescriptions. For students, CMI offers the opportunity to interact with a computer, obtain immediate reinforcement, and be rewarded for their efforts.

Limitations

The major limitation of a CMI system seems to center on whether it is cost effective. The evidence suggests it is not. As Patterson and Patterson (1983) state, "The idea of achieving the same results at less cost, or doing more with the same cost is not possible under CMI. If CMI is to be sold on the basis of cost effectiveness, its selling point is the belief that with added experience comes added effectiveness" (p. 138). Criteria of cost effectiveness have been postulated by Pogrow (1983a) and Milner (1980). They are: CMI should (1) directly improve student learning outcomes, (2) reduce personnel time devoted to the activity, (3) result in instructional time savings, and (4) reduce the cost of instructional transactions without impairing effectiveness.

The research that has been done on CMI has primarily focused on student outcomes and reduced personnel time. These studies, limited in number, were conducted mostly in the 1970s when a few mainframe computer programs were being developed or in the early 1980s when the microcomputer was first introduced as a CMI tool. The results on student outcome are contradictory. Brown (1982) contends that research has not demonstrated that computers provide more efficient or effective instruction since few studies reported significant differences in student achievement when compared with other instructional methods. Riedesel and Clements (1985), in their survey of the literature, report that the results of classrooms using CMI compared to non-CMI classrooms favored the former in terms of student achievement. They acknowledge, however, that the results have not been uniformly positive or statistically significant.

Respecting the criterion of reducing personnel time, the research again is not consistent. The difference may be attributable to one's definition of time. That is, is one speaking of time related to reducing clerical tasks or time devoted to operating the computer and using the reports generated by the CMI system? One of the strengths of the CMI system, as has been reported, is the reducing of teacher's clerical tasks. Pogrow (1983a), in contending that CMI is not cost effective pertaining to personnel time, uses the latter definition. Teachers, he feels, have to spend an enormous amount of additional time digesting and implementing the diagnostic, prescriptive, and monitoring information generated by the computer. Further support for this assertion comes from Baker (1978) who observed that teachers involved in the early phases of the Sherman School CMI project were hard pressed for time to perform both managerial and instructional functions. Overall, it seemed, they had difficulty attending to all facets of their responsibilities. In the use of microcomputer CMI systems, teachers or support personnel will be obliged to spend time (1) learning the techniques needed for storing, retrieving, and summarizing records; (2) entering data regularly on student files; (3) creating backup records at regular intervals to avoid losing all or part of the stored data files; and (4) combining student files from several disks, if the system uses floppy disks, with multiple copies of each disk located within a school or classroom. The cumulative time spent by personnel performing these tasks can add to the cost of operating a CMI system.

The criterion of instructional time savings pertains to the question, "Will individual self-paced instruction reduce the length of time spent on instruction?" If the answer is "yes," then instructional costs can be reduced. Milner (1980) feels this is possible. Empirical validation, however, is lacking. More research, it seems, is necessary today to study the impact of CMI systems, especially those supported by microcomputers.

Another limitation is the restrictiveness of some CMI systems. This occurs when the program is designed to teach objectives from a prescribed course of study, text, or strategy of instruction. For small districts not having a curriculum with predetermined objectives and test items, such a system may meet a local need. If resources are limited, the district would be hard pressed to develop from scratch their own bank of objectives and test items to measure those objectives. For large districts having an established curriculum with instructional objectives determined, a CMI system that permits incorporation of these objectives is needed. In selecting a commercial CMI program, potential buyers need to know if the program is restrictive or open as to local input of objectives and the creation of a valid test-item data bank.

CMI ISSUES

Issues confronting CMI users center on instructional strategies, testing, the role of the teacher, administrative issues affecting students and faculty, the integrating of CMI with the school/district management information system, and the CMI philosophy (Willis, Johnson & Dixon, 1983; Riedesel & Clements, 1985; Hofmeister, 1984; Kohl, 1985; Telem, 1983).

Instructional Strategies

What learning mode should be used in a CMI system and how should assignments be made that would best facilitate student mastery of the instructional objectives? Willis, Johnson and Dixon (1983) observe that CMI is compatible with most teaching strategies, but no guidance is provided on which learning mode is best suited for given learners. The developers of CMI programs having a prescribed curriculum make the determination that certain objectives call for individual projects, peer learning, programmed instruction, or lecture/discussion. For other objectives they may advocate the use of such learning modes as planned experiences, using a computer-assisted program, reading texts, or watching an audiovisual presentation. The users of a CMI system may want to have some say in the choice of learning mode since they know best the learning style of their students. To be fully effective, a CMI system should allow for this provision.

The size of the assignment given students can affect how well they learn and the extent to which the computer can serve as a good support tool. Learning tasks broken down into several long assignments have the disadvantage of the student not being able to get adequate feedback from the computer to help guide their learning. Too many short assignments, though, can be counterproductive by breaking up the content unnecessarily and preventing students from integrating the information to discern the whole. Complex subjects such as math and science that require beginning concepts to be mastered before advancing to higher skill areas are amenable to short assignments. Longer assignments seem more conducive to courses less concerned with the acquisition of large masses of detailed information than with the broad understanding of the subject. Most CMI software programs available today are programmed to handle short assignments. The use of CMI in English and literature classes, which seek to have students read, ponder, and discuss their assignments, has not yet materialized. In the final analysis, teachers, it seems, should be the determiners of the types of assignments made regardless of whether a CMI system is used or not.

Testing

Issues identified concerning testing in CMI are the testing of low-level objectives, the specification of entry and exit criteria, item sampling and difficulty, and testing versus teaching.

Testing and Objectives.   The accusation has been made that "Results only," meaning the acquisition of facts, is the motto of the computer-managed classroom (Kohl, 1985). This concern is aptly summed up in the words of Mr. Gradgrind in Charles Dickens's book *Hard Times*: "Now, what I want is Facts! Teach these boys and girls nothing but Facts! Facts alone are wanted in life. Plant nothing else, and root out everything else." All too often in assessing instructional objectives, the multiple choice and/or true-false tests used measure only simple recall or the recognition of information. Though facts are important, learning should go beyond the knowledge level of Bloom's *Taxonomy of Educational Objectives* (1956). The taxonomy, proceeding from the simple to the complex, has six hierarchical categories of learning objectives:

1.   Knowledge—Are students able to recall or recognize information?
2.   Comprehension—Are students able to explain ideas?
3.   Application—Are students able to use ideas?
4.   Analysis—Are students able to see relationships (the "take it apart" level)?

5. Synthesis—Are students able to combine ideas (the "put it together" level)?
6. Evaluation—Are students able to make judgments?

An indictment of mastery learning and its use in CMI is that too often tests are used that measure knowledge that is easy to test rather than knowledge that is important to test (Willis, Johnson & Dixon, 1983). To offset this criticism, developers and users of CMI should assure that the test-item bank prepared to measure the instructional objectives is not limited to items only in the knowledge level of the cognitive domain.

Entry and Exit Criteria.   Entry and exit criteria pertain to the criterion-referenced tests administered to students at the entry (preassessment) of a new course or unit of study and at the end (summative) of the prerequisite course or unit. If students successfully pass the exit test, it is assumed they will encounter no difficulty passing the entry test. If a high proportion of students were to fail the preassessment test, questions should be asked about the quality of the summative or exit test. For example, did this test measure the full range of objectives set for the course or unit? Were sufficient items included for each objective to assure students have mastered the skill or concepts taught? Users of CMI will want to be alert to the relationship that exists between tests used to assess mastery in a sequence mode of instruction. They should be aware that students may pass a course or unit without having mastered all the learning objectives requisite to the new learning.

Item Sampling and Difficulty.   Content validity is crucial to CMI tests. It refers to the extent the test measures what is taught or what is emphasized in the unit of instruction. It is determined by comparing the test items to the content of instruction emphasized or taught by the teacher. Sax (1974) states that decisions based on content validity determine whether students have mastered in, excelled in, or failed items or tests measuring specific course objectives. Since CMI tests are typically criterion referenced, content validity should be a matter of paramount importance, especially as to the test's adequacy of content coverage or item sampling. With many instructional objectives the question becomes, "How many items should be included on the test to adequately measure each objective?" The inclusion of too few items makes for a limited and biased sample of what the student is learning. The use of a table of specifications is advocated when constructing CMI tests. Doing so should ensure that a proportional number of test items are included to measure fairly each of the objectives in a unit or course of instruction.

The item difficulty of CMI tests is dependent upon the nature of the concepts and skills students are learning. The rule of thumb is, "If the learning tasks are easy, the test items should be easy. If the learning tasks are of moderate difficulty, the test items should be of moderate difficulty. No attempt should be made to modify item difficulty, or to eliminate easy items from the test, in order to obtain a range of test scores. . . . Care must be taken to match item difficulty to the difficulty of the learning task described in the learning outcome" (Gronlund, 1981, 144). Generally, CMI commercial programs do not contain information on the difficulty of the mastery tests. This does not preclude the possibility, however, of users conducting an item analysis to determine test item difficulty.

Testing versus Teaching.   Kohl (1985) has questioned the use of CMI programs, contending they are tools that make it easier to test rather than teach. Noting there is a dichotomy between testing and teaching, he portrays each in these words: "Teaching is an ongoing process—a dialogue between teacher and student—whose goal is to empower the student. Testing is an attempt to make the dynamic process of learning static, to fix moments when one 'has learned' rather than acknowledge that learning is cumulative, that it grows out of experience, and that ultimately what is learned is what one loves or needs in order to survive" (pp. 19–20). Educators also speak of the mechanical acceptance by students of memorizing lesson material and being tested on it as one of the ceremonies of humiliation in the classroom.

The accent on testing, to the detriment of teaching, is underscored by Durkin, a national reading expert (Durkin, 1985), who told a conference of educators that a lot of time is spent assessing reading comprehension, with little time spent teaching. Most of the new reading programs being introduced, she contends, focus on testing rather than teaching students how to read.

Administrators and teachers who endorse the adoption and use of CMI should recognize that it is a tool, one of many that may be used in the classroom. Its purpose should be to improve the quality of student learning, not to make learning mechanical. The educational philosophy of administrators and teachers has much to do with how CMI is used. If the accent is on having students do what they are told to do rather than challenging them to think and not just memorize, CMI may serve its purpose.

The Role of the Teacher

The role of the teacher using CMI is directly affected with regard to the testing function just discussed. Another issue centers on whether CMI diminishes the role of the teacher as a decision maker. The testing and prescriptive functions of CMI programs outline diagnostically what students who fail to achieve mastery should do to correct deficiencies. Do these prescriptions mean that CMI has excluded teachers from the decision-making process? Hofmeister (1984) feels otherwise. He feels that successful CMI programs support teachers as decision makers because they can modify both the testing and prescriptive processes. To do this, however, a CMI program must be flexible, allowing teachers to choose from alternative teaching-learning strategies. Otherwise, teachers need to exercise their own judgment by prescribing those strategies they feel are best for the learner.

Another concern affecting teachers who are included in a CMI program deals with their understanding and acceptance of individualized instruction. Those who have had little to do with this mode of instruction may feel threatened by CMI. In-service training, it seems, should be instituted for these teachers before they are requested to use such a system.

Administrative Issues

A number of administrative issues will arise when a CMI system is introduced in a school or district. Some (adapted from Willis, Johnson & Dixon, 1983) are:

(1) What action should be taken when students who take an exit test for a course or unit fail to meet criteria? Should students merely study the same material again? Will detailed information on exactly what they are to study be provided? Or will new remedial information be assigned?

(2) Should teachers who develop CMI materials for a course or unit receive compensatory credit for their effort? If yes, should the credit be in the form of reduced teaching load or extra salary?

(3) What should be done when the teaching load of faculty is reduced because a CMI program has proven successful in being able to monitor the work of students enrolled in several sections of a foundations or introductory course? Should those teachers who have managed the CMI program be given credit for teaching these sections or should they be given additional teaching responsibilities?

The administrative decisions made on these and other issues that arise stemming from the use of CMI must be dealt with at the local level. Every effort, it seems, should be made to ensure that the decisions are fair and equitable. All parties involved in the issue should also be included in the deliberations.

CMI and the Management Information System

Telem (1982) makes the case that CMI should be integrated with the management information system of a school or district. To support this argument, he states that the CMI data base would provide information that could be used by various decision makers at not only the district level but also at the state, regional, and federal levels. At the school, CMI, together with student scheduling, grading, and attendance, would comprise one of the instructional administration's subsystems.

Though Telem's idea may have merit, it may be premature, especially when concerns are still expressed over the quality of CMI software, the cost effectiveness of CMI, and the logistical problems relating to setting up an integrated system that would embrace district, regional, and federal levels.

The CMI Philosophy

Kohl's (1985) appraisal of CMI systems is that they have the same educational philosophy, which he describes as:

> Learning can be measured and recorded; learning can be judged according to discrete quantitative measures; these quantities can be fit into a discrete scale of 1 to some number; the goal of education is to get the highest possible rating on this scale on both individual and group levels; teaching consists of setting discrete measurable tasks, giving tests and recording results; and the nature of the teaching process is irrelevant—it is the results that count (p. 19).

Riedesel and Clements (1985) describe the CMI philosophy as "the school-as-a factory approach" (p. 96), the skills-management approach borrowed from the business world. Elements of this approach are similar to those espoused in mastery learning, that is, specific objectives are written, diagnosis and prescription occur, performance is monitored, and mastery is determined. Consequences identified with this philosophy, which are similar to those mentioned by Kohl, are:

> First, it stresses assessment of observable, fractionalized behaviors; and most individualization concerns only the rate of progress. Further, materials can become confused with the original purposes and become the ends instead of the means. The approach can tend to emphasize content rather than process, the logical rather than the psychological, the mechanical rather than the meaningful, and organized structure rather than room for incidental growth. Finally, some professionals may trust the "system" rather than their own judgment, and they may lose control over their program (Riedesel & Clements, 1985, p. 96).

It is not uncommon for schools and districts to disseminate to parents and the community their statement of educational philosophy. A pertinent question becomes, "Does the printed philosophy square with practice?" The answer has much to say about the implementation of a CMI system. That is, if the philosophy does not reflect a view of individualization, the new practice is at variance with what the administration is conveying to its "publics." At the planning stage of considering CMI, administrators should be assured that their school/district philosophy is compatible with the CMI philosophy. They should also be aware of the criticisms associated with the CMI philosophy and be prepared to take steps to address these criticisms.

SUMMARY

Computer-managed instruction (CMI) is a tool school officials are using increasingly to manage the instructional program. It has been defined as the procedure employed to manage the instructional process by assisting teachers in diagnosing instructional needs, testing and monitoring student achievement, prescribing learning activities, and matching instructional materials to teaching/learning activities. Mastery learning and the individualization of instruction are the concepts underlying CMI.

CMI functions have been categorized as supervisory and executive. Clerical tasks such as assigning, recording, arranging, and reporting are associated with the former, while executive functions include planning, evaluating, commanding, coordinating, organizing, and controlling instruction. CMI programs range from the simple to the sophisticated. Electronic grade books, which permit teachers to maintain student and class records, typify low-level programs. Sophisticated programs include both supervisory management and executive functions.

Before adopting a CMI program, school administrators should be assured that their instructional program reflects the assumptions underlying CMI—that is, are the philosophies underlying both programs congruent? Is the instructional cycle of teaching defined sequentially? Does the management and evaluation approach taken include the collection and analysis of quantitative as well as qualitative information? Further, it should be determined if the costs of a CMI system can be justified. If the decision made is to adopt a CMI program, assurances should be had that implementation guidelines are followed and that the benefits outweigh the limitations and the issues raised regarding its use.

7

SOFTWARE
CONSIDERATIONS

One of the first lessons school administrators learn about a computer is that without software, the written programs that instruct the computer can do nothing. The computer is just an inanimate piece of machinery; it is like an automobile with an empty gas tank, sitting and going nowhere. Before developing or buying financial, personnel, and student information software, one of the most important activities school administrators and their staffs must do is to specify the data requirements. These specifications should grow out of the needs assessment conducted to determine what types of information are needed to manage the schools. In districts with central data-processing services, these specifications are communicated to the director, who typically is responsible for selecting or having internal programmers write the software that enable defined tasks to be executed. Regarding the use of microcomputers, district and school computer coordinators appear to have the responsibility for selecting and purchasing the best software for instructional and administrative purposes (Barbour, 1986).

To assist school administrators to be knowledgeable about software and issues, the following topics are discussed in this chapter: types of software, writing software programs, costs and cost effectiveness, training, care and maintenance, selection and evaluation, and legal aspects.

TYPES OF SOFTWARE

Two major types of software exist for computers—systems software and application or user software (Figure 7.1). *Systems software* refers to the computer's operating system, which is typically provided by the manufacturer. Well-known systems used with microcomputers are MS-DOS (*Disk Operating System*), PC-DOS, Apple DOS, and CP/M. The operating system is the link between application programs and the computer and its peripheral devices. Its function is that of a general manager coordinating the hardware and the application software to make sure everything runs smoothly. Some of the functions of the operating system are to load the user's software into memory; monitor the storage and retrieval of programs and data; create, open, and close data files; enable backup copies to be made of data files and the systems and applications software; communicate with the user on the status of the system; and perform job control and accounting procedures whereby information is provided on the date, time, and number of minutes to run a job.

Applications software refers to programs written to meet the needs of users. In the educational setting microcomputer application software has been written for the classroom teacher (computer-assisted instruction and computer-managed instruction), the administrator, and the guidance counselor. Microcomputer software used for management purposes may be subdivided into task-specific software and general-purpose software. Task-specific software programs are prestructured to do a specific task like

FIGURE 7.1 Types of Computer Software

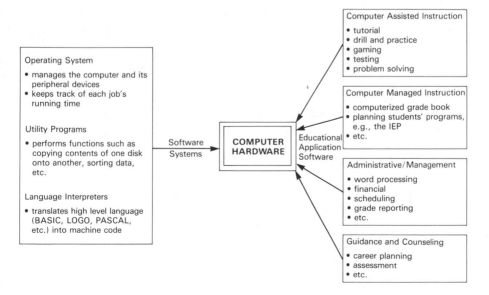

inventory accounting or attendance accounting. The user has only to input data into the prespecified format. Most administration software made available to schools is task specific.

General-purpose programs allow the user flexibility in customizing a program to fit local needs. School administrators wishing to computerize paperwork have the choice of word-processing programs, data-base management systems (DBMS), and electronic spread-sheet programs. Word-processing programs (Chapter 8), because of their ability to edit textual material, can be a boon to administrators in facilitating the writing of letters, memos, announcements, and special reports. Data-base management systems (Chapter 10) permit school administrators to establish electronic data files on students, faculty, equipment, and purchase orders. Electronic spread sheets (Chapter 9) may be used for budgeting and forecasting purposes, such as projecting enrollments.

For the busy school administrator who wants to use a microcomputer for office and school management, word-processing, spread-sheet, and data-base programs have real merit because of their flexibility. In the past an administrator would have to buy these programs separately, learn them separately, and use them separately. A major limitation was the incompatibility of these programs, meaning information generated from one program could not be combined with information from another program to create a complete, unified report. This problem has been addressed by the development and marketing of integrated software programs. *Integrated software* can be defined as a "set of programs that use mostly the same keys to perform the same functions and permit files created on one program to be used by any other program in the package" (Peterson & K-Turkel, 1984b).

Integrated microcomputer software programs offered for purchase may be fully integrated or linkage programs. Fully integrated software may consist of a single program that combines several general-purpose programs or programs that use an operating system that permits the transferring of data between compatible programs. Linkage programs serve to link or transfer data between existing programs. *Memory Shift* from Northern American Business Systems and *Des Q* from Quarterdeck Office Systems, developed for use on the IBM-PC, are examples of linkage programs (Pogrow, 1983b).

Examples of programs combining general-purpose software are Appleworks (Apple Computer), Symphony (Lotus Development Company) and Framework (Ashton-Tate). LOTUS's Symphony uses windowing environments that permit handling word processing, data-base management, spread-sheet and graphics files as if they were pieces of paper on a desktop. Framework's desktop, in contrast, organizes pieces of paper, whether notes on different topics, data bases, graphs, or spread sheets, into an outline similar to what students do in school. Under the major headings, related information is grouped together as subheadings. In turn, these can be expanded by adding yet a lower level of subheadings. The PFS family (Software Publishing Corp.) may be used individually, but all work together to get an integrated package because the programs are compatible. PFS:FILE, the file data management software; PFS:REPORT, the companion program to FILE, which sorts and prints files by various categories; PFS:GRAPH, the program that makes bar, pie, and line graphs; and PFS:WRITE, the word processor, can all be integrated. For example, a report created in WRITE can contain graphs and charts from GRAPH and data from FILE. Names and addresses from FILE can be merged with letters created in WRITE to make a simple and efficient mailing list.

An advantage of a single fully integrated program is that the user has only to learn one program, not three or more. Another advantage of integration is the compatibility that exists between programs or functions, which permits text or data to be transferred easily from one application to another. To illustrate, using Appleworks, an administrator who has set up a budget with the spread-sheet program can readily transfer it, making a few keystrokes, to the appropriate spot in the budget report being written with the word-processing program.

Currently available for use in schools are integrated administration software programs which combine such applications as scheduling, attendance, and grading. Examples of these types of integrated programs are: The School System (Columbia Computing Services, Inc.), Schoolmaster (Olympia Computing Company, Inc.), Attendance and Scheduling Program (Charles Mann and Associates), ESM-100 (Educational Software and Marketing), School Management Applications (Scott, Foresman and Co.), Assistant Principal (Monument Computer Village Data Center), and Harts (Systems in Education). An important consideration for the use of such programs is the need for adequate data storage. For microcomputers this can be attained by using a hard disk system. Instead of a floppy disk drive, a Winchester drive would be employed. It operates similar to the floppy disk drive but is engineered to yield greater storage capacity.

Pogrow (1983b) has suggested a procedure to help administrators determine whether integrated administrative software is needed. This may be done by charting a map on paper that shows the information flow of a school or district. Figure 7.2 illustrates the initial procedure of recording the needed information. It is essential that the map reflect the information broken down into specific data elements such as the demographics needed for a student directory. Once all the informational needs have been recorded on the map, the analysis step occurs. The analysis should reveal clusters of people and applications that need to share the same information. These findings permit the administrators to conduct the next step of linking clusters to types of software and types of integration needed. Integration possibilities are (1) general-use software such as a word-

Kinds of Information Needed	Users of the Information	Data Elements	Applications or Use of the Information
1. Daily attendance	Principal Assistant Principal Attendance Clerk Counselor	Student's name, address, phone and absences by day and period	Make home calls Send out absentee slips/daily report Compile term and semester absentee reports
2. Enrolled students	Yearbook advisor Counselors Attendance clerk Principal Assistant Principal	Student's name, address, phone, gender, ethnicity, grade in school, class schedule	Master file Registration Attendance Student directory
n.			

FIGURE 7.2   A School Information Flow Map

processing program with a data-base management system, (2) specific application software, such as an attendance and scheduling program, and (3) both task-specific and general-use software. In deciding whether or not to use integrated software, the administrator needs to take into consideration the added cost and complexity of the software compared to the time saved in not having to duplicate the data-entry process for a number of different programs (Pogrow, 1983b).

WRITING SOFTWARE PROGRAMS

Application software programs for educational institutions are generally written by three groups of programmers: (1) individuals in the employ of the institution, (2) consultants hired by school administrators, or (3) programmers working for large publishing firms, computer manufacturers, or in the cottage industry. The term *cottage industry* applies to self-employed software producers who sought to capitalize on the market created when educators began buying microcomputers in record numbers. The advantages and disadvantages of each method are summarized in Table 7.1.

To assure obtaining quality administrative/instructional software, educators are gravitating more and more to programs written by educational publishers and computer manufacturers. Findings from a recent study of schools revealed that 60 percent bought their software from publishers and/or vendors outside the school district (For Your Information, 1982). Primary factors underlying this trend are the prohibitive costs

TABLE 7.1   Methods of Software Writing: Advantages and Disadvantages*

PROGRAMMERS	ADVANTAGES	DISADVANTAGES
Internal	1. Individual (teacher or administrator) is knowledgeable about the data specifications for the program. 2. Modification and maintenance of program can be performed readily.	1. Individual may not be adequately informed of specific application. 2. Program, being specific to user's specifications, limits generalizability. 3. Individual may lack high-level skills to do sophisticated programming. 4. Costly design and debugging is relatively expensive. 5. Program documentation is usually lacking or inadequate.
Consultants	1. Consultant can assess objectively the informational needs of the school and/or school district. 2. Consultant can write software tailored to meet the user's specifications.	1. Program(s) will be no better than the user specifications provided to the consultant. 2. Expensive, with costs increasing with the complexity of the problem. 3. Support for maintenance and modification difficult to obtain once program is complete.
External (programmers from publishing and computer manufacturing firms and in the cottage industry)	1. The lowest cost since development costs are absorbed by a number of users rather than one. 2. Programmers are highly skilled, being knowledgeable about specific or general applications for target users. 3. Maintenance support available.	1. Flexibility limited if programs are specific and not general. 2. Content of program may not be appropriate. 3. Backup diskette policy may not be clear. 4. The user of the computer program or system has no control over procedures that are included in the software.

*Adapted from Stern, R. A., & Stern, N. (1982). *An Introduction to Computer and Information Processing.* New York: John Wiley & Sons, p. 305.

school districts would have to expend to develop and debug their own computer programs and the issues of poor documentation (operating instructions) and unreliability when programs are written by amateurs not versed in how students learn or the organizational concerns of schools. It has been estimated that the time required to design and code a computer program may range from 100 to 300 hours per hour of running time. Translated into dollars, the development costs of a program that administrators, teachers, or students might use for only one hour at a time is between $2,000 and $100,000, depending on the program's sophistication and complexity (Walker, 1984).

COSTS AND COST EFFECTIVENESS

Computer growth, we found in Chapter 2, goes through a series of stages. It is during the initial and expansion stages that expenditures for computer hardware and software and personnel salaries reflect a steady and steep rise. To control runaway growth, school administrators are encouraged to monitor and evaluate the computer resource. To do this, costs for hardware, software, salaries, supplies, and so on should be analyzed periodically. A 1980 report on the data-processing budget in education (Shaw, 1980) showed that hardware and personnel salaries accounted for 79 percent of the budget. Software expenditures comprised only 9 percent. The increased use of microcomputers commencing in the early 1980s appears to have changed dramatically the proportion of the budget expended for software and the training required to use these programs. One source has stated computer hardware costs account for about 30 percent of the budget, with the remaining 70 percent going for software programs and staff training (Truett & Gillespie, 1984).

With 95 percent of microcomputers in school districts being used for instructional purposes (Gangel, 1983), software expenses for computer-assisted and computer-managed instructional programs account for a large proportion of the computer budget. Large districts acquiring more microcomputers for classroom use are experiencing escalating software expenditures. As an example, the Houston Independent School District's software expenses increased nearly five times, from $55,000 in 1980 to $250,000 in 1983 (Sturdivant, 1984). For the nation as a whole, $130 million was spent during the 1984–85 school year by school districts (Computers, 1985) for educational software. Applying 5 percent to this figure, which reflects the administration uses of microcomputers, approximately $6.5 million was spent for administrative software.

The cost of commercial task-specific software programs may range from less than $100 to many thousands of dollars depending on whether the program is for classroom management purposes or a student management or financial accounting program for use in a school or school district. Costs also tend to vary according to whether the software has been designed for a mini or microcomputer. Most general-purpose microcomputer software programs cost between $100 and $800, with programs having less power or fewer features in the lower range. Integrative software packages tend to range from $200 to $800. Though price of a software program may not be a determinant of its quality, some credence may be given to the statement, "The higher the cost, the better the quality."

Criteria for determining the cost effectiveness of software are (1) Does the software program serve multiple uses? (2) Does the program process data cheaper than doing it manually? and (3) Is a dollar return realized on the investment? A comparison of task-specific to general-purpose software has shown the latter to be more cost effective due to its multiplicity of uses. This is possible since these programs allow the administrator more flexibility in designing formats for data input, data files, and information output. This flexibility and the fact that similarities exist among different administrative informational tasks permit general-purpose software to meet a variety of data-processing needs.

Respecting the second criterion, Pogrow (1983a) presents the net time savings principle, which is:

> The time required to assemble the data for computer entry, plus the time to enter the data and make necessary modifications to the computerized data, must be less than the amount of time required to assemble the data and calculate the results manually (p. 124).

To determine the costs to do data-processing tasks manually, a time management study can be conducted (Naumer, 1984). Baseline data would then be on hand to compare these costs to those expended to do the same activities using either a mainframe computer, minicomputer, microcomputer, or a mainframe or minicomputer networked with a number of microcomputers. Time allocated by staff and faculty to perform attendance, grading, scheduling, and other activities by hand would be logged on a time-management chart over the time frame necessary to complete the job. The cost to do each of these tasks manually would be determined by multiplying the hourly wage of the persons engaged in the various activities by the number of hours they devoted to their portion of the overall job. Computerized costs to do the same activities would be compiled on the time expended to assemble the data, enter it into the computer, make modifications in format, and print out the finalized product. The cost of the hardware, software, and the time allocated to train individuals to use the program should be noted separately as a start-up cost. The results of the cost-effectiveness analysis for each of the administrative/management tasks performed in a school or school district will enable superintendents and school principals to determine which tasks should be considered for computerization.

School administrators wishing to determine whether moneys invested for computer hardware and software are cost effective should determine what benefits accrue by having this resource. In other words, does the resource not only pay for itself but bring a benefit to a school or district in terms of increased productivity, a better product, or a savings in time and funds? As an example, have heating costs been reduced by introducing a computerized system to manage heat control? Also, by computerizing attendance has a percentage increase occurred in average daily attendance? Within the classroom it can be asked if increased productivity has occurred when teachers use management software to help facilitate the instructional process. In one small high school a microcomputer acquired by the principal for the library netted the school a savings of $2600. This figure was the difference between the computer hardware/software costs and the $7100 saved in reducing the cost of replacing damaged, lost, and stolen books (Corbett, et al., 1982).

SOFTWARE TRAINING AND USE

One of the hidden costs of the computer resource is the training of personnel to use software programs adequately. This applies particularly to the investment of personnel time to learn the various microcomputer software programs. Whether the program is task specific or general purpose, the school administrator should recognize that at the outset release time must be granted to individuals from their regular duties to obtain training. Training options are (1) courses offered by vendors who sold the software; private trainers, including hired consultants; or districts, colleges, and universities and (2) self-instruction using tutorial programs, computer source books and references, and training materials included with the software. Greater returns will likely be realized by enrolling school personnel in a formal course or training program.

For each software program to be learned the administrator needs to determine which people need the training. Provision should be made to have at least two people trained for each program used. Doing so will ensure having a knowledgeable backup person in the event of illness or absence of the other user (Beach & Lindahl, 1984). The extent of training needed is dependent upon the complexity of the program, the extent to which the software program is user friendly and has good documentation, and the degree to which the individual is computer literate. Suggested time estimates and formal course training costs to teach novices the use of a microcomputer and a general-purpose software program at the rate of $10 or $20 per person per hour are shown in Table 7.2. Total cost for twenty-two hours of instruction ranges between $220 and $440. This cost reduces to a range of $160 to $320 for learning future software programs since individuals would be competent in setting up the microcomputer and in using its operating system.

Beyond the sixteen hours of instruction needed to learn a general-purpose software program, an additional fifteen to thirty hours of practice time should be devoted by the trainee to developing program proficiency.

TABLE 7.2 Time and Cost Estimates for Learning a General-Purpose Software Program

NATURE OF INSTRUCTION	TIME ESTIMATES	POTENTIAL COST
Orientation to the use of the microcomputer	2 hours	$20–$40
Instruction in using the disk operating system (DOS)	4 hours	$40–$80
Introductory instruction to the program	8 hours	$80–$160
Advanced training in the program	8 hours	$80–$160
Total	22 hours	$220–$440

Totally, thirty to forty-five hours of formal instruction and practice time are necessary for an individual to become completely trained to use an administrative software program.

Administrators wishing to design their own data files or financial summaries using general-purpose software must expend additional time designing templates for this purpose. For data-base management programs Naumer (1984) implies that four to eight hours are needed to design a template (Figure 7.3) and test it with ten records. Designing a template for a spread-sheet program would require a similar number of hours, depending, though, on size and complexity. What administrators should recognize from this discussion is that software and personnel training costs may readily equal or exceed computer hardware costs.

SOFTWARE CARE

Many microcomputer system and application software are on floppy disks. Instructions for the care of these and all data disks are included in the manufacturer's manuals and all software package manuals. Upon receipt of these materials, school administrators should carefully read these cautions. For convenience, the major dos and don'ts of software care are summarized below:

DOS

1. Do place the self-adhesive tab sold with the write-protect software master program over the small cutout at the upper right of the disk to prevent its being erased.
2. Do make a backup copy of the write-protect software program disk and all other important data disks.
3. Do slip disks into their protective sleeves when not in the disk drive.
4. Do keep disks dust-free by storing them in a specially made file box or similar container.
5. Do keep food, liquid, dirt, and whatever might come under the heading of debris away from your disks.

DON'TS

1. Do not expose your disks to magnetic fields or extreme heat or cold.

```
      JONES, JOHN P.               5590570 > E9 < EVALUATE GRADUATION PROGRESS
GPA: 3.356  TRACK: GEN GEN  SEP: 141901

AREA                REQD  SCHD SUBJECT         AWRD  PEND  WT 1 2 S  3 4 S  AB GR

*COMMUNICATIONS     3.00  3.50                 3.50  .00
                                 SPEECH          .50  .00  01 A A              1 11
*         DIFFICULT 2.00  .00                    .00  .00
     ENGLISH        2.00  3.00                  3.00  .00
                                 ENGLISH 9      1.00  .00  03 A A A  A A A     3 09
                                 ENGLISH 10     1.00  .00  03 A A    A A       2 10
                                 ENGLISH 11     1.00  .00  03 A-A-   A A       3 11
*     FOREIGN LANG  1.00  .00                    .00  .00
*SOCIAL STUDIES     2.00  2.50                  2.50  .00
                                 SOC STUDIES    1.00  .00  03 B B B  B+B B     1 09
                                 WORLD HISTORY  1.00  .00  03 A A-   A A       2 10
                                 ECONOMICS       .50  .00  02        C B       1 11
*     AMERICAN HIST 1.00  .00                    .00  .00
 MATHEMATICS        1.00  3.00                  3.00  .00
                                 GENERAL MATH   1.00  .00  03 C C+C+ B-B-B-    1 09
                                 ALGEBRA 1      1.00  .00  03 C C+   B B+      2 10
                                 GEOMETRY       1.00  .00  03 B B-   B B+      2 11
*COMPUTER SCIENCE   1.00  .00                    .00  .00
 SCIENCE            1.00  2.00                  2.00  .00
                                 SCIENCE        1.00  .00  03 B+A-A- B B+A-    1 09
                                 BIOLOGY        1.00  .00  03 B B    A B       2 10
 HEALTH              .50  .50                    .50  .00
                                 HEALTH          .50  .00  01 B B+             1 10
*PHYSICAL ED        1.00  2.00                  2.00  .00
                                 PHYSICAL ED    1.00  .00  03 P P P  P P P     2 09
                                 PHYSICAL ED    1.00  .00  03 B C    A B       1 10
*WORK-SERV-GOAL     1.00  .00                    .00  .00
*VOCATIONAL         1.00  .50                    .50  .00
                                 TYPING 2        .50  .00  02        A A       2 11
*ARTS               1.00  .50                    .50  .00
                                 DRAMA           .50  .00  02        A A       2 11
 ELECTIVES           .00  7.50                  7.50  .00
                                 CRAFTS          .50  .00  03 B+B+B+ WP        2 09
                                 WOODWORKING     .50  .00  03        A A A     2 09
                                 AUTO MECH      1.00  .00  03 B B    B B       2 10
                                 JAZZ BAND      1.00  .00  03 B B    D B      14 10
                                 TYPING 1        .50  .00  01 C C              1 11
                                 PHYSIOLOGY     1.00  .00  03 B B    A A       1 11
                                 ACCOUNTING     1.00  .00  03 A A    A A       1 11
                                 ENGLISH 1      1.00  .00  03 B-B    B A       8 12
                                 GEOGRAPHY      1.00  .00  03 A A    A A       1 12
*TOTALS            15.00 22.00                 22.00  .00

   NEXT SCREEN --------------- 5590570 > E9 < TRACK: GEN GEN   AREA: CO
```

FIGURE 7.3　Student Demographic Data　From Information and Instructional Services (1984). *SIS Student Information System.* Salt Lake City, UT: Utah State Office of Education.

2. Do not force your disk into the disk drive or try to force the disk drive door closed over it.
3. Do not bend or crease your disks.
4. Do not use paper clips on your disks because the clips may be magnetized and can crease and scratch the disks.

SOFTWARE EVALUATION AND SELECTION

The selecting of administrative software is a tough, frustrating, and time-consuming task. The sheer number of task-specific and general-purpose programs now available to choose from can overwhelm administrators seeking to implement a data-processing system into their school. One publication (The Educational Administrator's Survival Guide, 1984) listed some 300 different types of microcomputer programs, with the greatest variety of choice being in the areas of business management, student records, attendance, grade analysis and reporting, and media center. It is a nearly impossible task for a single administrator or a single school district to evaluate them all. With new releases continually being added to the selection pool, there is no way administrators can keep up with them all. Further compounding the selection dilemma is the compatibility problem. Assurance must be obtained that the software chosen will be compatible with the computer hardware to be used in terms of the operating system, memory, number of disk drives, and peripherals required. Faced with these realities, the busy school administrator cannot help but ask, "Do I have the time and the expertise needed to search out, review, and test software programs preparatory to making a choice?" If the answer is no, what then are the alternatives? Will the approach be one of accepting the recommendations of salespersons or administrative colleagues? Might a clearinghouse for administrative software be consulted? Should a gut reaction choice be made based on what one hears and reads? Should consultants be hired to obtain their recommendations? What about having a districtwide steering committee organized to address administrative/instructional computer uses in the schools and to make software recommendations?

A guiding principle governing software selection is that it should be done rationally and systematically, applying sound criteria. A recent editorial in *Educational Technology* (Technically Speaking, 1984a) lamented the present system of software selection. They noted that selections are based first upon gut reaction and second, upon the recommendation of a friend. This is no different, they contend, than what happens in the educational system at large when it comes to solving the practical problems of schooling. They state:

> . . . rational criteria for software purchase are feasible only when an instructional system itself is rational. It makes no sense, on the one hand, to spend countless hours evaluating computer software while, simultaneously, everything else in the school system is being run according to whim, caprice, "gut reactions," and local or state politics.
>
> Perhaps computer software selection can serve as a catalyst in moving more educators to think rationally about what they are doing. If so, then the computer will have a greater effect on the improvement of education in this world than anyone can imagine. (p. 6).

The implication is that the software selection process should continue to be done systematically, applying rational criteria. Steps in conducting such a process are as follows:

Step 1. *Analyze the results of your informational needs assessment.* A principle governing the selection of administrative/management computer software is that the programs recommended for adoption reflect the informational goals of the school district. As indicated in Chapter 2, a needs analysis should be conducted to determine these goals. Determining the information flow of a school or school district is one way to do this. Once all the information needs have been identified, the question should be asked of each, "Can it be computerized?" For the kinds of information for which computerization is feasible, a ranking of each by order of importance should be conducted. School administrators and computer coordinators, by having established priorities based on the rankings, are in a better position to determine which types of software should be purchased. If the intent is to computerize office paperwork, a word-processing program is called for. If budgeting is a concern, a spread-sheet or business-management software program should be selected. If the priority is to computerize attendance and class scheduling, attention should be focused on a data-based management system or a task-specific program designed to perform this function. A benefit of the needs assessment is that it provides focus and direction in determining what the computer software and hardware requirements are in initiating a data-processing system.

Step 2. *Prepare an adoption list.* The purpose of this step is to narrow the number of possible software programs that an administrator or selection committee wishes to preview. In compiling the list, reference should be made to software catalogs, directories, and buyer guides. Recommendations of administrators who have had experience with given programs also can be added to the list. Knowledge about a program, its cost, and hardware requirements can be obtained from these sources.

To pare down the list, those responsible for selecting the software should obtain answers to the following questions: How reputable is the program? Is there evidence of field testing? How many years has the program been on the market? What do reviewers and users have to say about its merits and features? How well established is the vendor?

Step 3. *Obtain or see demonstrated a preview copy.* If a local computer store has a copy of the software you are interested in, see it demonstrated. Learn what you can about its functions from qualified sales personnel. Another option is to invite sales representatives of large publishing companies to come to the school or district to give a demonstration. If these options are not available, seek to obtain desired copies of administrative/management software programs from noncommercial preview centers. If you place an order for the program of interest with a software dealer or company, exercise the 30-day approval policy if it is offered. It permits the return of the software if it does not meet selection standards. It may be that a demo disk only is sent which features highlight excerpts of the program. This procedure is followed by companies that do not want their product pirated. Reviewing a demo disk, though, is a second-best approach to conducting a complete and thorough evaluation of the software package. When working with the software dealer or a company, check out the warranty and support provisions of the program. Determine, for example, if

- Updates on documentation and the software are provided routinely.
- Training to use the program comes as part of the purchase price.
- The software is guaranteed to be free from defects in workmanship and materials.
- The program can be exchanged if it won't load or run properly or contains errors.
- The name of field test sites are provided to permit contacting successful users of the program.
- A toll-free number is provided if help is needed from the software company.
- Damaged disks can be traded or replaced.
- A backup policy exists if the program is write protected.
- A discount is provided for purchasing multiple copies or a licensure agreement exists if the program will be used by many schools in a district.
- The company is financially sound, meaning it will still be in business when support services are needed. Heath and Camp (1984) estimate that there are more than 2000 software producers active in an industry that has many sudden arrivals and departures. Fallout seems greatest among small firms in the so-called cottage industry.

Before placing a software order, assurances should be obtained that the school or district has the necessary hardware and operating system to run the program. For schools opting to use a microcomputer to computerize office tasks, the minimum hardware configuration needed to run administrative software programs is a standard typewriter keyboard, an 80-character-wide monochrome display monitor, a microcomputer with two disk drives and 128K random access memory (RAM) and a 132-column letter-quality printer. Add-ons to be considered are a hard disk with a minimum of 10 megabytes capacity to handle scheduling and attendance requirements and a card reader to facilitate inputting data such as student test scores.

Step 4. *Study the preview material.* Preliminary to running the program, the documentation accompanying the software should be read and an evaluation made as to its quality. *Documentation* refers to the written explanation of the development, workings, and operations of systems and application software. The purpose of the application documentation is to provide the user with a step-by-step description of what must be done to operate the program. Sometimes this information is built into the program for the user to call up. The written-use documentation, however, is a reference manual. Typically, it contains the title of the program, author(s) information, a table of contents, the development and purpose of the program, a sequential outline of operations, examples and illustrations of input screen displays and output report formats, and an index. Technical documentation should also be included to provide information on the hardware configuration and storage capacity requirements. The quality of the documentation can often be used as a criterion of the quality of the software. This should not be the only criterion, because some software programs have more than proven their worth regardless of poor documentation. A case in point is the word-processing program Word Star, considered a standard in the industry.

In critiquing the documentation, determine if it meets the following criteria (adapted from Newman, 1983):

Completeness. Does the documentation cover all aspects of the program, not neglecting the basics?

Usefulness. Does the documentation contain a general information component, a reference manual component, and a tutorial component which serves to lead the user through the most common uses of the program?

Organization. Is the documentation organized in a logical and easy-to-use manner? A good table of contents and index are essential.

Appearance. Does the documentation have quality printing? Is the text sharp and legible? Are the illustrations of the visual displays and reporting forms clear and useful?

Comprehensibility. Is the documentation text easy to read and comprehensible, using simple straightforward language?

System specificity. Does the documentation make provision for the operating system you intend to use? Does it also make reference to specific function keys on your keyboard?

Step 5. *Test the software program.* The proof of the pie, it is said, is in the eating. The proof of software is in its execution. This can only be determined by running the program. As this is done, the reviewer should make note of the procedures to input, process, and output the data. Attention should be focused on error handling, ease of use, security, size of data fields, speed, helps, design format, and type of reports that can be produced.

Step 6. *Make your decision.* The culminating step of the software review is deciding whether to recommend adoption of the software outright, recommend with qualification, or to reject. If the process has been done rationally and systematically, applying sound criteria, a judicious decision should result. To facilitate making this decision, an overall evaluation can be made using the rating form shown in Figure 7.4. Circle the number that represents the rating to be given. Total scores on the eight dimensions will range between 8 to 40 points. If the cumulative rating is 32 points or higher, serious consideration should be given to purchasing the program.

SOFTWARE DIMENSION	RATING				
	NOT ACCEPTABLE (1)	POOR (2)	AVERAGE (3)	GOOD (4)	EXCELLENT (5)
Warranty	1	2	3	4	5
Dealer support	1	2	3	4	5
Documentation	1	2	3	4	5
Ease of use	1	2	3	4	5
Error handling	1	2	3	4	5
Graphics quality	1	2	3	4	5
Value for money	1	2	3	4	5
Overall performance	1	2	3	4	5

FIGURE 7.4   A Software Rating Form

LEGAL ISSUES

Pertinent legal issues affecting school administrators with respect to the use of computer technology are software piracy, the illegal duplication of copyrighted software; invasion of privacy; and the confidentiality and security of computer data files. The school administration should be knowledgeable about these issues to assure that compliance exists with copyright laws and legislative enactments.

Software Piracy

Software publishers are adamantly opposed to the illegal copying of their products. The results of two nationwide studies revealed that from 8 to 17 percent of the responding schools had large-scale illegal copying of software (Chion-Kenney, 1984; Becker, 1986). Violations such as this account for 97 percent of thirty-nine publishers surveyed stating that they took measures to protect the copying of all or some of their software. About half of them indicated that some of their software is multiple loaded, but were reluctant to publicize these products. Twenty-six of the thirty-nine vendors frowned on the school practice of using a backup or archive diskette as a second copy. This practice, they noted, violated not only the law but company policy (Williams, 1985). The International Communications Industries Association (ICIA), an association of publishers and dealers in computer software and audiovisual materials, has been applying pressure on school districts by challenging or threatening to challenge several districts for alleged illegal duplication of copyrighted software programs. The superintendent of the one district involved has indicated that policy guidelines on software would be adopted to provide tighter control (Brady, 1985).

Copyrights and license agreements are two ways software publishers have legally sought to protect their product and their investment. The current copyright law, enacted in 1976 and referred to as Title 17, USC, copyrights, deals only cursorily with software. With the passage of the Computer Software Copyright Act of 1980, a general framework of protection was given to owners of copyrighted software. Purchases were restricted to making a single archival or backup copy of the software. In seeking to sell, modify, or make multiple copies of the software, the purchaser would be infringing on the sales or profit of the copyright holder and thus be in violation of the copyright law. Administrators wishing to know more about this law are referred to the article written by G. Becker (1984).

Computer developers and publishers not wishing to sell their software outright have resorted to licensing agreements. Upon purchase of the program and the signing of the agreement, the licensee is permitted to use the software under the proprietary rights of the owner. This means the licensee agrees not to sell, transfer, disclose, display, or otherwise make available the licensed programs or copies or portions thereof to any other entity. By allowing the licensee to use the program without the transfer of title, the ownership rights of the publisher or vendor are protected.

How binding are these licenses? What happens if they are ignored? Peterson and K-Turkel (1984c) asked these questions of attorneys who specialize in this kind of law. The answers were mixed, but the supposition is that licenses are binding. Two court cases initiated by Alston-Tate respecting the use of Lotus 1-2-3 were ruled in their favor.

Notwithstanding these legal efforts to protect software, developers have been losing millions of dollars in revenues from home computer users and professionals. The latter group includes former software company programmers, crooked software distributors or jobbers, and educators who have limited budgets but need software for use on multiple computers in classrooms or on a district local area network. The copyright law has restrictions on the use of software with multiple computers and networks. To permit school officials to make multiple copies of a licensed disk legally, one company has marketed what is known as a site license. It allows a school to make copies of each licensed software package for each computer on the premises or to load the software onto a hard disk for the school's computer. A site license is needed for each item of software.

The magnitude of the revenue loss due to pirating has been estimated to be $800 million for 1985. Future Computing, Inc., of Dallas, a unit of McGraw-Hill Information Systems Co., estimated piracy cost the software industry $1.3 billion in lost revenue between 1981 and 1984. They believe there is currently one pirated copy of business software in use for every copy authorized by the publisher (Software Piracy Puts Big Dents in Revenue, 1985).

Since owner copyrights and software license agreements have not thwarted pirating, a number of developers have resorted to the use of a software protect code or encryption system in their disks to prevent illegal copying. Copy protection devices, though, are vulnerable, for programs called "nibble copiers" have been designed to copy supposedly copy-proof software. Another approach to software protection is the use of a special disk which is customized with a unique fingerprint. The process has been developed by Vault Corporation and carries the name PROLOK on its special disks. Invisible to the legitimate user, the fingerprint eliminates the threat of mass bypass schemes such as nibble copiers. Unprotected programs are unaffected by this process and may be copied and run in the normal manner.

A self-policy for educators, instructional software publishers, and vendors has been endorsed and published by the International Council for Computer Education (ICCE). The document, entitled *ICCE Policy Statement on Network and Multiple Machine Software*, outlines responsibilities for each of the three groups. Educators accepting the statement would be expected to:

- Strictly observe copyright laws and publisher license agreements.
- Be responsible for trying to prevent the manufacture or use of unauthorized copies on school equipment.
- Formally designate and authorize an educator to sign software license agreements for the school.
- Formally designate an educator to be responsible for the enforcement of district policy and licensing agreements.
- Expose students to legal, ethical, and practical problems caused by the illegal copying of software.

Responsibilities expected of software developers would be to develop sales and price policies that are sensitive to the needs of educators. This would mean always providing a backup copy and allowing schools to preview software before they decide to buy. Vendor expectations would be to (1) provide special prices for schools that buy many copies but do not require multiple documentation and (2) work with hardware vendors to provide an encryption process to discourage theft. Also addressed in the statement is the request that software producers make available network-compatible versions of software.

School districts are asked to adopt a policy on software copyright and communicate it to software publishers. A suggested form, drafted by the International Council for Computers in Education, is shown in Figure 7.5.

One state, California, has adopted the ICCE policy for its districts (Across the Nation, 1985). Other districts, such as the North Allegheny School District in Pennsylvania (Weintraub, 1986) and the New York City Schools, seem to be developing their own policy to handle student or faculty incidents of illegal computer activity. The intent of these policies is

Suggested District Policy on Software Copyright

It is the intent of _____
to adhere to the provisions of copyright laws in the area of microcomputer programs. Though there continues to be controversy regarding interpretation of those copyright laws, the following procedures represent a sincere effort to operate legally. We recognize that computer software piracy is a major problem for the industry and that violations of computer copyright laws contribute to higher costs and greater efforts to prevent copies and/or lessen incentives for the development of effective educational uses of microcomputers. Therefore, in an effort to discourage violation of copyright laws and to prevent such illegal activities:

1. The ethical and practical problems caused by software piracy will be taught in all schools in the District.
2. District employees will be expected to adhere to the provisions of Public Law 96-517, Section 7(b) which amends Section 117 of Title 17 of the United States Code to allow for the making of a back-up copy of computer programs. This states that " . . . it is not an infringement for the owner of a copy of a computer program to make or authorize the making of another copy or adaptation of that computer program provided:
   a. that such a new copy or adaptation is created as an essential step in the utilization of the computer program in conjunction with a machine and that it is used in no other manner, or
   b. that such a new copy and adaptation is for archival purposes only and that all archival copies are destroyed in the event that continued possession of the computer program should cease to be rightful."
3. When software is to be used on a disk sharing system, efforts will be made to secure this software from copying.
4. Illegal copies of copyrighted programs may not be made or used on school equipment.
5. The legal or insurance protection of the District will not be extended to employees who violate copyright laws.
6. _____ of this school district is designated as the only individual who may sign license agreements for software for schools in the district. (Each school using the software also should have a signature on a copy of the software agreement for local control.)
7. The principal of each school site is responsible for establishing practices which will enforce this policy at the school level.

FIGURE 7.5   Attachment 1 from the International Council for Computers in Education (ICCE) Statement on Software Copyright Policy   The attachment is a suggested form for a letter to software publishers describing school districts' policies and intentions regarding the illegal copying of software.

to serve as a deterrant or to keep the honest person honest. The New York City Board of Education policy stipulates the following: that (1) duplication of copyrighted software or documentation is *prohibited*; (2) software publishers *must be contacted* to verify procedure for back-up; (3) a publisher's *written permission is required* to download or network programs to other microcomputers; and (4) all students and Board of Education employees *may not* use school computers to duplicate copyright software (News Briefs, 1986). Overall, it seems school districts are making a serious effort to control copyright abuse. A recent survey indicates that approximately 80 percent of all school systems in the country have adopted some guidelines to protect the copyrights of publishers (Pattie, 1985).

Reducing the cost of software programs to stop computer software piracy is the position taken by the editor(s) of *Educational Technology* (1984a). They state:

> We believe that the computer software copying problem will begin to disappear as software prices fall. And they will fall. They are falling. In the end, then, competitive factors in the market place will do more than copy-protection schemes, law suits, and exhortations to stop the copying epidemic (p. 6).

A third approach taken to deter software copyright violations is the enacting of legislation. The first such law enacted in the U.S. was in Louisiana. Known as the Software License Enforcement Act, it establishes the enforceability of so-called "shrink wrapped" licensing agreements. Once a consumer breaks the seal on a packaged software program, the agreement, which appears on the outside wrapper, takes effect. This means the customer agrees not to duplicate or transfer the purchased software. Software manufacturers, as a consequence, expect to sue software pirates more easily. Other states, particularly California and Georgia, expect to introduce similar legislation (Talab, 1985).

The implication for school administrators, as the educational leaders in the schools, is that they must be ever diligent in upholding the legal rights of software companies and vendors. Finkel (1983) reminds us that as educators we have a responsibility to stop stealing software and respect the publishers' right to a fair return on their investments.

Privacy and Security of Data Files

The information revolution brought on by the computer has magnified the public's concern over personal privacy. Awareness is had that financial, medical, employment, legal, psychological and educational histories of millions of Americans are on file in data banks maintained by governmental agencies, hospitals and health care centers, banks and credit offices, and educational institutions. Concerns are: How secure is the information? How accurate is it? and Who has access to the data? Privacy and security are the major issues surrounding the widespread collecting and filing of personal information on individuals from birth to death. Though privacy and security are closely intertwined, since security is needed to protect privacy, there are important differences. The concept of privacy relates to property, the person, and information (Privacy and Computers, 1972). Information privacy is the key issue surrounding the collection, storage, and transmittal of information on individuals. It has been defined by Westin (1967) as "the claim of individuals, groups, or institutions to determine for themselves when, and to what extent, information about them is communicated to others" (p. 12). Security pertains to measures instituted to restrict unauthorized access to sensitive information by building safeguards into management and the hardware/software aspects of the computer system. Privacy, then, is a social issue, while security is a technical and management problem (Garrison and Ramamoorthy, 1970).

Information privacy encompasses at least three dimensions, namely, the rights of individuals with respect to the (1) collection of data, (2) accuracy of the records maintained, and (3) confidentiality of the information (Mandel, 1984). To protect individuals' privacy, Congress passed a number of privacy acts during the 1970s. The Privacy Act of 1974 was the first, but was protective only of individuals in the employ of the federal government. The act provided that an agency could only release information by written consent of the individual or through a legal process such as a court order. Further, a person had the right to inspect his/her personal information in a data bank and to correct erroneous information.

The information practices of federally funded educational institutions came under regulation when the Family Educational Rights and Privacy Act also became law in 1974. Previously, school practices and policies pertaining to releasing student information on grades, test scores, attendance, and so on were varied, haphazard, and often formulated on the spot. Frequently overlooked was the obligation to protect students against harm from those who would misinterpret or misuse the data. What the act did was to (1) permit student and parent access to student records, (2) require institutions to provide the right of due process to challenge information that was inaccurate, misleading, or in violation of student privacy, (3) require the student's or parent's written consent before personal information in records could be disclosed, (4) require keeping a record of third parties reviewing the student's file, (5) prohibit third parties from disclosing any information in the record if student consent was not obtained, and (6) require institutions to inform students of their rights.

The language of the law respecting parental right to access their child's records is as follows:

> The parents of students under eighteen years of age attending any school . . . higher education, community college . . . [have the right] to in-

spect and review any and all official records, files, and data directly related to their children, including all material that is incorporated into each student's cumulative record folder, and intended for school use or to be available to parties outside the school or school system, and specifically including but not necessarily limited to identifying data, academic work completed, level of achievement (grade, standardized achievement test scores), attendance data, scores on standardized intelligence, aptitude, and psychological tests, interest inventory results, health data, family background information, teacher or counselor ratings and observations, and verified reports of serious or recurrent behavior patterns.

Much, if not most, of this information may be stored in a school district's computer data bank. School administrators wishing to comply with the law are obligated to ensure safeguarding of information privacy by instituting security measures. Computerized employee personnel records, too, are to be protected. District policy should be established to prevent data errors and unauthorized uses such as using confidential personal information about employees that adversely affects their employment status. Regarding abuses of personnel data banks, Mandel (1984) states:

> Release of medical records, personal references, psychological tests, performance evaluations, and even salary information are possible sources of personal embarrassment and even economic harm to an individual. As a result of the volume of data collected and its potential for misinterpretation and abuse, the personnel file may pose the greatest modern risk to individuals' dignity and freedom (p. 180).

To protect student and employee computer data files against unauthorized access or disclosure and against unintentional or intentional modification, security is vital. Security must focus on the control of, access to, and use of information. Figure 7.6 shows the phases of access control. A critical problem for schools today is to keep confidential records protected against hackers. Many bright student hackers seem challenged to gain access to a school's data banks following the precedence set by the high school youth in the movie *War Games*. What security measures are available to school administrators and their staff to protect the computer system? Figure 7.7 illustrates procedurally how the information rights of individuals can be protected. Access control methods advocated by IBM experts (*Staying in Charge* 1983) include (1) locks on computer room doors, on tape and disk libraries and on terminals, consoles, and printers, and (2) the use of a password that controls the release of a transaction, data element, or document. Krauss and MacGahan (1979) cite four basic systems: reusable passwords, once-only codes, limited-use passwords, and question-and-answer sequences.

The use of a password or prearranged set of questions requires no special hardware and is the least expensive means of identification. The weakness of passwords is that they tend to proliferate like a chain letter.

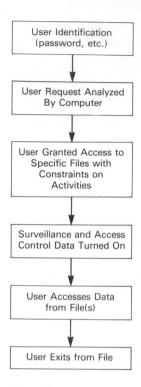

FIGURE 7.6   Phases of Access Control   Adapted from Garrison, W. A., & Ramamoorthy, C. V. (1970). *Privacy and Security in Data Banks.* Austin, TX: Electronic Research Center.

Individuals also tend to forget them, so they resort to using easily remembered words like one's birthday, anniversary, or name. A tendency also exists to write the password down where unauthorized persons may find them.

Other methods are to (1) use a card entry system to keep unauthorized persons away from the data files; (2) remove and lock up confidential data stored on tape or disk; (3) not use a dial-up system; (4) use special software packages; (5) employ a data switching system, and (6) use a relational data-base management system. Typically, special software like V.M. (Virtual Machine) from IBM and Top Secret from C.G.A. Software Products group are used with minicomputers and mainframes. What V.M. does is to make a single computer system operate as if it were two or more separate systems, thus reducing the chance of unauthorized entry. Top Secret, a commercial product that can be modified for school use, is leased at a starting price of $9000. It functions to define precisely which individuals have access to what information and on what day and at what time they can use that information.

Data switching is a security procedure developed for use with computer systems that have terminals hooked into a mainframe or minicomputer. The procedure is commonly known as data PABX or data private automatic branch exchanges. It serves to prevent certain users from getting access to restricted information and resources. Data PABX acts similarly to a telephone switchboard, as a "referee" between terminals contending for access to data files. It serves to connect a terminal only to its authorized category or categories (Saver, 1983).

Relational data bases permit accessing information from a master source. They offer the convenience of updating all established student and employee files once the master source is updated. Another feature of relational data bases is the ability of user to create a whole range of files containing different fields. This provision permits information to be kept confidential, since a secretary would not be given access to the entire student or personnel file but only to separate files containing just those fields that he/she must have in order to make any updates.

The important points school administrators need to remember about privacy and security are that procedures should exist in their school districts to (1) safeguard student rights by adhering to statutes and regulations, (2) maintain the confidence of student and employee information, (3) preserve data security against deliberate, unauthorized access, modification, or destruction efforts, and (4) maintain data integrity, the integrity of the administrative hardware/software system, and the personnel responsible for the operation of the system.

Principle	Implementation	Security Measures
Right to Know	Notification	Restrict assess using locks
Right to inspect	Interview Printout	Use of passwords and question and answer sequences
Right to challenge and protect	Review Verification Correction Rebuttal Purging	Use of card entry system Remove and lock up data stored on tape or disk
Right to limit dissemination	Informed consent Confidentiality Data security	Refrain from using dial-up system
Assurance of Compliance	Auditing Testing	Use software security programs

FIGURE 7.7 Protection of the Information Rights of Individuals. Adapted from Garrison, W. A., & Ramamoorthy, C. V. (1970). *Privacy and Security in Data Banks*. Austin, TX: Electronic Research Center.

SUMMARY

Software pertains to the programs written, systems or application, that instruct a computer what to do. *Systems software* refers to the computer's operating system and is the link between application programs and the computer and its peripheral devices. *Applications software* refers to programs authored to meet user needs. They may be task specific, performing a given function like student scheduling or attendance accounting; general purpose, which allows the user to custom fit a program (word processors, data-base managers, and electronic spread sheets) to meet local needs; or integrated, which may consist of a single program that combines several general-purpose software features. Application programs may be written by employees of the school system, consultants hired for the purpose, or by programmers in the employ of publishing firms. To assure having quality programs, educators tend to buy commercial programs.

Issues of concern to school administrators regarding software pertain to the cost effectiveness of various programs, the procedures to employ in training personnel adequately to use adopted programs, the care of purchased software, and what criteria to employ when evaluating and selecting programs for the local setting. Legal issues of concern are software privacy, the illegal duplication of copyrighted software, the invasion of privacy, and the confidentiality and security of computer data files. To help school administrators explore these issues, guidelines and criteria are presented.

8

SOFTWARE
FOR MANAGING
THE ADMINISTRATIVE
OFFICE

Software for use in helping manage school and school district offices, as indicated in Chapter 3, includes word processors, merge programs, and time manager or electronic calendar packages. Word processing is the major automated office tool to help administrators manage the information in their offices. Accessory programs that can be used with most word-processing programs are spelling or dictionary programs, thesaurus and grammar programs, and merge programs. Merge programs are used to print mailing labels, produce reports summarizing data, or combine text from other entries when printing. Personalized letters become possible when merging a letter with the list of names and addresses of those to receive the communication. Electronic calendars serve as time managers to help administrators keep track of appointments, schedule meetings, and remember important dates such as birthdays, anniversaries, and holidays. A suggested procedure for evaluating and selecting a word-processing program follows. It is applicable to selecting accessory and time manager programs. For each category, a sampling of programs that school officials might review is presented.

EVALUATING AND SELECTING
A WORD-PROCESSING PROGRAM

The task of selecting the right word-processing program can be a difficult one due to the array of packages available on the market. For example, the Buyer's Guide to Word Processing in a recent issue of *Personal Software* (Buyer's Guide 1984) listed 113 programs marketed by 99 vendors. School administrators, for whom the concept is new, may be overwhelmed by the terminology of the field, the confusing gaggle of functions, and the claims of productivity made by the software vendors. What questions should the administrator ask to help determine which of many programs is the one to buy, especially when they do essentially the same job? As Bahnick (1983) says, "Good software can be a pleasure to use, whereas, poor software can make usage a frustrating experience" (p.42). The steps outlined in Figure 8.1 are presented as a workable procedure to help school personnel evaluate what word-processing program is best for them.

Step 1: Determine User Requirements

Word processing is used by individuals to meet their specific purposes. Three classes of users have been identified: writers, managers/professionals, and secretaries (Professional Computing Word Processing Programs for the IBM Personal Computer, 1983). The writer/author is involved in writing long and continuous articles. Managers/professionals, in general, limit their word processing to memos, short letters, and reports. The time they spend using a word processor will be considerably less than

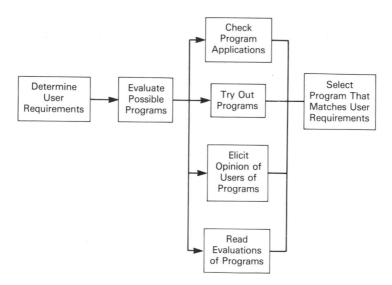

FIGURE 8.1   Steps in Selecting a Word-processing Program

that spent by the writer or secretary. Secretaries handle complicated typing projects delegated to them by their managers. What word-processing requirements are recommended for the manager/professional and secretary? The following guidelines may be of help (adapted from Professional Computing Word Processing . . . , 1983):

The Manager/Professional.   School superintendents and principals fit into this class. They should look for a program that would permit them to gain access to file information to facilitate the decision-making process. Such a program would allow easy access among files and would enable financial, legal, student, and personnel management documents from other programs to be accessed, edited, and combined with the text documents. The capability of having the screen split into two windows to view two files simultaneously for editing is desirable. Advanced features such as detailed text formatting and list processing are not essential.

The Secretary.   School secretaries should have a program that allows for easy editing. Form letter merger and list processing are essential, as are multiple formats per document used for technical and outline typing. If the secretary is to use a word processor at least for three or more hours per day, the program should be an efficient one, even if it requires time to learn.

In the school setting it is incumbent that the administrator and office staff list all the paper tasks they want the word processor to perform. Miller (1984b) advocates asking such questions as: "How will I use this program? Will I use it for one-off memos, formulating indexes, updating standard letters, creating original reports, or writing a book?" (p. 126). Talley (1983) suggests that school users analyze the types of documents they need to produce. To facilitate this analysis, she asks users to answer such questions as:

> Will the document include any or all of the required letters, reports, ledgers, or forms? If the documents will be primarily letters, are there standard paragraphs which will be used frequently in a variety of letters? How long are the letters? Will certain people be contacted frequently? How often will you do mass mailings? If the word processing package will be used to produce reports, what will be the average length of a report? Do the reports include graphics? How many copies of each report will have to be produced? What form of printed output will be used: single sheets, letterhead, custom forms, continuous forms, labels? Will you need to merge letters with mailing lists? Will electronic mail be used? (p. 76)

If the analysis revealed that a microcomputer would be used minimally for word processing, the evaluation/selection process would stop at this point. On the other hand, if the analysis revealed that the office paper requirements merited the acquisition of a word processor, Step 2 would be implemented.

Step 2: Evaluate Possible Programs

Preliminary to evaluating prospective programs, a number of word processors (the software) need to be identified. They may be compiled from users of given programs, lists found in computer journals, and software offered by computer vendors. Having the names of several programs, it becomes possible to evaluate them by employing the following procedures (Figure 8.1): (1) Check each program's applications—what it can do or not do, (2) try out the program, (3) elicit opinions of users of the program, and (4) read evaluations of the program printed in computer journals. If a committee exists in a school district to evaluate administrative/instructional software, the evaluation can be done by them with recommendations going to the administrator/user. Based on the results of a recent survey, it appears that district and school computer coordinators are assuming a primary responsibility for the evaluation and purchase of software for instructional and administrative use (Barbour, 1986).

Figure 8.2 provides a checklist of characteristics that may be found in word-processing programs. As a program is evaluated it should be possible to determine the features needed by the user. The task of determining what applications a given word-processing program can perform becomes simpler for the novice user if reference is made to reviews in computer journals that indicate which text and formatting characteristics the software has. Filling out the checklist, therefore, becomes relatively straightforward. After analyzing the data on the checklist for the various programs under review, the most promising should be identified. They would then be subjected to a tryout to assess the degree user requirements are met. The match should be as close as possible. As Schuford (1983) states:

> A word processing program is just a tool and just as you choose a hammer that fits your hand you should choose a program that fits both the job to be done and your working style. That means you should try out the software before you buy it (p. 178).

In testing out the program, check the command structure or those keys that are used to initiate such tasks as editing a draft document and loading or printing a document. Talley (1983) feels the most important element in ease of use of a word processor is command structure. Commands should be simple and mnemonic, such as a control character and "EF" for "find the end of a file." Some command key sequences may be confusing, which would not enhance the use of the program if it were acquired.

What about the user friendliness of the program? Danny Murphy, former president of the Association of Information Professionals (AIP), in

INSTRUCTIONS: For each of the major characteristics of word-processing software, place a check mark in the space provided for each application that exists.

I. CURSOR CONTROL
    ____By character
    ____By word
    ____By line
    ____By page
    ____Skip to beginning/end
    ____Horizontal scrolling

II. TEXT CONTROL
    ____Right and left justification
    ____Centering specified lines, titles and texts
    ____Automatic underscore
    ____Column layout
    ____Tab and ability to change margins
    ____Tabs inside a document
    ____Phantom hyphenation
    ____Move block
    ____Copy block

III. PAGE CONTROL
    ____One-line heading
    ____Multi-line heading
    ____Heading and footing
    ____Setting pages for various lengths
    ____Manual page breaks
    ____Automatic pagination

IV. DELETE
    ____By character
    ____By word
    ____By string
    ____By screen
    ____By block
    ____Continuous deleting
    ____Recover deletions

V. INSERT
    ____Typeover
    ____Insert character
    ____Insert line
    ____Insert from buffer
    ____Key phrase

VI. SEARCH AND REPLACE
    ____Find word/phrase
    ____Find and replace times
    ____Global find and replace
    ____Use wild card
    ____Ignore upper/lower case

FIGURE 8.2 Checklist of Microcomputer Word-processing Software Applications Adapted from Talley, S. (1983). Selection and acquisition of administrative microcomputer software. *AEDS Journal, 17(1,2), 78.*

VII. *FILE CONTROL*
____Save/load entire file
____Save/load partial file
____Auto backup
____Save file and continue edit
____Delete file
____Merge files
____Display file directory

VIII. *PRODUCTION CONTROL*
____Underline
____Boldface
____Subscript and superscript
____Single, double, or triple spacing
____Sequential printing of multiple files
____Print multiple copies
____Print single sheets
____Interrupt/resume
____Pause for text entry
____Start/stop as designated
____Screen display of formatted text
____(Is easily configured to one's printer)

FIGURE 8.2 (continued)

speaking of microcomputers as a productivity tool for executive and middle managers, has said, "If a program is not user friendly—if it's complicated, difficult to learn or hard to analyze—it's not going to be used regardless of the hardware on the desk." Amy Wohl, President of Advantage Office Concepts, a consulting group in Bala Cynwyd, Pennsylvania, concurs with this assessment (Miller 1984b). She states:

> Once you've put the disk in and loaded the program, you'll know how to use the package by just reading the screen. That won't be true for the most complicated tasks, but if you can't start a program, get text up on the screen, edit it, then send it to the printer without reading the manual from cover to cover, then it's probably not the ideal package for you. (p. 126)

The quality of documentation, as noted in Chapter 7, is critical in enabling an individual to use the word-processing program. While testing out the program, spend some time reading the manual. Is it first rate? Does it have quick reference guides? An index? Are good illustrations provided of the program's features? Are the command functions explained clearly? In making this assessment, try to get a feel for how much training time would be needed for one to become a competent operator. As the program is being tested, also determine if it can interface easily with other software such as mail merge or a spelling checker or dictionary.

If possible, seek the opinions of those who have used the programs you feel might meet your needs. Obtain from them their evaluation of the program's strengths, limitations, and idiosyncrasies. Also elicit their impressions of the program's documentation, tutorials, reliability, and cost effectiveness.

Many educational and general computer journals include evaluations of software, typically in a buyer's guide selection. Publishers such as Seybold Publications, Inc., and Software Digest, Inc., provide in-depth evaluations of software. To ensure a thorough evaluation of the software under consideration, these or other reviews should be examined.

Step 3: Select the Program that Best Matches the Requirements

Regarding the recommendation of a program for selection, the user should keep these points in mind:

1. The program should be machine compatible, assuming the computer hardware has already been purchased.
2. Avoid getting trapped into buying a program just because it is popular. Buy the program that is right for you.
3. Do not feel compelled to buy a software program from the company that sold you your microcomputer. Do so only if it meets your evaluation criteria.
4. Cost should not be the only criterion. Simpler programs generally cost less; sophisticated programs cost more. The rule of thumb should be, Buy the program that does the job for which it is intended.
5. User friendliness is important but not the most important selection criterion. User friendliness can be equated to the number of functions a program can perform—fewer functions, easier learning; many functions, more learning. In selecting the program, be sure you get the needed functions.

AUTOMATED OFFICE SOFTWARE

The pool of word-processing programs educators may choose from is staggering. They have been written for all brands of microcomputers found in the schools. Here is a sampling of word processors used by educators: (1) Apple Writer II, MacWrite, Apple Works, Lisa Write, and Microwriter for various Apple models or the Lisa and Macintosh computers; (2) Atari Writer and Letter Perfect for the Atari; (3) Superscript and Palantir Word Processor Version 2.0 for Radio Shack computers; (4) Word Pro 4 for Commodore models; (5) Leading Edge Word Processor, Friendly Writer Version 3.10, Textra Version 3.1, and Wordvision for IBM PC, PCjr., and XT computers; and (6) Bank Street Writer, Bench Mark, Easy Writer II, Final Word, Homeword, Multimate, WordPerfect, WordStar, PFS Write, and Microsoft Word, which have versions for different microcomputers such as IBM PCs and Apple computers. Costs range from $50 to $700 with the expensive programs being able to perform more functions.

A sampling of office microcomputer software that provides mailing lists using an Apple or IBM PC includes: EZ Label, Mailing List, Mailing List Program, Mail Room, Name List, and School Mailer. The average cost for one of these programs is nominal, around $75.

Time-manager programs generally seem to have been written for the IBM PC, supposedly to meet the needs of business managers who use this hardware. A sample of typical software programs includes: Calendar Management, Calendar Plus, IntePlan, Shoebox 2, Sked 2, and Time Manager. The average cost of one of these programs is $169.

Information on any of the software programs that serve to automate office functions may be found in published journals and reports catering to computer users.

SUMMARY

Software for managing the administrative office includes time-manager or electronic calendar programs, merge programs, and word processors. Word processors have become the major automated office tool. School officials may utilize the following steps in evaluating which word processor to buy: (1) determining whether the program is to be used by writer/authors, managers/professionals, or secretaries; (2) evaluating prospective programs by trying them out to assess what each program can or cannot do, eliciting the opinions of users of the programs considered, and weighing the written evaluations of these programs; and (3) selecting the program that best matches local needs and requirements.

9

SOFTWARE FOR MANAGING BUSINESS OPERATIONS

FACTORS AFFECTING SOFTWARE SELECTION

Business-application software is available for mainframes, minicomputers, and microcomputers. Size of the district, existing data-processing practices, hardware configurations, and the results of a needs assessment are factors that may affect the decision of a district as to whether to modify existing programming or to develop or purchase new software.

Size of District and Hardware Configurations

Large districts, especially those with enrollments over 25,000 students, have tended to rely on a mainframe computer to process their business applications (Educational Research Services 1982). Minicomputers, too, have been used widely for this purpose by large school districts. According to Pogrow (1984b) districts with over 6000 students would do well to look at a financial software package developed exclusively for a mainframe or minicomputer system. Small school districts (less than 2500 students) and medium-sized districts (2500–6000 students), because of differing needs and limited computer budgets, typically would not require such expensive, sophisticated fiscal programs. Options open to these approximately 14,000 school districts are the contracting of computer services or the use of microcomputers.

In the area of property control and fixed asset reporting, Bass and MaRous (1983) state that school districts exceeding 15,000 students most likely are using a mini or mainframe computer due to their physical size and financial reporting requirements. For smaller school districts a microcomputer system might be considered, irrespective of whether their property and fixed assets program are organized on a district or individual basis.

Microcomputers have now impacted on school and business offices and are considered to have the potential to greatly enhance the computerization of business applications (Dembowski 1984b). Districts that advocate distributed computing to permit local schools to use microcomputers to handle in-house administrative tasks, yet interface with the central office mainframe or minicomputer, affirm this potential.

Microcomputer software for business applications includes data-base managers, spread sheets, and task-specific programs (Figure 9.1) Data-base managers have been used at both the central district office and the local school levels. Spread sheets have been used to handle fiscal accounting and to make student enrollment, revenue, staffing, and salary projections. These two general-purpose programs are invaluable to school districts of any size but are ideal for the very small districts (fewer than 1000 students) that wish to computerize their business applications (Pogrow, 1984b).

The majority of task-specific programs have been written to handle the "big five" accounting functions of accounts payable (A/P), accounts receivable (A/R), general ledger (G/L), payroll, and inventory control. A few commercial programs exist to facilitate food and transportation management, but the trend in these areas has been toward in-house development. Financial packages that integrate all or most of the "big five" accounting functions are also available from a number of vendors. These programs have advantages over software designed to process a single function only. For this reason they should be considered seriously by school districts wishing to employ microcomputer technology. Pogrow (1985) indicates that only thirteen companies produce financial-management programs capable of managing the entire range of school and district accounts and funds.

The quality and quantity of task-specific programs varies depending upon the vendor and the brand of microcomputer. Pogrow (1984b) laments the lack of programs designed to meet the needs of medium-sized school districts that are reasonable in cost yet perform the functions of packages developed for mini and mainframe computers. To assure meeting local information and procedural requirements, task-specific programs may have to be modified. This necessitates districts having personnel trained to do this.

BUSINESS APPLICATIONS	TYPE OF SOFTWARE		
	DATA-BASE MANAGER	SPREAD SHEETS	TASK SPECIFIC
A. Financial			
1. Accounts payable/receivable		X	X
2. Accounting—financial/cost/petty cash/cash flow		X	
3. Budget monitoring		X	X
4. General ledger		X	X
5. Investments		X	
6. Payroll			X
7. Purchasing	X		X
8. Student activity/dept. accounting		X	X
B. Inventory Control/Fixed Assets			
1. Schools—books/supplies/equipment/ uniforms	X	X	X
2. Facilities—supplies/equipment	X	X	X
3. Warehousing-monitoring inventories	X		
4. Property control/fixed assets			X
C. Food Management			X
D. Personnel			
1. Assignments, development, evaluation	X		
2. Custodial scheduling	X		X
3. Payroll data/reports/overtime	X		
4. Staff statistical analyses	X		
5. Substitute teachers/interns/student teachers and data/records	X		
E. Planning/Projections			
1. Budget development		X	
2. Enrollment projection		X	X
3. Revenue projection		X	
4. Salary projection/negotiations		X	X
5. State aid forecasting		X	
6. Staffing/facilities projections		X	X
F. Transportation			
1. Bus routes	X		X
2. Bus passes	X		
3. Student car registration/parking/ sticker number	X		

FIGURE 9.1   School Business Applications by Type of Software   Adapted from Leahy, P. E. (1983). General use of microcomputers for school management. In F. L. Dembowski (ed.), *Administrative Uses for Microcomputers* Vol. 1 (pp. 8–15). Reston, VA: Association of School Business Officials International.

Needs Assessment

Preliminary to selecting any software package, districts should conduct a needs assessment to identify priority business applications. This task can be facilitated by using a priority/decision matrix (Figure 9.2). The matrix reflects applications at district, school, and special program levels in relation to having a minimal, basic, or advanced program of business computer services. A *minimal* program would retain manual processing, with complex operations being computerized. A *basic* program com-

LEVEL		Minimal	Basic	Advanced
District	1. Needs and expected outcomes 2. Staff/equipment requirements 3. Number of students/staff served 4. Developmental/operational cost estimates 5. Overall priority ranking	1. _____ 2. _____ 3. _____ 4. _____ 5. _____	1. _____ 2. _____ 3. _____ 4. _____ 5. _____
School	1. _____ 2. _____ 3. _____ 4. _____ 5. _____	1. _____ 2. _____ 3. _____ 4. _____ 5. _____	1. _____ 2. _____ 3. _____ 4. _____ 5. _____
Special Program(s)	1. _____ 2. _____ 3. _____ 4. _____ 5. _____	1. _____ 2. _____ 3. _____ 4. _____ 5. _____	1. _____ 2. _____ 3. _____ 4. _____ 5. _____

FIGURE 9.2 Priority/Decision Matrix for Computerizing School Business Applications Adapted from Vigilante, R. P. (1983). Decision making in software acquisition. In F. L. Dembowski, (ed.), *Administrative Uses for Microcomputers* (pp. 25–31). Reston, VA: Association of School Business Officials International.

puterizes each business application as a separate entity. The *advanced* program integrates the computerized applications into a districtwide administrative data base with a computer network functioning to permit entry/retrieval from authorized users. Within each cell of the matrix an overall priority ranking would be made based upon district needs and expected outcomes, the number of students and staff to be served, and the costs estimated to develop and operationalize the computerized system (Vigilante, 1983).

The next step following the determination of priorities is the specifying of the types of software packages needed. To assure selecting quality software that does the task and is reasonable in cost, a request for proposals or RFP for software may be prepared. The purpose of an RFP is to use the competitive bid process to find which vendor can supply the software to meet best a district's specific priority needs. This process may go counter to the recommended procedure of purchasing hardware after identifying the desired software. In practice, this process is usually reversed. With respect to business software, the brand of microcomputer can dictate both the quantity and the quality of programs available for purchase. The premier microcomputer for school business applications seems to be IBM's PC, XT, or AT, and its look-alike computers. Factors supporting this choice are the large selection of software packages written for the machine, its capability for memory expansion through both the mother board and expansion slots, and the number of machines in use (Dembowski, 1984b). The hard disk on the IBM XT or AT also provides more memory, writes new data onto the disk, and retrieves stored information many times faster than the floppy disk. Compared to a 10-megabyte hard disk which can store twenty-five books worth of data, the floppy disk holds barely 260 pages of information. For districts intending to use a microcomputer exclusively for business applications, the hard-disk machine seems to be the answer (Peterson & K-Turkel, 1985).

Existing Data-processing Practices

One outcome of the needs assessment is the awareness that the existing central district office program, whether manual or automated, is adequate. To introduce a microcomputer system when this is the case would, in the words of Bock (1983), be "wasteful... redundant and counter-productive" (p. 60). Criteria that may be used by district officials to assess the effectiveness of their existing program to a contemplated microcomputer system are: Would the latter system (1) save time, (2) save dollars, (3) provide reports in a more timely fashion, (4) provide reports not now possible, (5) improve the accuracy of reports, and (6) improve decision making (Jones, 1983)?

The purpose of this chapter is to present selection/evaluation guidelines for school officials seeking to acquire general-purpose and/or accounting software as part of a microcomputer business system. Preliminary to examining any software, officials should prepare two documents that evolve from the needs assessment. The first would include all data elements that would be entered into a given program such as payroll or accounts payable. The second document would list all required reports, district and state, that relate to the accounting function. As each software package is evaluated, assurances must be acquired that its features match the requirements listed in both documents (McCaleb, 1982). To facilitate the selection process, evaluation questions unique to electronic spread sheets and the "big five" accounting packages are included. Evaluation criteria for selecting a data-base manager may be found in Chapter 10.

SELECTING/EVALUATING ELECTRONIC SPREAD-SHEET SOFTWARE

The selection of a spread-sheet program can be a frustrating experience for school administrators. Currently over forty-five different programs are available from vendors. Though all spread sheets have the same purpose, they differ markedly as to ease of learning, ease of use, versatility, performance, and error handling. Costs may range from $100 to $695, but price does not necessarily reflect what buyers may get for their money. In choosing the appropriate spread sheet, an assessment should be made of both present and future needs. If requirements change or expand, the software selected should be powerful enough to handle the projected changes.

A fundamental question school officials must answer is, "Should we purchase an integrated program?" The answer depends in large measure on whether the intended school officials are to be casual or serious users. The casual user may be the upper-level business manager or a staff member who merely enters information into a financial model to obtain a printout of the updated results. For the casual user, ease of use becomes more valued over functionality. Thus, features such as ease of start-up, ease of learning, and ease of use become paramount. The serious user, in contrast, is likely to be a staff analyst who gets involved in constructing models for reuse. Heavier demands consequently will be made of the program's features and functions. Functionality becomes more important than ease of use, especially if the intent is to assemble data, perform calculations, perform "what if" analyses, manipulate data, display information graphically, and produce the results in a memo or report (O'Keefe, 1984).

Spread-sheet programs should be compared on such variables as learning aids, commands, matrix size/screen layout, on-screen formatting, editing capabilities, math/statistical functions, data transfer, sorting capabilities, and report/printing options. To assist school officials in selecting a spread sheet that best meets local district needs, evaluation questions (Talley, 1983; National Software Testing Center, 1984) are presented under each of these categories.

Learning Aids

- Does the program have a written tutorial as well as a tutorial on the disk? Are sample spread sheets on the disk? Is a reference card/folder and/or key template available? Does the manual provide a table of error messages?
- Can on-screen help be called to the screen or is it continuously displayed? Do on-screen indicators include current cell contents, current cursor location, name of current file, formula for current file, and remaining memory?

Commands

- What type of commands does the program use—mnemonic, control (ctrl) key, or slash commands? Is the program menu driven?

Matrix Size/Screen Layout

- Are the number of rows and columns included in the matrix adequate for local need?
- Does the screen layout provide for variable column width, third-dimensional spread sheets, multiple views of one model, simultaneous views of more than one model, synchronized scrolling, horizontal and vertical windows?

On-Screen Formatting

- Does the on-screen formatting permit numbers to be displayed with dollar signs, floating dollar signs, percentage signs, scientific notation, commas, general decimal, and two-place decimal for dollars?
- Can a standard border be suppressed if desired?
- Can text be entered into cells centered within cells, right-justified within cells, left-justified within cells, and extended past cell boundaries?

Editing Capabilities

- Does the system enable the user to insert a row or column, delete a row or column, move a row or column, overwrite a row or column, edit a single cell, copy a range of cells, go to a specific cell, do block manipulation, conduct a search, and replicate/copy on an absolute, relative, and mixed addressing basis?

Math/Statistical Functions

- Do mathematical functions include sum, square roots, integer, absolute value, common and natural logarithms, sine, and modula?
- Do statistical functions include standard statistical calculations, for example average, standard deviation/variance, linear regression, count or tally, and minimum/maximum?

- Do logical operator functions include (1) less/greater than, (2) equal to, (3) less/greater than or equal to, (4) not equal to, and (5) if-then-else?
- Does the system permit automatic and/or manual recalculations?

Data Transfer

- Does the system permit (1) saving data and/or model only, (2) saving and/or loading partial spread sheets, (3) merging spread sheets, (4) reading and/or writing data interchange format (DIF) files, and (5) reading and/or writing ASCII files?

Sorting Capabilities

- Does the system have a variety of sort parameters such as by row and column?
- Is the speed of the sorts acceptable?

Report/Printing Options

- Are reports wider than eighty columns?
- Does the system use standard printer interfaces, for example, parallel or serial?
- Does the system print (1) screen display, (2) cell formulas, (3) numbers with dollar signs and commas, (4) borders, if desired, and (5) selected portions of the spread sheet?
- Does the program allow printer codes to be inserted and cells with zero values to be omitted?

Miscellaneous

- Is the program hard disk compatible? With the trend toward hard disks for business applications this feature becomes more critical.

Depending on the use they'd be put to, school administrators may want to evaluate such spread sheets as: Planner, Lotus 1-2-3, MicroPlan, MultiPlan, PFS: Plan, Super Cal 3, and VP-Planner (Peterson & K-Turkel, 1986).

EVALUATING/SELECTING BUSINESS SOFTWARE

The "big five" business accounting functions are accounts payable, accounts receivable, general ledger, payroll, and inventory control. Other business applications affecting schools are salary schedule/negotiations and food services. When evaluating/selecting software performing accounting functions, school officials need answers to specific questions pertaining to use in their setting and program strengths and limitations. For example, will task-specific accounting software meet such local requirements (adapted from Pogrow, 1982b; Pogrow, 1984b) as

- Accommodating fund or municipal accounting rather than cash accounting, which is commonly found in business. A fund accounting system shows obligations in the form of commitments or encumbrances, not at the time checks are issued for payment, but at the time purchase orders are issued. Districts that are mandated by state law to use this form of accounting must be sure the accounting program being evaluated allows for this requirement.
- Being compatible with the specifications outlined in *Handbook II Financial Accounting: Classifications and Standard Terminology, Revised* adopted for use by most school districts across the country.
- Allowing for custom formatting of account numbers to meet local needs.
- Generating audit trails to detect unauthorized changes and locate errors. A microcomputer system can facilitate making an audit trail by permitting data recall using reference numbers. Paper documents can be matched readily using these numbers, thus permitting data files to be searched quickly. Predefined checks and balances should also exist to correct input errors automatically or to flag them for manual correction. For transaction entries the system should automatically generate an internal file or produce a hard copy of all transactions compatible with the accounting system used by a county administrative office responsible for managing the investment of district funds and/or approving payments.
- Restricting entry/access of data/general ledger/check-writing files to authorized users only.

Task-specific and integrated business software have been written for microcomputers and minicomputers. Some of these programs have been written for small businesses. For school districts wishing to introduce microtechnology, this means a program may not fit local needs 100 percent. As an example, the field needed to describe an inventory item may be larger than the program allows. Also, the reporting capability may not produce a particular local- or state-required report. For a variety of reasons a program may have to be modified in one way or another. Realizing this, school officials can prepare for this eventuality.

When evaluating a business accounting program, school administrators should be sure it will run on their machines. Though the proper microcomputer model may be owned, the internal memory may not be large enough; or double-sided, double-density floppy disks, or whatever else is required, may be lacking. With respect to any program, local business application requirements need to be matched against the functions and capabilities of the program. To facilitate this process for local reviewers, relevant evaluation questions (McCaleb, 1982; Pogrow, 1982b; Frankel & Gras, 1983) unique to each of the "big five" accounting functions are presented below.

Accounts Payable (A/P) Evaluation Questions

- What is the maximum number of accounts the program will handle? Will it permit future expansion?
- Does the package automatically generate purchase orders (POs)?

- Can the system accommodate partial payments of POs?
- Can a PO payment be distributed to several accounts?
- Does the system prevent modification of PO information after receipt of goods?
- Can one enter payment due dates and maximum payment data for automatic A/P management?
- Are items automatically posted to A/P when goods are received (the invoice-linked system)?
- Can one request a prepayment register before checks are written to make certain all amounts are correct?
- Does the system keep track of uncashed checks?
- Can the system automatically reduce payment due if payment is made within the discount period?
- Does the system prevent checks from being altered after payment has occurred?
- Are checks automatically numbered or must one use preserialized checks with their accompanying tracking requirements?
- Can payments over a certain amount be flagged for personal approval before checks are produced?
- Can payments be deferred to particular dates?
- How flexible are the output formats for check printing and remittance notices? Does one have to buy special forms or can the format be altered as needed?
- Can partial payments be made on each invoice?
- Are payments automatically posted to the general ledger?
- Can the system report unpaid bills according to the length of elapsed time?
- Does the system have a subsidiary file?
- Can one store discount terms in each vendor's file, or can discounts be entered automatically as each invoice is received?
- Can the system report year-to-date (YTD) transactions by vendor?
- How easy is it to add, modify, or delete vendor accounts?
- Can one project cash requirements through any given date, either by invoices or vendors?
- Can one list past-due invoices on command or at periodic intervals?
- Is it possible to retain the following data for each vendor:
  - _____ invoices outstanding?
  - _____ total purchases and discounts taken for this year and last year?
  - _____ number of outstanding transactions and the cumulative outstanding balance?
  - _____ date and amount of last payment?
- What are the error correction features of the system? Can one enter predetermined limits to provide checks and balances during the payment process? Does the system check for valid vendor numbers, invoice codes, or order amounts?
- When errors are discovered, does the system provide an edit list and a clear audit trail?

Accounts Receivable (A/R) Evaluation Questions

- Is the maximum number of accounts the system handles adequate for both current and future requirements?
- Are the number of transactions that can be tracked during an accounting period for each account adequate for local purposes?
- Does the system:
  - ____ report on a balance-forward or an open-item basis?
  - ____ retain all transactions for the end-of-period listing?
  - ____ provide automatic error detection with mandatory edit listings?
  - ____ have an easy data entry process?
  - ____ adjust debits and credits easily to consumer bills?
  - ____ flag any account in which consumers have exceeded their credit limit?
  - ____ permit making account inquiries by video screen rather than by having all information printed out?
  - ____ enable preset credit limits to be established for each consumer's account?
  - ____ have flexible formats for input and output or is special programming required?
  - ____ have adequate reporting capabilities in terms of invoice status report, consumer status report, and so on?

General Ledger (G/L) Evaluation Questions

- What is the maximum number of accounts, and transactions to each, which may be handled in any period? As accounting needs expand, will there be enough room?
- Is the chart of accounts flexible? How easy is it to add, delete, or modify accounts?
- Is posting due automatically? Can you post and list the general ledger at any time?
- Is trial balance automatically produced?
- How easy is it to purge transactions from accounts?
- Will the system accept a single entry transaction?
- Are balance sheets and statements of charges in financial position produced automatically?
- Does the system automatically enter the second part of the double-entry transaction?
- Can the operator enter a transaction to an account that doesn't exist?
- What types of journal entries are supported?
- How often must accounts be closed?
- Are there automatic capabilities such as closing income and expense accounts to retained earnings?
- Can one post transactions to the previous fiscal year (or other period) after the accounts have been closed?
- Are historical records available, such as storing and reporting net balances for each ledger account for the past year, two years, or three years?

- How much flexibility is there in formatting account numbers? Are hyphens inserted automatically? Can letters be used? Can leading zeros be inserted automatically?
- Does the system provide reporting features that fit one's preferred format? Can one define
  - ____ dollar precision for rounding as required?
  - ____ column locations and headings?
  - ____ subtotaling and grand totaling locations?
  - ____ a way to carry forward subtotals and totals to other statements?
- Does the system supply the desired reports, for example,
  - ____ balance sheet?
  - ____ trial balancing
  - ____ year-to-year comparisons?
  - ____ tracking by month, quarter, or year?
  - ____ income statement?
  - ____ department/school financial reports?
- Does the system provide automatic backup of ledger accounts on storage disks after the account is closed?
- Is historical on-line data available to permit such comparisons as this month with last month, this month with same month last year, or this quarter with last three quarters?

Payroll Evaluation Questions

- Does the system
  - ____ accommodate the number of employees currently active? Will it permit further expansion?
  - ____ permit essential personnel data on each employee to be entered? Is it easy to add, modify, or delete employee files and/or job cost control accounts?
  - ____ accept variable pay types? Does it fit one's compensation policies and methods?
- Can employees be paid from more than one account?
- How many and what types of employee benefits can be accommodated?
- Are provisions made to calculate voluntary and statutory deductions? Are these items retained for end-of-period reporting and governmental tax form requirements? Can new deductions be added easily, if needed?
- Are federal, state, and Social Security withholding calculated automatically?
- What provisions are there for updating tax tables?
- Are notices of withholding, such as W-2 forms, produced automatically?
- Are payments posted automatically to the general ledger? If not, does the system provide the appropriate output to complete the G/L?
- Can the system handle a sufficient volume of transactions for one's needs and distribute them properly to appropriate ledger accounts?
- Does the system
  - ____ print automatically checks and information stubs?
  - ____ prevent checks from being altered after payment has occurred?
  - ____ prevent checks from being edited after they have been posted?
  - ____ report unpaid bills according to the length of elapsed time?

- How flexible are the input and report output formats? Can one define them or are they fixed?
- Does the system
  _____ produce the reports one needs, for example, payroll edit list, deduction register, check register, payroll distribution report, payroll history report, overtime and sick report, payroll register employee master file listings, etc.?
  _____ provide historical cost reports to meet future budgeting requirements?
  _____ automatically post all gross pay and reimbursements to the budgetary accounting system?

Inventory Control Evaluation Questions

- Is the maximum number of items that can be tracked by the system adequate for local purposes? Is the part numbering flexible?
- Does the system
  _____ enable items to be added or deleted easily?
  _____ permit basic information such as cost, reorder point, etc. to be modified readily for each item?
  _____ provide suitable sales order listings and sales analyses as required?
  _____ provide automatic shipment reminders?
  _____ produce an average inventory valuation on command?
  _____ calculate carrying costs?
  _____ produce period reports in the right G/L format? Can the report formats be changed as needed?
  _____ enable predetermined levels of safety stock to be set?
  _____ permit economic order quantity and cost data, item cost, and carrying cost for each item to be entered?
  _____ allow the user to query the inventory information from the monitor screen rather than having all the data printed out?
  _____ provide the type of reports needed for local use such as item stock; status reports; inventory file listings showing name, number, quantity, value, and periodic shipment date; price list; back-order status reports; items out of stock and to be reordered; and so on?
  _____ handle inventory adjustments adequately?
  _____ permit regular checkpoints to be entered to alert the user automatically when a reorder is needed?
  _____ enable purchase orders for required parts to be produced automatically?
  _____ integrate satisfactorily with the accounts receivable and general ledger systems?

Eighty-four publishers were identified that offered 286 business software programs to education institutions. The "big five" programs were the most popular, accounting for over three-fourths (76.6%) of the total. In rank order, payroll/personnel ranked first (18.2%), followed by general ledger (15.4%), accounts payable and inventory/warehouse (14.7% each), and accounts receivable (13.6%). Interestingly, only thirteen (15.5%) of the publishers offered package programs for the "big five."

The business software marketed by the above vendors had been written to run on one or more of nine different microcomputers. Of the 286 programs, 90 (31.5%) ran on the IBM PC or XT with Apple (72 programs/25.2%) and Radio Shack (55/19.2%) following next in frequency. Twenty-eight programs (9.8%) being sold by four vendors were written solely for a minicomputer.

The results of this survey imply the following: (1) The IBM family of microcomputers appears to be the preferred business machine, (2) the number of publishers who offered a complete package of "big five" accounting software is small but growing, and (3) the use of minicomputers to perform complete accounting functions for a district seems to be increasing.

Salary Schedule/Negotiations Evaluation Questions

School district officials have the option of using spread sheet software to project salary schedules or to purchase a task-specific salary schedule/negotiations package. If the latter choice is exercised, potential users should seek answers to the following evaluation questions (adapted from Fredenburg, 1983):

- Does the program handle the following types of salary schedules: hourly schedules by hours per day times days per year or hours per week times weeks per year? Annual salary schedule? Salary and credit hours schedule?
- Is the scattergram matrix adjustable up to twenty-five steps and twenty columns? Can the program retain at least one scattergram, a base salary schedule, a new salary schedule, and a salary index at one time?
- Does the program
    ____permit automatic advancement of personnel on the scattergram, with top-step personnel remaining in place? Is total Full Time Equivalent (FTE) also provided by the scattergram?
    ____automatically generate the new salary schedule as follows: percent increase at every cell? flat dollar amount increase at every cell? combinations of percent and flat dollar increases permitted by step? Flat dollar on salary index base automatically increased by index of every cell?
    ____produce the average dollar increases by FTE by class of employees, preferably top step versus those not on top step? Also, are the average dollar and percent raises generated for all employees with the display of these raises by class of employee (top step versus those not on top step)?
    ____provide menu access to different negotiating groups so that it is not necessary to reboot the program when a change of groups is made?
    ____have the printing capability to (1) set up the print format once for automatic recall, (2) provide a printout of dollar differences between any two salary schedules displaying differences by cell, and (3) date stamp all printouts?

SELECTING FOOD SERVICES SOFTWARE

Food services microcomputer software currently seems to be one of two types. The first type is geared to the individual elementary and/or secondary school and focuses on student/adult meal accounting. The second type is designed to manage a school district's food services program. The Food and Nutrition Services (FNS) of the U.S. Department of Agriculture has been in the forefront to promote the development of the latter type. They began this effort in 1979 in conjunction with the Gaston County School District in Lowell, North Carolina. From this venture five software programs were developed (Scofield, 1983): inventory control, a warehousing/distribution and accounting system; pre- and post-costing where both quantity and cost comparisons would be made on an inventory item basis; free and/or reduced-price meal applications; participation and revenue reporting reflecting daily participation and revenue information from the individual schools; and nutritional analysis of the menus served.

Continuing efforts have been made by a number of school districts in the country and by state educational agencies to refine or rewrite the originally developed FNS programs. State agencies, by actively promoting computer initiatives, have had a number of private vendors involved in developing computerized programs to help manage the food service operation. It is expected that more commercial programs will be available in the near future to schools and school districts desiring to implement microcomputer technology. A sampling of food services software available to managers of school/district food services programs is shown in Figure 9.3.

SUMMARY

Primary factors affecting the type of software school administrators might select to manage their business operations are the size of the district and choice of hardware. Though no firm rules apply, it has been suggested that districts having less than 6000 students may find software developed for use on microcomputers adequate to meet their needs. Differences exist as to what size a district should be to consider using a minicomputer or mainframe. Districts having over 25,000 students seem more apt to use a mainframe, while school systems exceeding 15,000 or more students might opt for either a minicomputer or mainframe dependent upon budget and program needs.

Most financial-management microcomputer software has been written for the IBM PC, XT, or AT. Available to school personnel are general-purpose software (data-base managers and electronic spread sheets), task-specific, and integrated programs. The majority of task-specific

FIGURE 9.3 A Sampler of Food Services Software Programs

NAME/COST	HARDWARE	DESCRIPTION	COMPANY NAME/ADDRESS TELEPHONE NUMBER
Automated School Fund Service System (no cost except for copying software)	Apple II+, IIe, III; IBM PC and CP/M based microcomputer	The Apple system includes the following integrated programs; free and reduced price applications, inventory control, participation and revenue, and pre- and post-costing of meals. The IBM PC and CP/M based system includes all of the above programs except the pre- and post-costing of meals program.	Food and Nutrition Service (FNS) c/o Regional Offices or Technology Transfer Section 3101 Park Center Drive Alexandria, VA 22302 703/756-3888
Cafeteria Inventory Control Manager ($200)	Apple II+/48K IIe/64K and IIc/128K	This program will keep track of a full year's inventory of stock items. It allows up to 500 food stock items and 250 commodity stock items. A maximum of 35 cafeteria inventories can be stored in the program report capability.	Precision Computer Systems S. W. Bliss and Associates, Inc. 5155 E. Blue Jay Lane Flagstaff, AZ 86001 602/526-5320
School Free/Reduced Meals Data Manager ($200)		Meal eligibility for students is determined by this program. Random verification letters printed, letters to parents regarding child's eligibility, and school notification lists are output features.	

Product	System	Description	Contact
Food for Fifty ($795)	IBM PC, PC XT, PC AT, Sperry 400	Nine diskettes which contain a data base of nearly 1200 tested recipes comprises this system. Automatically provides scheduled and sized vendor-order sheets, costs and extends recipes, and performs menu-mix analysis. The program can be combined with any other food-cost and production-control system from the vendor.	The CBOARD Group, Inc. Suite 300 First Bank Building Ithaca, NY 14805 607/272-2410
Food Services Management Software	IBM PC HP 125	An integrated menu-driven system, this package includes six distinct modules: revenue recording, payable recording, inventory recording, general ledger, recipe module, and menu function module. The package is designed to handle ten or fewer cafeterias or food service preparation locations.	Weidenhammer Systems Corp. 220 North Park Road P.O. Box 6218 Wyomissing, PA 19610-0218 800/422-8397 (in PA) 800/345-2221 (outside USA)
Lunch Cruncher ($405 for all micros except Apple, which is $375)	IBM PC/256K, DEC Rainbow 100/256K, TI Professional/ 256K, Victor 9000/256K, NCR Worksaver/512K, Burroughs B-20/ 512K, Apple II, II+, IIe, IIc/164K	Specific programs in the Lunch Cruncher are sales and income, invoice and expenses, purchases and inventory.	School Lunch Computer Services, Inc. 66 Witherspoon St. Princeton, NJ 08540

FIGURE 9.3 *(continued)*

NAME/COST	HARDWARE	DESCRIPTION	COMPANY NAME/ADDRESS TELEPHONE NUMBER
Nutribyte ($395 for Inven Tally $495 for Meal Money, or $795 combination)	Apple II, IIe IBM PC, PC XT	Two modules make up the Nutribyte food management system: Inven Tally and Meal Money. The integrated Nutribyte system maintains a file of recipes, plans daily menus, generates grocery lists for ordering, and provides a complete cost analysis.	Masbo Cooperative Corporation 99 School Street Weston, MA 02193
School Lunch (manual, two program disks and data disks $112)	Apple II/48K, card reader ($350) recommended, which reads in all student data going through lunch line	This program can account for all money, lunches sold, lunches eaten, and moneys paid by the students and adults in a school. A nondescript lunch card is essential to the program as it serves to process students through the lunch line and serves as a backup record in case of power or equipment failure.	Educational Computing 755 North 700 East Logan, UT 84321 801/752-3983

Product (Price)	Computer	Description	Publisher
School Lunch Network (Acctg., $189.95; Application, $99.95; Inventory, $249.95)	Apple IIe/128K IBM PC/128K Radio Shack TRS 80 Model III/128 K	Modules in the integrated network are: school lunch accounting system, application approval and verification system, and school inventory system.	Millar & Co. Software G. Bret Millar 1342 Davis Avenue Logan, UT 84321 801/753-6079
Second Secretary ($300)	Apple II, II+/48K	Besides helping to organize school registration, print class lists, and generate current enrollment reports, this program does lunch accounting. It records all cash transactions and establishes a lunch account for each student that is monitored.	Silicon Solutions P.O. Box 2302 Provo, UT 84603 801/373-2224

programs have been written to handle the "big five" accounting functions of general ledger, payroll, inventory control, accounts receivable, and accounts payable. Integrated programs that combine most if not all of these functions are also on the market. The quality and quantity of any of the three types of programs offered to schools vary dependent upon the brand of microcomputer and the publisher.

Prior to selecting any business software it is recommended that school officials first conduct a needs assessment to identify the priority applications. Next, a request for proposal (RFP) might be drafted to help find the vendor who can provide the software that best matches the stated specifications. Prior to making a final decision, school officials should apply guidelines developed for evaluating general-purpose software and financial-accounting software programs.

10

SOFTWARE FOR MANAGING THE EDUCATIONAL PROGRAM

A computer-based information system (hardware and software) has proven to be a real boon to school administrators in managing the educational program. To provide information on the current status of the schools, it was noted in Chapter 1 that data-processing systems (DPS) have been established. At the school level this constitutes a student information management system (Figure 1.6) designed to handle such operational tasks as: attendance accounting, registering and scheduling students, producing report cards and grade reports, maintaining student demographic and health records, monitoring student progress toward graduation, and reporting student performance on school- and/or district-administered standardized tests. Student information management systems have been operated manually or by (1) a microcomputer housed in a school building, (2) a district mini or mainframe computer, (3) the use of a commercial service bureau, or (4) the use of a state-supported and -administered system.

THE SOFTWARE CHOICE

School administrators wishing to introduce a computer-based information system should remember that the first step is the conducting of a needs assessment (Chapter 2). Knowing what the data specifications are, consideration can then be given to determining which of the above approaches seems most feasible in terms of personnel, cost, and support services. If the decision is to go with a microcomputer housed in the school, attention has to be given to the choice of software. Viable approaches are to (1) have the software custom written, (2) adopt prewritten software, or (3) adapt the prewritten software to the locally determined data specifications. If prewritten commercially produced software is the option chosen, the administrator has to ask the question, "Should the software be task-specific or general software (Chapter 7)?" Task-specific software has the advantage of being easier to use since the data forms and the files have already been set up. The disadvantage is the inflexibility, since the program has to be used as written. General-purpose software, such as file management and relational data-base managers, provides the flexibility to meet local needs and specifications. The user determines the form layout and the nature of the files to be set up.

Regardless of whether the decision is to opt for task-specific or general-purpose microcomputer software, school administrators will be confronted with literally hundreds of programs to choose from. In the process they will face a bewildering array of titles, price tags, program descriptions, and program claims. The purposes of this chapter are to introduce school administrators to the types of task-specific and general software on the market that will enable a student information management system to be implemented and to introduce some evaluation aids to facilitate the selection process.

Task-specific Software

Software specifically designed for managing the education program exist as attendance, student scheduling, and grade reporting programs. Packages that execute all three of the tasks are called *integrated programs*. Integrated programs seem to be the wave of the future since they permit the use of a central data file to serve multiple purposes. This capability has the advantage of saving time in entering data and producing reports.

A factor to consider in the selection of any of these programs is, Can the task be done more quickly manually? Administrators can learn much from the experience of one principal who, after spending literally hundreds of hours and much money to get an inexpensive scheduling program to work, sat down and scheduled the students in three days. The moral of her story (Pogrow, 1982a) was:

> Taking enough time (and money) to select the right program in the beginning can save you the most time (and money) later on; and do not use a computer for what you can do as well by yourself (p. 21).

Some general questions school administrators and their staffs should answer when evaluating microcomputer student management software are presented below (Pogrow, 1982a; Huntington, 1983; Dembowski, 1984a):

- Are the reactions of school users of the program positive? Talk to two or more administrators who have used the program at least a year to get their feedback. If the vendor is reluctant to furnish names of users, look elsewhere.
- Is the program free of "bugs"? The rule of thumb is, "The longer a program has been out on the market, the more likely it is to be free of 'bugs'" (Pogrow, 1982a, p. 24).
- Does the software vendor offer adequate support in case of trouble, such as a hot line for user questions? Examination of the vendor's policy and the opinions of users of the program should clarify this issue.
- Are all required program files (program, compiler, DOS) on one floppy disk, hard disk or RAM disk? Program operations can be speeded if this feature and auto boot are part of the software.
- Can all data files be stored in ASCII format, the industry standard for storing data? With different types of microcomputers and different software programs, ASCII storage permits the transferring of data files from one machine or program to another without having to key in all the data again.
- Is the program integrated with other application programs? Integration of attendance, scheduling, and grade-reporting software reduces the number of programs to buy and serves to expedite the analysis and reporting of these management tasks.
- Regarding a tryout of the program using a demo copy or the actual program, (1) Is it easy to start up? Were the start-up instructions adequate to quickly boot up the program? (2) Is it easy to learn? Was the manual well written, providing examples and tutorial aids? Were the help screens well organized and easy to understand? (3) Is it easy to use? Was it easy to enter the data? Do disks have to be swapped frequently? Are help screens provided? (4) Is it structured to handle effectively error trapping or the automatic deleting of entry errors when wrong keys are hit or required procedures are not used? If an error occurs, does the program display a clear message with a remedy for the problem or does the program not allow the error or wait until the user hits the right response key? To test this function, purposely make errors to assess the program's capability to address errors and not lose data in the process of recovery. (5) Does it have adequate storage capacity? The use of a hard disk capability should be considered if a school's enrollment exceeds 1600 or the program is to be used in the central office (Pogrow, 1982a). One advantage of having the hard disk is eliminating the need to switch program disks if an integrated program is used.

Attendance Software

Elementary and secondary principals are required by state law to keep attendance records of enrolled students. The accuracy of these records is important, since the ADA or ADM reported to the state education agency is generally a factor in determining the level of financial aid for the schools. The manual approach to attendance accounting requires each teacher to report student absences during the periods of the day. Office personnel then prepare a roster of student absences for the day and by period that is printed and circulated to administrators, teachers, and counselors. Though the accounting procedures of a computerized system are essentially the same as those of a manual system, the process can be expedited.

Attendance software programs generally require a card reader or optical scanner to enter the absences into the computer. This permits the reporting of student absences by specified categories for each period of the day, with the parents' names and phone numbers printed out. Form letters (Figure 10.1) can be produced to inform parents when an excessive number of absences have occurred. Some programs enable the home to be called to notify the parent that the student is not in school. Schools using these programs have reported cost savings. Summary reports that reflect term (six or nine weeks), semester, and total year attendance can be produced readily. In some instances computer reporting of attendance data is accepted by state departments of education as the official attendance report.

Eighteen publishers were identified that offered task-specific attendance software. Their average cost was $625. The majority of the programs were written for the IBM PC or XT (50%), followed by Apple computers (22.2%). An inconvenience of many of these programs was the use of multiple disks, though one of the more expensive programs had hard disk capability. When evaluating any of these or other attendance programs, the administrator should be assured that the software has features compatible with locally determined specifications. Determine, for example, if:

- Daily attendance is kept by full and half days, including tardies and early dismissals.
- Period-by-period accounting and checks for cuts is routinely done.
- Predetermined absence categories meet local need or can be user determined.
- An adequate number of absence categories exists.
- Telephone call lists are produced.
- Parent homes are automatically dialed to deliver and receive messages.
- Form letters can be produced, using absentee categories, to be mailed to parents' homes.
- Mailing labels can be produced.
- Attendance can be tracked for over 180 days to accommodate eight or more periods with the number of students per period being over 100.
- Reports produced provide for: (1) daily attendance information by period and course; (2) summary attendance data by student, teacher, course, school, date range (weekly, monthly, term, semester, and total school year), home room, and grade level; (3) ADA, ADM, excessive absences, and other statistical analyses; and (4) needed information required for the state education agency.
- Year-round scheduling appropriate to the specific setting can be handled.

```
MR./MRS. TIMOTHY HOLLAND                          DATE:   5/19/86
702 EAST LAWN DRIVE
NEPTUNE
NJ   07753


RE: HOLLAND, KENNETH M.
    870024     NEW JERSEY INSTITUTE OF TECHNOLOGY


DEAR  MR./MRS. TIMOTHY HOLLAND

PLEASE BE ADVISED THAT YOUR SON IS IN DANGER OF FAILING IN
HIS ACADEMIC PROGRAM DUE TO EXCESSIVE ABSENCES FROM SCHOOL.  FOR
THE PERIOD FROM 09/ 9  TO 06/ 5 HE  HAS BEEN ABSENT   6.0 DAYS
AND TARDY   0  TIMES.
THIS POOR PATTERN OF ATTENDANCE IS UNACCEPTABLE BY OUR SCHOOL
STANDARDS AND MUST BE IMPROVED IF THE STUDENT IS TO MAINTAIN
A GRADE AVERAGE SUFFICIENT FOR PROMOTION.  EVERY ATTEMPT HAS BEEN
MADE TO IMPROVE THE STUDENT'S HABITUAL TARDINESS AND/OR ABSENCE.
NO SIGNIFICANT IMPROVEMENT, HOWEVER, HAS BEEN SHOWN.


IN ACCORDANCE WITH SCHOOL POLICY,  THE FOLLOWING MEASURE(S) MUST
BE TAKEN IN AN ATTEMPT TO REVERSE THE EXISTING PATTERN:


        (  )   ADDITIONAL COUNSELING

        (  )   PARENT CONFERENCE  (PLEASE CALL FOR AN APPOINTMENT)

        (  )   REFERRAL TO ATTENDANCE DEPARTMENT FOR LEGAL PROCESSING

        (  )   PLACEMENT IN LOSS OF CREDIT STATUS

        (  )   PLACEMENT ON PROBATION

        (  )   OTHER:


TO INSURE A SATISFACTORY SCHOOL EXPERIENCE FOR YOUR SON,
PLEASE MAKE EVERY EFFORT TO HAVE HIM ATTEND SCHOOL REGULARLY.

IF YOU WOULD LIKE ANY FURTHER INFORMATION,  PLEASE CONTACT OUR
ATTENDANCE OFFICE.


THANK YOU FOR YOUR COOPERATION.
```

FIGURE 10.1 A Standardized Attendance Letter to Be Sent to the Parents of Students With Excessive Absences From Micro Scholastic Records Student Attendance System of Micro Educational Systems, Inc., Howell, NJ

- Storage capacity is adequate for the number of student records needed.
- The program can be integrated with other applications like grade reporting.

Automatic dialers, according to some users, have proven effective in improving a school's average daily attendance or ADA. Gains from 1 to 10 percent have been reported (McGinty, 1985). The prices of self-dialing attendance systems offered by vendors range from $750 to $10,000. The expensive systems provide more calling lines, greater number capacity, enhanced reporting capability, and the ability to deliver many messages. Benefits for administrators of an automatic dialer that seem to weigh against the initial purchase cost are increased revenues due to potential gains in ADA and the freeing of counselors or other office personnel charged with making attendance calls to do other tasks.

Grade Reporting Programs

The computerization of grade reporting was one of the first applications of a student information management system introduced into the schools. Computerized systems have reduced the clerical work of teachers, given administrators information that is succinctly organized 'and has materially helped to increase the efficiency of grade analysis and reporting.

It is safe to say that the more flexible and extensive the grade reporting system is, the more capable the computer software and hardware must be. Though a particular computer-based information system (hardware and software) may be capable of handling a report card program, the machine may not be able to deliver output to the user on a timely basis. Minimally, a grade reporting program should be able to:

- Print personalized report cards that would show a student's grades for each course enrolled.
- Generate self-sticking permanent card labels.
- Compute individual and group statistics on student grades.
- Prepare output reports such as honor roll lists, failure lists, and grade distributions by class and teacher.

For schools and districts that currently do not have a computerized grade reporting system, local marking and reporting requirements must be met by any software program that is being considered for adoption. Some points administrators may wish to check when evaluating grade reporting programs pertain to date selection and analysis. For example, does the program:

- Accommodate a school's total enrollment?
- Accommodate the total number of courses a student can actually take in a school year?

- Accommodate term (six or nine week), semester, and final grade reporting?
- Accommodate the total number of marking periods in the school year?
- Permit optional weighting of letter grades?
- Allow for alphabetic, numeric, and a combination alphanumeric reporting?
- Allow for plus and minus grades?
- Allow for report card comments based on locally determined or predetermined statements?
- GPA calculation method correspond to the local method?

Care should also be given to evaluation of the reporting features of the software, for example, does the program provide:

- Permanent record card labels and/or an end-of-year student transcript?
- Mailing labels?
- Frequency distribution of grades by teacher and department?
- Student grade listings by grade, teacher, course, and/or school level?
- High and low honor rolls for each class?
- Student class ranking for each grade level?
- Student failure, incomplete, and/or withdrawal lists by course and section?
- Alphabetized cululative GPA listings by grade level and school?
- Marking period attendance report?
- Progress reports/warning notes?

Task-specific grade reporting software marketed by vendors seems limited. The average cost of four programs examined was over $600. The current trend is toward the use of integrated programs.

Student Scheduling

The scheduling of students in courses is an application specific to middle, junior high, and high school levels. The availability of scheduling software has done much to enable principals and their administrative/counseling staff to prepare the master schedule and take into account such variables as class size, room usage, graduation requirements, and student/parent course requests.

The features of nine task-specific programs on the market ($940 average cost) ranged from straightforward listings of class enrollments through the actual registration/scheduling of all students on an individual and block schedule basis. The more sophisticated programs allowed students' desired schedules to be compared with their previously earned credits and their school's graduation requirements to assure assigning them to classes on a priority basis. Such programming assures that students will have opportunity to enroll in classes necessary for their graduation. In scheduling students into classes it is expected a program will (1) balance class loads and sections and distribute classes and students fairly; (2) produce homeroom, class, and study hall lists; and (3) avoid course conflict in the student's schedule.

Administrators considering the purchase of a scheduling program should be mindful of the following concerns (adapted from Pogrow, 1984a), for example, can the program:

- Perform block scheduling? Such programs help reduce the number of data entries by not having to enter for each student courses that are uniformly required. Block scheduling, for example, enables all students required to take American history to be registered together or as a block.

- Attend to student alterations? Once the initial scheduling occurs can the program handle transfers, withdrawals, and requested course changes or must this be done manually?

- Run fast enough to meet local needs? A factor affecting the speed of a program is the language in which it is written. Assembly or machine language programs typically are the fastest, followed by programs written in COBOL, Pascal, and BASIC. Printed schedules for the entire school should be able to be run overnight. To assess a program's speed, learn from the vendor how many minutes it takes to schedule 800 students.

- Be networked? This capability has value for large schools that have several computers hooked up to a central hard disk drive. Networking enables more than one user to access the scheduling information simultaneously.

- Create and build the master schedule based on having a resource allocator?

Local requirements again must be considered by administrators when evaluating any scheduling program for possible adoption. Assurances should be obtained that the program can:

- Accommodate a semester, tri-semester, quarterly, or a combination time frame.

- Accommodate a five- or six-day scheduling cycle.

- Assign lunch periods and study halls.

- Handle the (1) maximum number of course requests a student might make, and (2) maximum number of students, teachers, periods, courses, and sections that are to be scheduled.

- Produce such products as student count, course tallies, conflict matrix, and student verification reports; study hall lists; student, teacher, and room schedules; and add/drop transactions.

- Generate a locator to permit locating students by time, period, room, or subject.

Integrated Programs

Reference has already been made that integrated task-specific programs have certain advantages over single-application programs. More vendors seem to be packaging their attendance, grade reporting, and scheduling programs in this format. A major advantage of the integrated program is its ability to reduce data entry time because it allows data from one application (attendance) to be transferred automatically to another application (grade reporting or scheduling) since the applications share a central data file.

Two questions, if answered affirmatively (adapted from Pogrow, 1983b), give reason to support the acquisition and use of integrated software by school administrators. They are: (1) Is there extensive overlap between the information used on two tasks? and (2) Are major portions of the records in one application used in another application? Respecting the first question, administrators likely would respond "yes," noting that overlap exists among their attendance, scheduling, and grade reporting tasks, since all three applications need such basic student information as student name, student ID, grade level, parent or guardian's name, mailing address, and telephone. This means common information can be shared using a central data file. Administrators probably would answer "yes" to the second question. Their reason for doing so is that attendance data stored on students in the attendance program's data file can be accessed by the grade reporting package to record on the student's generated term or semester report card the number of absences occurring.

The "floppy hop" and hard disk procedures (adapted from Pogrow, 1983b) are employed by software vendors to integrate task-specific application software. Under the former system, each application program generates its own data file. These files may be accessed by the different programs. For example, if the registration data file is to be accessed for grade reporting purposes, the registration program disk has to be replaced in the other disk drive by the grade reporting program disk. Though this method permits easy backup and incurs little cost, it has the disadvantage of causing confusion as to which disk should be where. The latter system, in contrast, stores all the application programs and their data files on a hard disk. This makes for convenience and ease of use, but the initial cost incurred to buy the needed hardware is higher.

The number of companies producing integrated student management software (attendance, grade reporting, and scheduling) seems to be increasing. Pogrow's (1985) survey of vendors identified twenty companies marketing programs for microcomputers and eight firms offering software for use on minicomputers and mainframes. This bodes well for school administrators, who now have a variety of choices, one of which should meet local requirements.

GENERAL-PURPOSE SOFTWARE

Task-specific software, we have found, is ready-to-run software that may perform a specific application like attendance accounting or student scheduling. Being completely prestructured, the user has only to enter the data called for in the prespecified format. Another option exists, though, for administrators who wish to custom design their own application formats to meet local needs. The type of software referred to is called a data-base manager. It is one of three kinds of general-purpose software, the others being word processors (Chapter 8) and electronic spread sheets (Chapter 9).

Data Managers

Data-base managers (also called data-base management systems or DBMS) are computer software programs designed to organize and maintain information that is contained in a data base. The data base is a collection of organized information recorded on records held in files that is stored on a computer disk. The data base can be visualized as an electronic filing cabinet having a set of files that can be shared. Once a data base has been created, the data-base manager permits the shared information to be edited, deleted, merged, and retrieved.

Data-base managers have proven to be a valuable tool for school administrators in helping manage the variety of records that are routinely filed in school and district offices. They have been used to help manage records on students, faculty/staff, equipment, property, purchases, expenses, attendance, and instructional and media materials.

To understand the features of a data-base manager, an understanding of such terms as *file, records, fields*, and *characters* is essential. Simply, a *file* is a collection of *records* that consist of a number of *fields* that are constructed of different *characters* (Blackhurst 1983). To illustrate (Figure 10.2), a file might be the personnel data collected on all teachers in a district. The file consists of the records of each teacher assigned to the various schools. Each record (Figure 10.3) contains fields of information about different variables such as name, address, school, salary, and so on. Characters are the individual letters or numbers that make up a given field. In the data base the fields are grouped into records, which are further grouped into files. To refer back to the filing cabinet analogy, picture the file as a particular file drawer having within it records or file folders. A field is a given piece of information in the record or the file folder.

Types of Data-Base Managers.   Though the term *data-base manager* is employed to indicate a computerized system for maintaining records of information or searching and gathering that data (Miller, 1984a), there are essentially two types of application programs: file managers and relational data-base systems. A *file manager* or *low-end data-base manager* permits the user to store and retrieve records made of fields. Similar to the file cabinet analogy used previously, a user is able to pull out a file folder from a cabinet drawer, look for the information that is wanted, and then place the folder back in the drawer. Basically, it is a storage and retrieval system

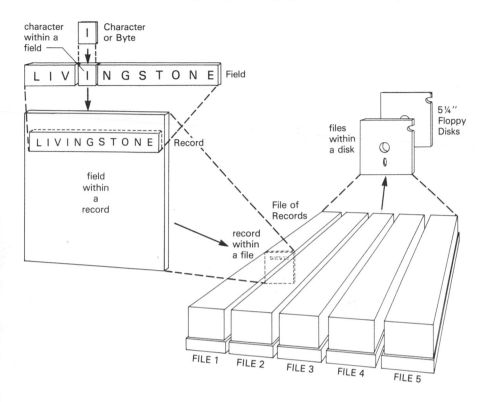

FIGURE 10.2 Physical Analogy of Several Characters Making Up a Field, Fields a Record, Records a File, and Files a Disk From C. D. Lewis (1983). *Managing with Micros.* Oxford, England: Basil Blackwell Publishers Limited, p. 91.

restricting the user to working with one file at a time. This means if a principal has accessed (opened) the student locator file, he/she must close it before being able to use or open the student attendance file.

A *relational* or *high-level data-base manager* has more power than a file manager because of its ability to compare information in one file (student locator) with information in another file (attendance) by "relating" two or more bits of information (class schedule and attendance) through one common item (student ID) or field. Data within the two files, in other words, can be manipulated.

The ability to open two or more files concurrently and move information back and forth among them is called *multifile capability*. As an example of multifile capability, suppose a principal had opened the student locator file to record 100. If he/she were to close that file and open the attendance file, his/her place would be lost. To return to record 100 the principal would have to close the attendance file, reopen the student locator file, and specify record 100. A relational data-base manager would enable

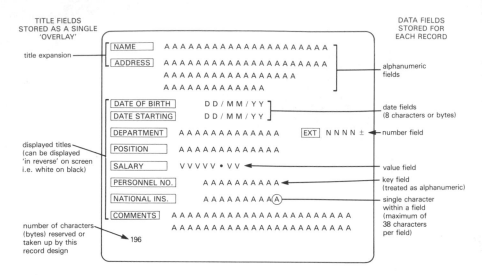

FIGURE 10.3 Designing the Record Screen Layout Showing Fields and Characters   From C. D. Lewis, (1983). *Managing with Micros.* Oxford, England: Basil Blackwell Publishers Limited, p. 93.

the principal to hold his/her place at record 100, look at the attendance file, and return back to the original position in the student locator file.

Another advantage of a relational data-base manager is its ability to create a whole range of files containing different fields. Consider the example suggested by Glossbrenner (1984) of the master personnel file. The master personnel file kept by a school district contains information on salary, supervisory comments, and other confidential information. The personnel director is charged with keeping this information private. How can this be done and still permit an office worker to update the files? The solution is to create a separate file that contains just those fields the worker must have to perform the updates. This restriction means the worker is unable to view any information from the total personnel file except the fields the new file contains.

Sophisticated or high-end data-base managers are able to generate programs, perform mathematical calculations, and do ad hoc inquiries. The built-in programming language of the program permits applications to be custom written, though the uninitiated user may wish to utilize the services of a programmer to write the applications. In comparing the differences between file managers and high-end data-base managers, Jeff Garbers, vice-president of product development at Microsoft, says (Miller, 1984a):

> I think a (high end) data base management system is distinguished by programmability, whereas a file manager is fairly self contained—everything

is there. You don't have to write a program, you just punch numbers from a menu to make things happen. . . . (p. 101)

The query function of a high-level data-base manager permits the user to check the data-base file not only to pull out selected pieces of information but to identify new relationships among data items. The strength of the inquiry function is to enable users to examine old or existing data in new and meaningful ways.

Using a Data-Base Manager.   The two major tasks involved in using data-base managers are, first, setting up the data-base files and, second, retrieving information from the created data files. Activities under the first task involve:

- Determining the specific type of information that is to be stored, sorted, and retrieved.
- Selecting the variables that are to be included in the defined data base.
- Determining the order in which each variable is to be entered into the data base.
- Designing the data entry form on the layout screen, which involves (1) naming the file and (2) setting up data categories on the layout screen such as name field, address field, and so on. Once the form is defined it is stored in the computer.
- Setting up records in the file by entering the desired data into each of the fields of the data form.

If the intent of a school administrator is to create a student master file, key variables would be demographic. Figure 10.4 illustrates many of the variable fields that might be included in a student's record. Before having the data entry form designed, the administrator should be confident that all essential fields in a student's record are included and that a sufficient number of characters have been allowed to enter the information. This advance planning can do much to reduce the risk which may exist in some programs of losing data by wanting later to add variables to the designed form or to change the form in some other way.

Activities associated with accessing or retrieving information stored in the data base are:

- Designing the type of reporting forms needed to print out information wanted from the data-base files.
- Creating an ISAM index or key word file. This requires selecting a few data entry fields to act as index keys on which the data files can be searched.
- Searching for a particular piece of information in a particular field.
- Sorting the records, using a primary and secondary key.
- Adding, modifying, and deleting data elements on the entry forms.
- Using a report generator, if included in the program, to produce documents that contain the desired titles, columns, labels, etc.

Information can be accessed from data-base files by the following methods: (1) sequential, (2) hashing, and (3) the index sequential access method (ISAM). The sequential method involves adding new records to the bottom of a file and finding a particular record by searching the file one record at a time from top to bottom. This method is acceptable only for small files. Hashing permits information to be accessed using a key. A key may be a field or set of fields, such as a student's ID number, that uniquely identifies a record in a file. The key, being numerically transformed, generates a number that points to the physical location in the data-base file where a record is located. Though quick access to a record is possible, the hashing method does not permit direct access of a record using secondary keys.

The index sequential access method (ISAM) permits the use of secondary keys such as a student's last name to access a particular record. To do this, an index is created. The index is a special file in which each data entry contains both the secondary key and a pointer to the actual data record. The data-base manager, using an ISAM, searches the index for a particular secondary key and then retrieves the data record pointed to by the index entry. Most data-base managers use the ISAM approach.

FIGURE 10.4   Sample Variable Fields of a Student Data Base

_____Name (the last name would served as a sorting index key)
_____Student ID number (an index access key)
_____Local street or building address
_____City and state
_____Zip code
_____Home phone
_____Business phone (male parent/guardian)
_____Business phone (female parent/guardian
_____Emergency phone
_____Parent or guardian
_____Birth date
_____Sex
_____Race
_____Entry date
_____Withdrawal date
_____Previous district
_____Previous school
_____Grade
_____Homeroom teacher
_____Bus route
_____Cumulative GPA
_____Cumulative course credits
_____Career goal

Data-base managers have versatility and for this reason have been advocated as a desirable approach administrators might consider when seeking to manage student, personnel, inventory, and other school records. Swartz, Shuller, and Chernow (1984) give the following advice to administrators who are committed to using a data-base manager:

1. Plan carefully before you set up any data-base file. Try out your record form manually before you set it up on the computer. Try out searches and report formats with a small number of sample records before entering all the records into the computer.

2. Phase in the electronic file gradually. Enter all new records into the computer, and enter old records as you have time. Continue to use the manual filing system until the electronic one is complete and has been found reliable.

3. Always make extra copies of electronic file disks, and store them in a different physical location from the originals. Disks cost a few dollars, but the information in a data-base file can be worth hundreds or thousands of dollars in labor costs alone.

4. Do not computerize all your records. Files that are always used in a straightforward manner will be easier to use in physical form (p. 227).

Selecting a Data-Base Manager. School administrators who are serious about wanting to acquire a data-base manager should ask how simple or complicated the information needs are of the school or district. If the needs are simple, involving only the storage and retrieval of a reasonable amount of information, a file manager may be the answer. Also, some of the data-base manager programs directed toward educational use may fit the bill. These programs are easy to use, doing a good job at low cost. On the other hand, if the needs are complex, involving complicated sorts, searches, math operations, and the accessing of two or more files at once to manipulate data, then a relational data-base manager is the ticket. Administrators caught in the dilemma of which type of data manager to choose would do well to ponder the counsel of Viet (1983) who said, "Don't buy more than you need, and try not to buy less (p. 22)."

To compound the problem even further, vendors now make available integrated programs that combine such functions as word processing, spreadsheeting, charting, or graphics with data-base management. The advantages of these programs have been discussed in Chapter 7. Lynn (1985) has touted integrated software as a versatile management tool that can be used by school principals. District office administrators, too, can be beneficiaries of an integrated program in projecting plans and making decisions on the assembled data. In the school setting the data-base component of the integrated program can be used to (1) assemble and update such lists as absentees, class rolls, faculty data, and names and addresses, (2) transform these lists into student and faculty data bases to extract information and create reports, (3) create a school/district achievement test data base to enable special reports to be prepared for counselors, teachers, and parents, and (4) institute computer-managed instruction (CMI) procedures whereby record-keeping functions of mastery learning can be maintained to help teachers assess the degree to which students have attained unit learning objectives.

The spread-sheet component would enable a principal to develop projection models for both short- and long-range planning which would include staffing patterns, budget estimates, enrollment projections, classroom equipment and supply needs, and facility maintenance. The graphics component allows the principal to use numbers from the spread sheet to create graphs or charts to depict visually school projections and trends. Written memos, letters, or reports that explain the data produced from the other three components can be prepared by the principal using the word-processing component.

What features should an administrator consider in a file manager or upper-end data manager? Pogrow (adapted, 1983c) helps answer this question by identifying essential and desirable features of data-base programs as summarized below:

Essential Features

- Ability to handle at least thirty fields.
- Mail/merge interface with a word processor.
- Multiple field sort and select criteria. Can sorts, for example, be made on both primary and secondary keys?
- Form and report generation capabilities.
- Math functions with calculated fields.
- File reorganization capability to permit adding another needed field to the file without losing any existing data.

Desirable Fields

- Note fields to allow a series of notes to be entered into the electronic record similar to the way comments and recommendations can be added to a regular file.
- Minimum restrictions on the use of the layout screens with respect to the number of records in a single file, the number of fields in each record, and the number of characters allotted for each field. One program with few limitations has the capability of storing 65,535 records per file with a maximum of 255 fields per record and a maximum of 120 characters per field.
- Nonunique key fields to provide a way of accessing records where the field is not unique, such as an individual's last name, realizing that more than one student could have the same last name.
- Menu or graphic icon prompts to indicate a procedure without having to seek help from oddly phrased computer instructions. Once a user becomes familiar with the procedures, these time-consuming prompts should be able to be bypassed.

- Hard disk capability to increase the speed of operation and record storage capacity.
- Ability to communicate with other specific application programs, through generating and reading ASCII files, and through producing files compatible with programs written in BASIC, COBOL, etc.
- State-of-the-art capabilities such as multifile systems, networking, and security provision. A "password protect" should exist to permit only authorized persons to access a file.

School administrators have a wide choice of file management and relational data-base software to choose from. Over twenty-five programs are marketed in each category, with the average cost of the former being $325 compared to $450 for the latter. Examples of popular or best-seller file management programs are Advanced DB Master, Friday, Nutshell Information Manager, Omnifile, PFS File/Report, and Visi File. Relational data-base software programs that appear to have acceptance are: DB Master, DataEase, D Base II/III, Info Star, Personal Pearl, Power Base, and R Base 4000. Data-base management software with special education applications are also available to educators. Seven programs administrators may wish to evaluate ($1100 average cost) are Administrative Planning System, Master File, Micro-Refer, Seer, Special Education Management System, SYSDATA: Special Education Information System, and Talley Special Education Management System.

The number of integrated software programs featuring spread sheet, word processing, data-base management, and, in some cases, graphics is still limited but growing. Programs identified ($600 average cost) were Appleworks, Aura, Enable, Framework, Homepak, IBM Assistant Series, Jack 2, Knowledgeman, Lotus 1-2-3, PFS Series, Open Access, VIP Integrated Library, Symphony, and Visi Series. The majority of these programs have been written for the IBM PC, XT, or AT and its compatibles, which limits the choice for schools having other machines.

SUMMARY

School administrators have literally hundreds of task-specific, integrated, and general-purpose software programs to choose from that may be used to help manage the educational program. Prior to the selection of any program the question should be asked, "Can the task be done more quickly manually?" If the answer is no, then care should be exercised to apply evaluation/selection guidelines developed to assess the quality and functions of task-specific (attendance, grade reporting, student scheduling) or integrated programs that might be considered for adoption.

Many schools have purchased data-base managers or data-base management systems (DBMS) to manage the variety of records that are maintained in school and district offices. Two types of programs available to school officials are file managers and relational data-base systems. The former is a low-end data-base manager that has as its purpose the storage and retrieval of one file (a collection of records) at a time. A relational or high-end data-base manager, in contrast, has more power because of its ability to compare information in one file concurrently with information in another file by "relating" two or more bits of common information. If a school's information needs are simple, a file manager may be adequate. However, if the needs are complex, involving complicated sorts, searches, math operations, and the accessing of two or more files concurrently to manipulate data, then a relational data-base manager is the answer.

11

SOFTWARE FOR MANAGING THE INSTRUCTIONAL PROGRAM

Computer-managed instruction (CMI) has been defined by Burke (1982) as "the systematic control of instruction by the computer. It is characterized by testing, diagnosis, learning prescriptions, and thorough record keeping" (p. 188). In the words of Leiblum (1982), CMI includes "all applications of the computer that aid the instructor in instructional management without actually doing the teaching" (p. 127).

What kinds of software reflect these conditions? Goodson (1984) states that CMI programs are instructional and include some report-keeping and report-generating ability. Since CAI (computer-assisted instruction) programs also include some kind of record keeping, such as keeping track of answer responses, this has created some confusion as to what differentiates CMI from CAI programs. Goodson, in seeking to illustrate this distinction, suggests we have a CMI program when the record-keeping capabilities go beyond basic score compiling and scorekeeping.

Within the context of the definitions cited and Goodson's distinction, CMI software can be interpreted to include computer-assisted testing (CAT) programs, electronic grade books or grade management packages, curriculum management systems, and programs designed to prepare individual education plans (IEPs) for use by special education teachers and administrators. All of these types of software meet Leiblum's criterion of aiding the teacher in instructional management. Curriculum management programs seem most to subscribe to Burke's definition since their features include testing, diagnosis, learning prescription, and record keeping. This type of program also appears to correspond closely with Goodson's description that CMI programs are instructional but have report-keeping and report-generating capabilities. A primary function of curriculum management programs is the monitoring of student progress toward specified (locally determined and/or publishing company determined) curriculum objectives.

Authoring programs, which permit the creating of classroom lessons, have also been viewed as CMI programs. In the words of Dennis and Kansky (1984), they provide a way in which teachers can answer the question, "What is the curriculum you want me to manage?" How does the authoring program aid the teacher in answering that question? According to Dennis and Kansky, this is done "by responding to more specific questions of various sorts used for a variety of reasons, etc. It allows the teacher to 'author' the curriculum by providing a non technical way of entering textual, questioning episodes, student controlled decision points, and system controlled decision points. Such programs would ensure the re-creation of the curriculum to keep it current" (pp. 145–146). Overall, it seems that authoring programs meet Goodsons's description, so they are included in this chapter as a type of CMI software.

Though computer-assisted testing programs are considered as a separate type of CMI software having specific applications, it should be understood that the testing function is an integral part of other CMI programs. The results of the test analyses in grade management, curriculum management, and IEP programs facilitate diagnosis, determination of learning prescriptions, and the generation of reports. Each of the types of CMI programs (Figure 11.1) that have been identified are discussed below.

COMPUTER-ASSISTED TESTING (CAT) SOFTWARE

Computer-assisted testing software developed for use with microcomputers can perform a variety of functions. Hsu and Nitko (1983) have identified various testing tasks which they have grouped into four categories (Figure 11.2). Many of these tasks, as noted previously, are incorporated in other than testing software packages per se. Hsu and Nitko also illustrate three types of testing applications using a microcomputer: item analysis, grade books or record keeping, and on-line testing. In our categorizing of CMI programs, electronic grade books are included as a separate type since the generating of class grades by the teacher may be based not only on teacher-made tests but also on homework assignments.

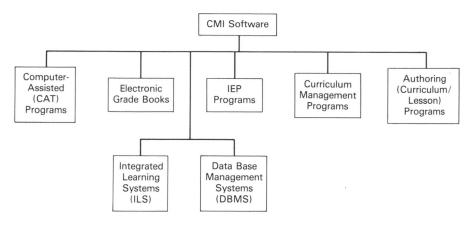

FIGURE 11.1 Types of Computer-Managed Instruction Software

Practical illustrations on how computer-assisted testing can be of help to teachers in test construction and test scoring and analysis are presented (adapted from Spivak and Varden, 1981) below. They enable administrators to recognize how the computer can be a friend to teachers in helping manage classroom tasks.

FIGURE 11.2 Testing Tasks that Can Be Performed by Microcomputer Software Programs   Adapted from Hsu, T., & Nitko, A. J. (1983). Microcomputer testing software teachers can use. *Educational Measurement: Issues and Practice*, 2(4):16.

Planning and Construction
1. Writing items
2. Developing a collection of items
3. Developing a collection of instructional objectives
4. Assembling items into a particular version of a test
5. Printing the final version of a test

Administration of Tests
6. Administration of diagnostic tests, tailored on adaptive tests, and standard fixed items.
7. Test coaching on the preparing of students to take such standardized tests as the ACT and SAT

Keeping Student Records
8. Developing a data-based class profile
9. Entering test results in a record or grade book
10. Placing the results of classroom performance in a more permanent record such as a report card
11. Developing a learning profile for individual students

Scoring and Interpreting
12. Scoring a test
13. Assigning grades to students
14. Computing item data for studying a classic performance or revising test items
15. Summarizing the test results for the class
16. Interpreting the test results for a group and for individuals

Test Construction/Generation

Suppose a teacher needs to check a student's ability to do multiplication. By following the directions of a given CAT program, a test can be created that would measure a student's skill in multiplication. What if one wishes to check a student's ability to understand the main idea of a story? CAT programs can enable a test to be generated to check that skill too. With the aid of a printer, a program can be directed to print tests. Let's say a teacher has stored in the computer's memory a copy of a test given last year. This year he/she would like twenty-five copies of that test. Can it be done? No problem. The computer can retrieve the test and print copies of it in minutes. On the other hand, let's say the teacher wants only ten items on that test or wants them arranged in a different order. Can it be done? Again, no problem. The right CAT program has the ability not only to generate a test but any parts of it in the format desired.

Test Scoring and Analysis

Is it possible to score one's own tests or standardized tests right in the school? Can scores be analyzed to tell what they mean and to have achievement profiles produced? What about using the test results diagnostically to tell us what student skills need to be developed? Computer programs are available to provide this help. For example, a child misses questions 5, 7, and 15 on a test that contains multiplication work. A CAT program can advise what practice work the pupil should concentrate on. Say a youngster misses questions pertaining to the formation of sentences. Again, the right CAT program providing an item analysis can tel! the teacher this skill needs to be retaught. An example of an item analysis report that can be produced by a CAT program is shown in Figure 11.3.

Computer-assisted testing (CAT) software available to schools may be test generation or test scoring and analysis packages only or a combination of the two features. Test generation programs, designed for use by the classroom teacher, have such names as Create a Test, Exam Builder, Test Writer, Tests-Made-Easy, Quick Quizz, Test Writer, Teachers Aide, Teaching Assistant, and Test Generator. The average cost of nineteen programs examined was about $80. These programs have the ability to:

- Develop a user test item/file bank that is stored in the system. Item formats may be multiple choice, true-false, matching, and short answer. Within the file/bank items may be organized by topic, chapter, or as specified. Item storage capacity may range from thirty-five to over one hundred items.
- Select items from the created file bank either randomly, selectively, or by key words to generated multiple versions of a test. The user may be able to specify the number of items wanted.
- Edit, whereby items may be added, deleted, or modified at any time. Some programs also enable lines, spaces, or whole pages to be deleted or inserted. The spaces provided permit students to record written responses.
- Print out student-ready test copies and an answer key.

NAME OR ID NUMBER	NUMBER OF ITEMS CORRECT	WRONG	PERCENT CORRECT	ITEMS MISSED
ARNDT JOHN	7	13	35	3, 4, 5, 8, 9, 10, 12, 13, 14, 16, 17, 19, 20
BENNARDO TONY	7	13	35	1, 2, 3, 5, 9, 11, 12 13, 15, 16, 17, 18, 20
HERTLEIN BOB	14	6	70	1, 8, 9, 10, 13, 17
KRAFT BILL	10	10	50	1, 2, 3, 4, 8, 9, 10 13, 17, 20
LESICUTRE BERNIE	13	7	65	3, 4, 5, 8, 9, 10, 13
LORENCE STEVE	12	8	60	2, 5, 8, 9, 10, 13, 17 20
MCGOWEN BILL	9	11	45	3, 4, 6, 7, 8, 9, 10 13, 14, 15, 19
REGAN BOB	15	5	75	8, 10, 12, 18, 20
SANTANA DAN	10	10	50	6, 7, 8, 10, 12, 13 15, 16, 18, 20
SMITH CRYSTAL	12	8	60	1, 2, 4, 5, 8, 9, 12 17
SUNG SHEEWON	11	9	55	1, 2, 3, 5, 7, 8, 10 13, 18
WOJCIECHOWSKI MIKE	9	11	45	5, 6, 7, 9, 10, 11, 12 13, 14, 15, 20
THE CLASS AVERAGE IS			**54 %**	

ITEM NUMBER	ANSWERS					RESPONSES FROM EACH ITEM			
	A	B	C	D	E	#R	%	#W	%
1	1	2	2	7*	0	7	58	5	42
2	1	1	2	7*	0	7	58	5	42
3	2	3	1	6*	0	6	50	6	50
4	7*	2	0	3	0	7	58	5	42
5	5*	1	0	5	0	5	42	7	58
6	3	0	9*	0	0	9	75	3	25
7	8*	0	1	3	0	8	67	4	33
8	4	6	2*	0	0	2	17	10	83
9	5	3*	4	0	0	3	25	9	75
10	2*	4	5	1	0	2	17	10	83
11	0	10*	2	0	0	10	83	2	17
12	3	2	6*	1	0	6	50	6	50
13	0	1	2*	9	0	2	17	10	83
14	0	2	9*	1	0	9	75	3	25
15	2	1	8*	0	0	8	67	4	33
16	1	1	1	9*	0	9	75	3	25
17	1	6*	2	3	0	6	50	6	50
18	8*	1	0	2	1	8	67	4	33
19	10*	1	1	0	0	10	83	2	17
20	5	2	5*	0	0	5	42	7	58

FIGURE 11.3　A Typical Item Analysis Report From Examination Evaluation Using the Microcomputer, JAC Software, Elgin, IL.

Test scoring and analysis software may have the ability to score standardized tests, but most of eight programs reviewed appeared to have teacher-constructed tests as the emphasis. The names attached to some of these programs—for example, Test Scorer, Quickscore, and Test Analysis—reveal their function. Their average cost was $200. Among the features of these programs are the ability to:

- Score objective tests and match scores against national or local norms.
- Do item analyses providing data on the difficulty level of each item and the degree to which the item discriminated in favor of students who scored high on the total test.
- Sort student responses by score, ethnic group, grade/age, and gender.
- Generate frequency distributions and individual, school, or district reports.

Test generation/scoring/analysis software provides users with a comprehensive package. Though more expensive, their acquisition and use by school officials outweighs the disadvantage of having to buy separate programs that may be incompatible.

ELECTRONIC GRADE-BOOK SOFTWARE

Electronic grade books seem to be the most popular type of CMI software available to teachers—at least, more of these programs are available to teachers. As a teaching aid, they have proven to be a reliable, relatively quick and easy method of recording information about students and printing out this information to meet administrative requests.

The purpose of electronic grade books is to produce student grades for six- or nine-week periods based upon individual classroom performance. Various kinds of reports can be generated such as progress reports, grade summaries, rosters with optional grade posting, and grade distribution plots containing statistical analyses. Characteristics that should be reviewed when evaluating grade books are shown in the checklist found in Figure 11.4. An example of an individual progress report with teacher comments is illustrated in Figure 11.5, while a typical grade summary report using student names instead of ID numbers is shown in Figure 11.6.

Software publishers offer a wide array of electronic grade books for teachers, who are the prime target for these programs. A survey of software catalogs and listings turned up forty-seven separate programs offered for sale by forty-five publishers. Their average cost was $56. These programs, including custom-written packages, appear to be used extensively in the schools. Though differences exist among the programs, basic features included:

- Providing record keeping, ranging up to 200+ students per class for up to twenty classes and up to sixty scores per student. Records would be maintained by name and/or student identification number.
- Recording student absences for any exam, quiz, or report.
- Weighting grades in averaging, creating new grades and changing old, adding extra credit, adding or deleting students, and dropping or restoring the lowest grade.
- Computing statistics such as the mean, median, mode, and standard deviation for any set of scores.
- Accommodating makeup grades, extra credit assignments, as well as regular test and quiz scores.
- Generating letter and/or numerical grades based on raw scores, percentages, or z scores.
- Recording the type of activity and the point value for each activity.
- Averaging grades on a quarterly, semester, and/or yearly basis.
- Producing class rosters (by name or grade), class profiles, class rankings, lists of students whose grades fall below the cutoff point, progress notes for parents, and the storing of teacher comments.

For teachers who are computer literate, innovative, and have access to a microcomputer, consideration might be given to using a spreadsheet to develop an electronic gradesheet program. A primary reason for doing so is

---

FIGURE 11.4 Electronic Grade Book Checklist of Characteristics

_____ 1. Backup disk?

_____ 2. Replacement policy?

_____ 3. Copy protected?

_____ 4. Special school license version?

_____ 5. Specifies student ID as well as name?

_____ 6. Maximum number of students per grade adequate?

_____ 7. Maximum number of grades per student adequate?

_____ 8. Maximum number of classes per diskette acceptable?

_____ 9. Provision made for weighted or unweighted grades?

_____10. Letter and/or percentage grade capability?

_____11. Editing capabilities permit changing scores, deleting scores, adding new names, inserting names, and deleting names?

_____12. Security measures exist to keep files secure?

_____13. Statistics include means, standard deviations, frequency distribution, or histograms?

_____14. Complete grade printout provided?

_____15. Individual student reports by name, ID, or assignment generated?

_____16. Class summaries provided?

_____17. Student missing assignment list capability?

_____18. Class ranking lists provided?

_____19. Provision made for preparing parent letters?

_____20. Teacher note capability?

```
                    PHYSICS I-SECTION 407 PROGRESS REPORT
 DEBBIE DAVIS              1ST SEMESTER 1ST NINE WEEKS    31 AUG 83 TO 10/31/83
 1 OCT 83
                              GRADE PERCENTS                  AVG X % = PTS
 ───────────────────────────────────────────────────────────────────────────
 TESTS            92  93                                       93  32  29.7
 LABS             EXC 95  92                                   94  32  30.0
 CLASS WORK       ABS 90  INC                                  45  16   7.2
 FINAL EXAM                                                        20

                                                           GRADE    83.6
                                                                      C+


 CONDUCT: ___SATISFACTORY                       (MRS.) RE KRAMER
          ___COULD USE TIME MORE WISELY         KINGWOOD HIGH SCHOOL
          ___COULD PAY MORE ATTENTION           540-5000
          ___DISRUPTIVE - DISTRACTS OTHERS
                                                ─────────────────────────
                                                  PARENT SIGNATURE



                    PHYSICS I-SECTION 407 PROGRESS REPORT
 LEONARD SPOCK             1ST SEMESTER 1ST NINE WEEKS    31 AUG 83 TO 10/31/83
 1 OCT 83
                              GRADE PERCENTS                  AVG X % = PTS
 ───────────────────────────────────────────────────────────────────────────
 TESTS            98  100                                      99  32  31.7
 LABS             98  98  100                                  99  32  31.6
 CLASS WORK       100 100 100                                  100 16  16.0
 FINAL EXAM                                                        20

                                                           GRADE    99.1
                                                                      A+


 CONDUCT: ___SATISFACTORY                       (MRS.) RE KRAMER
          ___COULD USE TIME MORE WISELY         KINGWOOD HIGH SCHOOL
          ___COULD PAY MORE ATTENTION           540-5000
          ___DISRUPTIVE - DISTRACTS OTHERS
                                                ─────────────────────────
                                                  PARENT SIGNATURE
```

FIGURE 11.5   Electronic Grade Book Individual Progress Report   From Grade Master, Encode, P.O. Box 5311, Kingwood, TX.

that the spreadsheet, in contrast to a fixed gradesheet program, provides the versatility a user desires to make modifications as need dictates, (McCutcheon, 1986).

CURRICULUM MANAGEMENT SOFTWARE

Comprehensive CMI programs appear to be rooted in a particular curriculum which has specified goals and objectives. These objectives may be locally determined and/or dictated by the program. The major function of the curriculum management program is the monitoring of student progress toward the attainment of these objectives based on student assessment and prescriptive lessons. To do this, the program has a common set of data bases, for example, objectives, curriculum structure, resource materials and activities, test items, student information, and teacher information (Smith R.M., 1981).

The steps listed below illustrate the procedural components that typically characterize curriculum management programs:

1. The curriculum must be spelled out in terms of a set of objectives. These objectives may relate to a course, subject area, or the competencies high school students must meet in order to graduate.

2. Test items must be prepared for each objective to create an item bank for the curriculum. The item bank permits the creation of placement or pretests.

3. Using a pretest, a student assessment occurs which helps determine if the objective has been mastered. Provision can be made to customize the test whereby the objectives to be tested are determined and the number of items per objective is specified.

4. Analysis of the test results has implications for grouping students according to mastery of the objectives and the nature of the corrective (remedial) or enrichment (mastery was attained) prescription.

FIGURE 11.6 Electronic Grade Book Grade Summary Report From Grade Master, Encode, P.O. Box 5311, Kingwood, TX.

```
                           CLASS 1 GRADE SUMMARY
  (MRS.) RE KRAMER                                              1 OCT 83
  PHYSICS I-SECTION 407   1ST SEMESTER 1ST NINE WEEKS   31 AUG 83 TO 10/31/83

       STUDENT          TEST      LAB    CLASS WORK FINAL EXAM      GRADE
                        32%       32%       16%       20%
```

STUDENT	TEST 32%	LAB 32%	CLASS WORK 16%	FINAL EXAM 20%	GRADE
1. DEBBIE DAVIS	93	94	45		83.6 C+
2. GEORGE HENDERSON	79	85	86		82.5 C+
3. CHRIS HOWARD	73	75	81		75.6 D+
4. CHARLIE JOHNSON	73	71	80		73.9 D
5. JIMMY JOHNSON	67	68	24		58.8 F
6. TOM JONES	82	86	87		84.6 C+
7. JAMES KIRK	96	96	99		96.8 A
8. MICHAEL MAC FARLAND	79	81	90		81.9 C
9. JAMES MC KINNEY	79	78	89		80.6 C
10.SEAN O'CONNOR	89	89	92		89.5 B
11.JOHN SMITH	78	81	88		81.4 C
12.AL SMITH	73	75	81		75.5 D+
13.LEONARD SPOCK	99	99	100		99.1 A+
14.BILL THOMAS	89	86	93		88.9 B
15.PEGGY THOMPSON	86	91	95		89.8 B
16.KATHY WESTFALL	81	86	87		84.1 C+

```
  CLASS AVERAGE                                               82.9 C+

                         NO. OF A'S = 2
                         NO. OF B'S = 3
                         NO. OF C'S = 7
                         NO. OF D'S = 3
                         NO. OF F'S = 1
```

5. Formative tests and teacher observation may be used to evaluate both student progress and the prescriptive strategies and materials used.
6. At the end of the instructional period a post- or summative test is administered to assess student mastery of the curricular objectives.
7. Reports are produced which might reflect individual and/or group performance on each objective tested for each test administered. Figure 11.7 illustrates a district summary of responses by objectives report.

For this reporting, twenty-six companies were found marketing curriculum management (the monitoring of student progress by objectives) software. Included were a number of textbook and/or test publishers (CTB/McGraw-Hill; Holt, Rinehart and Winston; Houghton Mifflin; Random House; Scott, Foresman; and Science Research Association) who have keyed the software to their products. Schools currently using curricular materials from any of these firms may wish to consider their

FIGURE 11.7 A District Summary of Responses by Objectives Report From Educational Assessment Test Scoring System, Applied Educational Systems (AES), RFS 2, Box 213, Dunbarton, NH.

			RANGE OF SCORES FOR QUESTIONS IN THIS OBJECTIVE	
REPORTING OBJECTIVES	# OF QUES	PERCENT CORRECT	LOW % CORRECT	HIGH % CORRECT
101 ADD FRACTIONS	4	72.5	62.9	80.0
102 SUBTRACT FRACTIONS	4	73.9	61.4	85.7
103 MULTIPLY FRACTIONS	4	66.4	57.1	75.7
104 DIVIDE FRACTIONS	4	70.0	54.3	80.0
105 FRACTIONS TO DECIMALS	4	57.9	35.7	75.7
106 FRACTIONS, DECIMALS TO PERCENT	4	63.6	47.1	74.3
107 PERCENT PROBLEMS	6	49.3	31.4	58.6
108 WORDS TO ALGEBRAIC EXPRESSIONS	3	77.6	74.3	82.9
109 EVALUATING EXPRESSIONS (AB/C)	5	63.1	27.1	80.0
110 SOLVING EQUATIONS (3+X=5)	5	66.3	54.3	77.1
111 GEOMETRY (ANGLES, AREA & PER.)	7	47.6	28.6	64.3
112 ROUNDING DECIMALS	1	67.1	67.1	67.1
113 PROBABILITY PROBLEM	1	61.4	61.4	61.4
114 PRIME NUMBER PROBLEM	1	44.3	44.3	44.3
115 ADD DECIMALS	4	84.3	77.1	88.6
116 MULTIPLY DECIMALS	4	80.4	70.0	87.1
117 DIVIDE DECIMALS	4	75.7	72.9	80.0
118 SUBTRACT DECIMALS	4	73.6	65.7	81.4
119 DECIMAL TO FRACTION	3	58.1	57.1	60.0
120 PERCENT TO FRACTION	1	61.4	61.4	61.4
121 ADDING SIGNED NUMBERS	3	83.8	82.9	84.3
122 SUBTRACT SIGNED NUMBERS	3	65.2	58.6	72.9
123 MULTIPLY SIGNED NUMBERS	3	76.7	68.6	81.4
124 DIVIDE SIGNED NUMBERS	3	75.7	70.0	84.3
125 SOLVE PROPORTIONS (A/18=3/9)	4	74.3	68.6	82.9
126 INTERPRET DIVISION SYMBOL	1	64.3	64.3	64.3
127 SQUARE ROOT (81^1/2)	1	85.7	85.7	85.7
128 COMPUTE AVERAGE	1	75.7	75.7	75.7
129 WORD PROBLEMS (PERCENT & AREA)	6	54.8	48.6	62.9

STUDENTS TESTED: 70   QUESTIONS: 98   OBJECTIVES: 29 software. Adoption, however, may delimit the program to use with a predetermined curriculum which could prove restrictive if curricular changes occurred.

The cost of the twenty-six identified programs ranged from $150 to $4000, with the average being $825. The low-range programs were delimited to monitoring student achievement toward goals and objectives, while the high-end programs were comprehensive, providing, in addition to monitoring, prescriptive lessons in several subject areas and extensive reports. The capacity of these systems was also greater, permitting more storage for student records, objectives, and test forms. Licensure provisions, too, tended to increase the purchase cost.

Features common to the comprehensive programs were the ability to:

- Develop a data base that would accommodate a given number of students, instructional objectives, teachers, test forms, and test administrations.
- Prepare personalized assignments for students, either displayed or printed, which would identify needed instruction and practice.
- Predefine the mastery level of performance in attaining mastery of the instructional objectives being measured.
- Prepare individualized lesson plans.
- Monitor student progress daily, weekly, or monthly.
- Cross-reference curriculum materials to instructional objectives.
- Produce individual, class, and building reports; mastery lists; and student take-home reports.

INDIVIDUAL EDUCATION PLAN (IEP) SOFTWARE

P.L. 94-142: The Education for All Handicapped Children Act of 1975 contains specific data collection and reporting requirements. These include the collecting of data for child count reports, the reporting of full-time equivalency to state departments of education, and the creating of individual education plans (IEPs). The IEP is central to the initiation of any special education program. Included in the IEP are such requirements as (1) the present educational level of the child; (2) a statement of annual goals, including short-term objectives; (3) specific services to be provided; (4) the educational program to be followed; (5) the date services are to begin; (6) the duration of such services; and (7) the evaluation measures to be employed to assess the child's progress toward meeting the objectives and goals specified.

The preparation of IEPs has required a considerable investment of time by teachers, secretaries, and other school personnel in school districts. One district estimated that it took as much as an hour to develop and prepare IEPs for each of their special education students (Guilbeau, 1984).

To reduce the time and expense involved in this preparation, a variety of CMI/IEP programs are now available for examination. Major components of many IEP packages (Bennett, 1982) provide that (1) curriculum goals and objectives relevant to the needs of handicapped children are stored; (2) an assessment of a student's current performance, using test items, is conducted; (3) the most appropriate objectives for the student, based on the results of the preassessment, can be determined; (4) teaching strategies, drawn from a stored list, can be selected to help teach the selected goals and objectives; (5) evaluation measures can be designed to test the student's progress toward the approved goals and objectives; and (6) the complete IEP is printed for use in instruction and compliance monitoring.

IEP programs vary in the features offered, which necessitates that in the selection process attention be given to the degree of local input allowed and the comprehensiveness of the package. Essential to the process is the checking (adapted from White, 1984) of the following features:

- *Printouts.* Can the package print only selected parts of the document? If so, on one or multiple forms?
- *Security.* Has provision been made for each IEP user to have a password? Is an auditing feature available that records when information was recorded and by whom?
- *Storage.* What is the maximum number of students the program can accommodate? Does the program have hard disk capability? Does the program allow interaction with a mainframe computer?
- *Compatibility with state networks.* Does the user's state have a network that electronically links local education agencies to a central bureau? If so, will the hardware already owned and the software considered permit communicating with this network?

The number of IEP packages offered by vendors has been increasing. They vary in complexity and cost. Of nineteen programs examined, a user could spend from as little as $50-70 to a high of $3995. The average cost was just over $1000. The low-cost programs were simple to operate, allowing users to create their own goals, but required the use of three separate disks: one for creating the master IEP form, a second to store goals and objectives, and the third to store the completed IEPs. Regardless of this inconvenience, teachers are able to create, edit (delete or insert student data as needed), and print the IEP document quite simply. The high-cost program was licensed for use and not only produced IEPs but generated remediation plans for the classroom and the home of each student.

A number of programs are based on different scales such as the Intellectual Abilities Scale (IAS), the Peabody Individual Achievement Test (PIAT), the Santa Clara Plus Inventor of Developmental Tasks, and the Brigance and Enright Inventories. If special educators endorse any of these instruments, adoption of the IEP-based software may be justified. Other programs, however, permit users to prepare and input locally determined goals, objectives, and prescriptive activities. In the selection process, consideration should be given to the reporting capability of the software to meet local and state reporting requirements.

AUTHORING SYSTEM SOFTWARE

Author-promoting system software is interactive, enabling teachers and other school personnel with little or no programs skills to create classroom or CAI lessons. The system asks the author what message to display, what answers to accept as correct, what feedback to display contingent on particular responses, and so on. The system then generates the lesson according to these specifications (Steinberg, 1984).

The advantages authoring programs have for school personnel who wish to design classroom lessons are: (1) programming expertise is not a prerequisite, (2) editing changes can be made by the author as needed, and (3) flexibility exists in working out formats to enhance individualization of instruction.

Disadvantages associated mostly with microcomputer systems are limited storage capacity and the limitations of program flexibility that are possible when using a programming language like BASIC.

Authoring programs enable more than a CAI lesson to be created. Procedures for managing a lesson are also possible, including (1) preassessment to determine before the lesson if the student has the prerequisite knowledge, (2) formative testing to monitor a student's progress toward the specified goals, and (3) criterion testing to determine if the student has met the minimum level of performance necessary to go on to the next lesson section or unit.

Thirteen publishers were found who offered school officials computer-authoring software. The average cost of fifteen programs was $430, but was skewed due to the $2000 cost of one program that touted the use of a powerful language to program computer-based training materials. Its authoring environment included on-line aids with editors for source, character sets, and graphics. Programs that provide both CAI and CMI applications may best meet the needs of educators who wish to use the software, not only to author courseware but to manage the instructional process. CAI applications would permit the development of courseware for most subjects. The text screens would enable the user to do word processing, test creation, prescriptions, and the updating of old lessons. CMI features would include the scheduling of next lessons, monitoring student progress, branching over remedial material, tutoring and evaluation, and the generating of student progress reports. The use of authoring programs facilitates the development of locally developed courseware, but the trend seems to be toward the purchase of commercial courseware. For this reason, authoring systems may be slow to catch on in the classroom environment.

INTEGRATED SYSTEMS

Integrated learning systems (ILS) are completely computerized packages that permit the hardware and courseware components to be used exclusively with each other. These systems had their beginnings with the mainframe and minicomputers, though today they have been adapted for the microcomputer. Other names associated with ILS are total instructional package and turnkey system. When used on a mainframe or minicomputer, they offer the advantages of a large storage capacity which permits the inclusion of a management record-keeping and reporting capability, and increased response time to a student's input. The major reason why many school districts do not use an integrated learning system is the cost associated with the purchase or renting of a minicomputer and/or the purchase of the ILS software service. Many systems, however, such as Dolphin, CCC-17, and Plato/WICA, have offered the complete teaching/learning package desired by some school districts.

DATA-BASED MANAGEMENT PROGRAMS

In lieu of specifically designed CMI programs, the use of data-based management systems (DBMS) may be applied to the development of programs to manage student information. Essentially, CMI programs inventory information, a task uniquely performed by data-based management programs. Besides having student demographics on file, DBMS programs can store student, class, or school performance in different curriculum areas. A fuller discussion of DBMS programs available for school use is found in Chapter 10.

EVALUATING AND SELECTING CMI SOFTWARE

The task of selecting CMI software is not an easy one, considering the many programs available on the market. A question many school districts ask when considering commercial programs is, "Will they meet our local needs and requirements?" Local circumstances may dictate preference of a custom program. If so, there are three ways (Smith R.M., 1981) this might be accomplished, for example:

- Hire a programmer and have a custom program written to match your instructional program.

- Buy a commercially available program, use what you want, and adapt your instructional process to the program.
- Buy a commercially available program, hire a programmer, and have the program modified to meet your needs (p. 7).

If time, money, and programming are not available for customizing, a school or school district may have to settle for a commercial program. Whether the intent is to utilize a commercial program or to customize it, a decision has to be made respecting which CMI software is best for local purposes.

CMI PROGRAMS: ARE THEY DOING THE JOB?

Consensus does not exist among users of microcomputer CMI programs as to their value. Less dissatisfaction seems to exist regarding the use of electronic grade books and CAT programs. More ambivalence is evident regarding the merits of curriculum management programs. Goodson (1984) identifies three reasons why dissatisfaction seems to exist among users: limited computer memory, too few reporting features, and programs that are too difficult to use.

Limited Computer Memory

Reporting and testing features in CMI programs use up a lot of memory. Microcomputers used for CMI typically have had a minimum memory size of 32K or 48K, with 128K now becoming more common. The secondary memory of CMI programs used to store information is generally done with floppy disks. R.M. Smith (1981) provides the following ground rules in terms of total system capacity:

- With little disk switching and a CMI program of medium complexity, about 100 students can be maintained.
- With much disk switching and a CMI program of medium complexity, up to 1000 students can be maintained (p. 6).

To increase secondary or disk memory, an option is to acquire a hard disk drive.

Too Few Reporting Features

Goodson (1984) contends that school administrators need more detailed reporting features than CMI programs generally offer. For the principal who has to manipulate information in different ways to provide the district office with specific records it requires, problems can arise. According to Hofmeister (1984) CMI information on pupil progress and resource information on instructional methods and materials can be used by district in-service training coordinators, curriculum supervisors, and instructional materials center staff. Specifically, the in-service training coordinators would use the information to plan in-service training and to assess the effectiveness of that training. Curriculum supervisors would review the information to determine areas of the curriculum that need revising and where consultant help to teachers and principals is needed. The staff of the instructional materials center would review the information in terms of what resource materials yet need to be acquired and how effective existing materials facilitate learning. The implication is that if CMI programs are to serve their purpose to improve the instructional program, they must contain the essential reporting features.

Too Difficult to Use

As Goodson (1984) remarks, "Educators may never spend much time using CMI software if they consider the program too difficult or cumbersome to use; if their students have difficulty using it; or if the results don't significantly improve a student's performance or add to their own information about the student" (p. 8). The method by which the entries are made is a major factor in determining if a program is going to be used. Hofmeister (1984) states that a program may become so aversive that it is dropped if teachers have to enter data by hand at a keyboard. The preference instead is the use of an optical card reader attached to the microcomputer to simplify data entries. R.M. Smith (1981) reflected this concern in his discussion of the advantages and disadvantages of alternative ways to organize a micro-based system for CMI. The most typical arrangement, he found, was the housing of the microcomputer in a central location operated by a trained aide who controlled all data entry and report generation. Teachers would submit data to the center on cards containing written codes on standardized forms or on mark sense sheets. A different alternative was the housing of computers in the classrooms of those teachers participating in the CMI system. This option appeared to have the advantage of involving the student in managing his/her own instruction but placed more responsibility on the teacher to monitor data entries.

Quality of Training

Related to the difficulty of any CMI program is the quality of training school faculty have received to use microcomputers for direct instruction or the management of instruction. The major criticism teachers have expressed about their training is that it was more programming oriented than application based. Recognizing this limitation, many states have made teacher training a high priority. Presently, eleven states and the District of Columbia require either all teachers or some teachers to take computer courses for graduation (Reinhold & Corkett, 1985). If the emphasis in computer training beccmes application based, the expectation is that more teachers will be introduced to computer-managed instruction programs and will be in a better position to select and use packages that make sense for them.

Examples of Successful Programs

Examples exist where CMI programs seem to be doing the job. Profiles of seven school districts having successful computer-managed instruction programs were reported by the Northwest Regional Educational Laboratory (R.M. Smith, 1981). Those districts ranged in size from 467 students in Wrangell, Alaska, to 190,000 enrolled in the Houston schools. Four of the districts used commercial programs; one did some customizing of a commercial program, while the remaining two districts developed their own software. The one factor that characterized the success of these separate CMI programs was the meeting of local needs.

New Developments

A new development that may make microcomputer CMI programs more attractive is the separating of the CAI and management sections into two separate programs rather than having them integrated. The large publishing companies that seem to be moving in this direction are applying this approach to broad curriculum packages such as in math and reading. Speaking of this development, Goodson (1984) says:

> This development could do much to solve CMI's historical problems. Memory would not be in short supply, so extensive reporting features could be offered without limiting the quality of the instruction. Administrators would be able to compile detailed information on the impact of computer-assisted instruction, for their own use as well as the districts (p. 8).

With the advances being made in computer technology and the quality of software improving, the prospects look good that CMI programs will make a greater impact in helping schools manage the instructional program.

SUMMARY

Software used to manage the instructional programs of schools includes electronic grade books, computer-assisted testing, curriculum management programs, IEP (individual educational plan) packages, authoring systems, integrated learning systems (ILS), and data-based management programs. These software may be categorized under the term *computer-managed instruction,* which has as its purposes the diagnosing of instructional needs, the testing and monitoring of student achievement, the matching of instructional materials to teaching/learning activities, and the recording of information about students.

When evaluating CMI software, school officials should be assured that a program will meet local needs and requirements, have adequate memory, offer detailed reporting features, and be simple to use. A new development that may make CMI programs more attractive is the separating of the instructional and management aspects into separate programs.

12

THE ROLE OF
DISTRICT/SCHOOL
COMPUTER POLICY

The microcomputer revolution of the 1980s has compounded what is required in the management of computer resources. Initially, the management model followed was that adopted from the business world. The mainframes of the 1950s and the minicomputer of the 1970s were centrally controlled and used for clerical data processing and paperwork automation. Instructional applications were limited. The computer was perceived as a piece of high-speed tabulating equipment that processed such business tasks as payroll, inventory, accounts payable, and accounts receivable. The clerical applications of automating student attendance accounting and grade marking subsequently followed. Over time, the use of these computers as managed by a district data-processing department reached Gibson and Nolan's (1974) maturity stage (Chapter 2). Under this management scheme, school principals and teachers assumed a passive role. For students, the computer was a purveyor of information and not the interactive machine it is today.

The microcomputer dramatically altered the perceptions individuals had toward computers. Being computer literate became equated in the public's mind with economic success. Schools, therefore, were expected to prepare students for the future by offering courses in how to use computers. This resulted in the computer becoming an *object* of instruction.

As the potential of the microcomputer was realized, other instructional and administrative applications for its use were implemented (Figure 12.1). For most educators and the public, instructional applications seem to be the most important, with the computer-literacy emphasis reigning as "king" (Technically Speaking, 1985a).

The microcomputer movement in the schools has shifted from Gibson and Nolan's initiation phase to the expansion phase (Chapter 2). The initiation stage was characterized by lax management, a loose budget, and little or no control over the direction instructional and administrative applications would take. Leadership, typically, was from the bottom up, with enthusiastic teachers taking the leadership, rather than from the top down. Due to the pressure to implement literacy programs, the acquisition and placement of hardware preceded the training of teachers and the development of the curriculum (Zuk & Stilwell, 1984). The expansion stage has been characterized by the proliferation of broader and more advanced instructional and administrative applications, the increased number of teachers and administrators becoming computer literate, and the continuing rise of expenditures for hardware/software acquisitions and personnel training.

Before schools and districts move into the formalization and maturity stages, greater control has to be exercised over the computer resource. Large districts with extensive resources have had the most success in this endeavor. The formalizing of a district/school computer policy is representative of the attainment of these stages. The policy would reflect district/school computing priorities as they relate to acquisition, funding, personnel, facilities, computer configurations, organization, privacy and security concerns, and evaluation of services (Figure 12.2). At present, school policies and procedures seem to be falling far behind the heavy investment made by school districts to acquire microcomputers for instruction. A survey conducted by the National School Boards Association of 263 representative school board presidents (School Policies Fail 1984) found that 96 percent of the districts used computers for instruction, but only 14 percent had board policies or guidelines for selection of software/hardware.

This chapter will focus on the elements of policy formulation, factors affecting computer policy, policy approaches, and the application of policy analysis in formulating computer policy. Though the microcomputer will be the primary focus of this chapter, the policy guidelines formulated apply equally to the projected use of mini or mainframe computers.

ELEMENTS OF POLICY FORMULATION

State and local educational agencies have and are yet making daily decisions on how microcomputers can be used best for administrative and

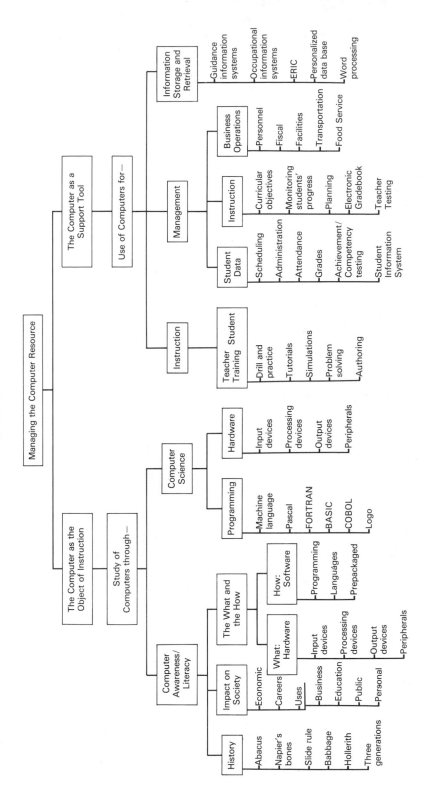

FIGURE 12.1 An Overview of Microcomputer Applications in Schools and Districts   Adapted from Schultz, K. A., & Hart, L. C. (1983). Computers in education. *Arithmetic Teacher, 31* (4), 36.

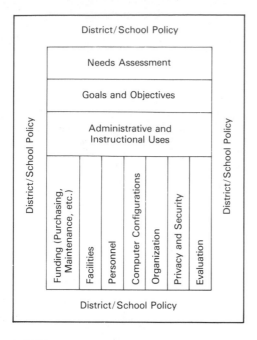

FIGURE 12.2 Dimensions of a District/School Computer Policy

instructional purposes. The formulation of a computer policy assures that the decisions made result not from inaction but from planned action. The purposes of a computer policy are to identify specific goals, establish mandates, provide guidelines, and outline problem strategy (Guba, 1984). The strategy provides school administrators with a plan of action or the guidelines within which they may operate. Good policy depends upon two judgments: knowing what is to be done and how it is to be accomplished. Critical to the success of both is timing (Rubin, 1984). This implies that school administrators should not delay formulating their computer policy if they wish to be "masters in their own house."

The formulated district/school computer policy should meet the following characteristics, for example, it should:

1. Acquaint the district's publics with the purposes of its educational computing program.
2. Provide the framework whereby the procedures for implementing the program will be specified.
3. Provide a legal reason for the allocating of funds and facilities to ensure making the policy work.
4. Be subject to review with the objective of modifying and improving it consistent with changing conditions. When under review, the following questions should be asked: What problem(s) does this policy answer? Are the computer goals desirable according to sound practice or individuals' visions

of where, directionally, computers in education are going? Are the mechanisms for implementing the policy sound and workable?

5. Be developed through a cooperative endeavor involving representatives from administration, teaching, support staff, and the community.
6. Be stated clearly and precisely.
7. Clearly define the lines of authority and responsibility for the execution of the policy.
8. Be interpreted periodically to keep the district's publics informed.

The nature of the computer policy is dependent upon the issues or problems it addresses. Ideally, the policy should be simple and straightforward addressing priority concerns. Rampy, White, and Rockman (1983) identified twenty-one policy issues concerning the roles of computers in education grouped under the categories of curriculum, courseware, teacher-related, other constituent's role (outside agencies), and acquisitions and funding. Today, a number of these issues have been addressed, such as state educational agencies calling for certification requirements for teachers. Administrators need to be selective regarding what issues to press for policy formulation. It should be understood that policy may be formal or informal, written or unwritten, formulated but ignored. The intent should be to propose policy only on critical issues that have both immediate and long-term implications for the continuance of a quality computer program.

FACTORS AFFECTING COMPUTER POLICY

Computer policy can be influenced by external groups or agencies and factors internal to a district. Prominent among external groups are state departments of education, legislative bodies, parent and organized community groups, and professional organizations such as the International Council for Computers in Education (ICCE) and teacher associations. State departments of education, by determining teacher certification and student computer-literacy requirements, have had a direct impact on local school district policy. State legislatures that appropriate funds for computer acquisition and use may write in certain conditions affecting how school districts apply the moneys. Parent groups, in promoting the interests of their children, may lobby for particular computer emphases. The ICCE, by publishing its suggested district policy on software copyright violation, is in a position to influence local policy. Teacher associations, too, seek to influence local computer practices. An example is the release by the National Education Association of software reviews that had their endorsement for use in the nation's classrooms. Controversy in the educational community resulted from this decision (Englade, 1984; Cramer, 1984).

Within the school district, organizational climate may dictate the direction formulated policy will take. The climate should be conducive to open communication that fosters a wholesome information flow between administrators, teachers, and others within the school district and with parents and other patrons outside the district. Of vital importance is feedback on the results of implementing a policy decision (Campbell & Layton, 1969). Since the internal climate and state policy impinge heavily upon a school district, the nature of these influences is discussed.

The Effect of Organizational Climate

To initiate and implement a policy respecting the administrative and instructional use of computers, an open and facilitative organizational climate seems essential. Managerial systems, including public schools, have been categorized by Likert (1961) as exploitative-authoritative; benevolent-authoritative; consultive; and participative. The authoritative systems are deemed the least desirable types of management in that communication is mainly downward, with goals and decisions determined or verified at the top. The consultive system leans toward a shared approach, with control remaining at the top. The participative system is preferred when change such as the introduction of microcomputers into the schools is to be accomplished. In this form of school management goals are set through group participation; communication flows in all directions (up, down, sideways); control is a shared function throughout the system; supportive behavior occurs in all situations; and rewards are determined through group decision.

Roberts (1978) has identified change facilitators under the categories of "strategic principles" and "process variables." Facilitators under strategic principles that can foster the use of microcomputers are *planning, support*, and *training*. Planning is oriented toward the people in the organization who will be expected to use computers. Support to assure successful implementation has to come from the superintendent and building principals, with adequate resources provided by them. Training must be provided that is tailored to local needs and reflects individual user differences.

The process variables that help create a climate for change are *participation, communication*, and *motivation*. Similar to Likert's participative system of management, the participation variable connotes shared decision making and the involvement of all personnel affected by computer use.

The health of an organization depends on the quality of communication. Open and active communication serves to reduce potential conflicts and strengthens constructive decision making. The motivation variable rewards accomplishment and encourages professional growth. Figure 12.3 depicts how communication is a vital link that facilitates the interface between the three administrative activity cycles of policy formulation,

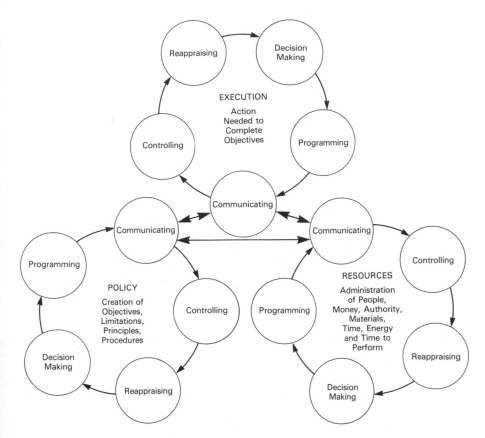

FIGURE 12.3   The Role of Communication in the Administrative Cycles of Policy Formulation, Policy Execution, and Administrative Resources   From Green, E. J., & Redmond, G. H. (1957). Comments on a general theory of administration. *Administrative Science Quarterly*, 2 (2), 240.

policy execution, and the resources administrators must provide to ensure the successful implementation of an established policy.

The organization of a computer committee is the strategy employed by many school districts to create a participative/shared environment to facilitate the formulation of a computer policy. This is compatible with the distributed or shared organization approach and is advocated in the contingency planning approach. The rule of thumb in organizing a committee is that it be representative of the various user groups in the district. Community representation may also be desirable. The actual number appointed by the superintendent should be small enough to assure having an effective working group. Though an outside consultant may be hired to help the committee in its task of developing an overall policy, caution should be exercised. Too heavy a reliance on the expert may negate having a true participative/shared approach.

The Impact of State Computer Policy

Increasingly, states have been adopting formal policies on the use of educational technology in the schools. Today, forty-seven states have formal policies incorporated in legislation, state board policies, or educational department mandates or regulations. This ground swell was a reaction to the grass roots movement that brought microcomputers into the schools. State officials took initiatives because of their belief that they had a pivotal role to play in coordinating the use of electronic technology to assure that its full benefits were realized (Chion-Kenney, 1984). Computer-literacy requirements affecting teachers and students were among the first formal policies initiated. These requirements have had a direct impact on schools with respect to the integration of computers into the curriculum. Presently, two states, Utah and Texas, and the District of Columbia require all teachers to take computer courses for certification, with nine additional states requiring some teachers (usually computer science and business education teachers) to meet this requirement. Though thirty-nine states have no certification requirements, many encourage teachers to enroll in state-sponsored computer workshops. Respecting student literacy, twenty-five states have legislated some form of requirement, for example, nine states require a computer literacy course, two states require schools to integrate computers into the classroom, five states stipulate schools must offer an optional computer course for students, while another nine states permit districts to determine how they will comply with mandated requirements (Reinhold & Corkett, 1985).

School districts have also been affected by state initiatives to implement a combination of statewide reporting and telecommunication systems. An example is the West Virginia Microcomputer Network Program, which links secondary schools to the state's department of education. This is accomplished through a statewide bulletin board. Schools are also linked to one another through a telecommunications system that allows them to share information, materials, and software (McGinty, 1984). States that have also implemented a student information system, available to local school districts via a microcomputer linkage, also affect decisions of local administrators as to what their computer policies should be.

Additional state policies may result from the recommendations made by 600 policymakers surveyed in twenty states. They identified further priority issues such as software exchange and dissemination, staff training, equitable access to computers, and what is computer literacy (Blaschke, 1984; State Policies, 1985). The implication for local school administrators is that they need to audit what is happening at the state level to assure that their districtwide computer policy is in compliance with state regulations.

POLICY APPROACHES

Organization and planning are key elements in the formulation and implementation of computer policy. Specific strategies that districts may apply in developing a policy are "backward mapping" and "policy analysis."

Organizational Approaches

Organizationally, school districts have had a centralized, decentralized, or distributed approach (Figure 12.4) respecting the acquisition, placement, and use of microcomputers for instructional and administrative purposes. The centralized (top down) approach is district-office-centered and typically is found in large school districts that have had a long history of using a mainframe or minicomputer to service the administrative needs of all their schools. The decentralized approach, being grass-roots-oriented,

FIGURE 12.4   District Organizational and Planning Approaches to Computer Involvement

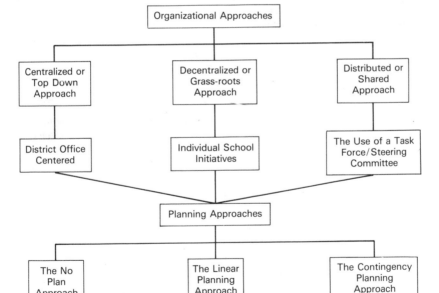

permits individual schools to take initiatives as to when and how microcomputers will be introduced and used by teachers and principals. This strategy appeared to be at its peak in the early 1980s as enthusiastic teachers and public-spirited patrons sought to implement computer-literacy instruction. The distributed approach seeks to combine the computer resources of the central office with the contributions that can be made from the building level. It is a shared or cooperative strategy that involves the use of a task force of key people from the central office and each school who have been involved directly in computer applications. This approach is amenable for school districts that have both microcomputers and a central mainframe or minicomputer and wish to link or network them together. Advantages and disadvantages exist for each of these approaches, as shown in Table 12.1. As school districts have gained more experience with microcomputers, the centralized or distributed organizational approach appears to have become more dominant.

Planning Approaches

Three planning approaches seem to have been used by school districts to introduce microcomputers into schools. They are (Figure 12.4) the no-plan approach, the linear or sequential approach, and the contingency planning approach. The no-plan approach may exist in either a centralized or decentralized organizational structure. It is characterized by uncertainty and ambiguity among district and school administrators as to where to begin with the introduction of microcomputers. The result has often been the acquisition of computers resulting from the initiative of vendors who offer low-cost or free hardware, software, or staff training. Termed the "getting on the bandwagon" stage by Cory (1984), the primary focus has been on the acquisition of as many computers as possible, regardless of what kind. Formal planning, typified by a needs assessment, was not a prerequisite. The attitude of most teachers and secretarial staff to these computers was generally ambivalence brought on by mistrust, fear, or curiosity.

The linear approach (Bozeman, 1984) represents steps that a district or school would take sequentially respecting the introduction and use of microcomputer technology. Specifically, they are: (1) Define district objectives on computer use, (2) outline procedures personnel would take to achieve these objectives, (3) specify time lines for each objective, (4) establish evaluation procedures to assess the degree to which each objective is attained, and (5) apply corrective actions for objectives not met. The success of this approach is conditioned on a district having (1) a common knowledge base about factors that affect decision making, (2) the resources to carry out the implementation sequences, and (3) clearly defined lines of authority. The linear approach is advanced as workable only if events have a high probability of occurring. Since districts are subjected to shifting external forces over which they have little control, such as uncertain financial resources, the contingency planning is suggested as a more viable option.

Contingency planning (Williams, Bank, & Thomas, 1984) recognizes that unforeseen events or actions taken that predate an event affect decision making. By seeking to anticipate these "trigger points," alternative strategies can be planned to deal with them. The application of contingency planning to computer technology, a rapidly changing field, would be characterized as incremental, ongoing, adaptive, and self-corrective. This approach is amenable to either the centralized or distributed organizational approach when schools seek to address the immediate and intermediate concerns about computer use. The planning process entails these essentials: (1) conducting a situation audit of the district's internal and external environments, (2) fostering support and commitment from the district's publics, (3) formulating a district/school computer policy, and (4) outlining the elements of an ongoing operational plan to effect the approved districtwide policy.

The primary purpose of the situation audit is to assess those forces, trends, and phenomena that may affect the formulation and implementation of a districtwide policy framework. The internal audit involves the inventory of existing hardware and software in the schools and the collection of information on how the computers are used, what personnel are involved, and how students, parents, teachers, counselors, and administrators perceive computers. External to the schools, an assessment would be made of those resources that are available in the community to support the educational use of computers. To encourage this support a network of interested persons would be established and activities sponsored such as computer fairs and demonstration sites.

The framework of a districtwide computer policy would evolve from the knowledge gained from the situation audit. An interschool task force committee would be organized and charged with determining program goals, suggesting implementation time lines, and proposing a budget. Once the policy framework had been developed, specific operational activities would be spelled out by the above committee or another committee. Central to the organizational plan would be a listing of operationally defined objectives and those activities that would facilitate the attainment of these objectives. A critical activity would be the training of staff to use computers for instituted instructional and administrative applications.

Planners need to be cognizant of impediments that may hinder or restrict the implementation of a district/school computer program. These variables may be internal or external to the system. They may be human oriented or affected by the rapidity of change occurring in the computer technology field. Human variables are related to individual resistance to

TABLE 12.1 Advantages and Disadvantages of Computer Organizational Strategies*

ORGANIZATIONAL STRUCTURE	ADVANTAGES	DISADVANTAGES
Centralized	1. Better purchasing benefits respecting price, service contracts, etc. due to quantity bid requests. 2. Standardization of computers and peripherals acquired. 3. Courseware/software evaluation and dissemination enhanced. 4. Computer expertise available to district schools for hardware maintenance and the answering of technical and procedural questions. 5. Coordination of training efforts. 6. Duplication of effort reduced. 7. Unified approach to computer literacy and computer-assisted instruction. 8. Management information system facilitated due to centralized fiscal, personnel, and student data files.	1. Individual school needs may not be assessed accurately. 2. Creativity of computer uses may be stifled at school level. 3. School dependency on the judgement and decisions of district personnel. 4. Inequity among schools due to how priorities are set. 5. Delimiting of teacher involvement in instructional applications.

Decentralized	1. School and community involvement is accented. 2. Local autonomy exists. 3. Innovation is fostered.	1. Lack of standardization may exist. 2. Hardware/software costs may be greater. 3. Duplication of effort may exist respecting the establishment of files, data processing, and reporting. 4. Instructional applications may not be coordinated between elementary, junior and senior high schools.
Distributed *or* *Shared*	1. Communication is increased between schools and the central office. 2. The collective administrative and instructional needs of the district are more readily addressed. 3. Funding for the computer resource is strengthened and costs reduced. 4. Broader support for the computer resource fostered among teachers, administrators, and patrons. 5. Climate exists for marriage of district's mainframe and mini- or microcomputers. 6. File-to-file transfers between individual schools and the district office are possible respecting attendance, scheduling, and grade reporting. 7. Management information and decision support systems enhanced.	1. Task force/steering committee agenda may get sidetracked. 2. Selection process may exclude key people from task force. 3. Mainframe/minicomputer/microcomputer networking requires sophisticated hardware and software control and a strict adherence to standards.

*Adapted from Stern, R. A., & Stern, N. (1982). *An Introduction to Computer and Information Processing.* New York: John Wiley & Sons, p. 52.

newness and change, the failure to define clearly staff roles, unclear performance standards, poor time management, limited or nonexistent feedback and follow-up training, and the lack of strong and continual administrative support. Other internal variables are failure to plan for contingencies, the lack of a reward and motivational system, financial constraints, and poor communication and cooperation between the various publics involved in managing and using the computer resource (Bender & Church, 1984).

One approach advocated to overcome barriers to implementing a computer resource program has been termed the administrative integration model (AIM). Developed by Bender and Church (1984), it reflects how primary, secondary, and tertiary interactions should occur among groups or individuals directly and indirectly affected by a proposed or implemented computer program. The model also specifies defining the roles of these respective interacting groups. Groups in the school setting might include school administrators, teachers, the resource staff, computer consultants, district and school computer coordinators, and parents.

Primary interactions involve the exchange of specific ideas, information, and feedback between such groups as administrators and computer coordinators who would be experiencing direct and ongoing communication. Secondary interaction groups—for example, resource staff and administrators—typically would not have continual contact but at various times may discuss different aspects of the computer program. Tertiary interactions generally entail communication provided by groups outside the school system who wish to provide new insights on ways the computer resource can be enhanced or improved. Parents and parent-teacher associations working with school administrators are illustrative of this type of interaction (Church & Bender 1985). Dynamic and effective interactions by groups who are knowledgeable about their roles may do much toward eliminating barriers that threaten the successful implementation and maintenance of a district or school computer program.

Backward Mapping

Backward mapping is a technique that stresses bottom-up in contrast to the top-down approach in formulating policy. Typically, the process used by most school districts in developing policy is to have top management outline the policy, reason through the actions and resources needed to execute it, and then ensure it is implemented at the bottom. Backward mapping (Elmore, 1979–80; Odden & Odden, 1984) instead first defines the problem, then identifies the setting where the problem is most directly affected, and then reasons backward (or upward) to specify appropriate policies at the top. An example of backward mapping is:

1. *State the problem.* Booting up computers in student labs cuts into the time teachers could expend in computer-assisted instruction.

2. *Determine where the problem is addressed most directly*. This occurs in classroom computing labs.

3. *Identify effective strategies to rectify the problem*. Consider the installation of a local area network or LAN.

4. *Moving up the system to ask how higher levels can help*. Invite the school principal to explore the merits of networking and whether finances are available to purchase a system.

5. *Continue the process up the policy-making ladder*. District personnel such as the data-processing director and/or computer coordinator, curriculum supervisors, the superintendent for curriculum and instruction, and the administrator of facilities would be asked what they could do to support implementation of effective computing practices. It is conceivable that members of the state educational department might be involved in giving input into the formulation of a computer policy that deals with networking.

Policy Analysis

Policy analysis is another technique school administrators may employ to develop district/school computer policies. Though differences exist between it and the backward mapping and the linear and contingency planning approaches, similarities are evident. The purpose of these techniques is to foster a systematic approach to the adoption and use of computers in the schools. The outcome should be policies that foster and produce quality results.

Policy analysis is defined as "the process by which systematically collected information is provided to decision makers" (Gray 1984, p. 72). MacRae (1979) states that it is intended to facilitate the choice of the best policy from a set of alternatives with the aid of evidence and reason. Policy analysis can serve to help school administrators understand the problems, issues, and needs (PINS) regarding the adoption and use of computers. The following steps are recommended to develop district policy (adapted from Gray, 1984):

1. A PIN (problem/issue/need) such as the use of microcomputers for instruction and administrative purposes emerges.
2. A policy analysis would be conducted involving (a) PIN clarification; (b) question development; (c) data collection, analysis, and synthesis; and (d) identification of alternative policy options and their implications.
3. The board of education would discuss the elements of each alternative.
4. A draft policy addressing the options chosen would be presented to the board for its approval or revision.
5. A public review of the policy would be scheduled.
6. The board would decide to adopt or revise the draft policy.
7. District and school administrators would be charged with implementing the policy and evaluating its impact.

To facilitate conducting a computer policy analysis, a computer use/PIN cluster matrix (Figure 12.5) is advocated. It enables questions to be asked about each of the PIN cluster topics as outlined in Table 12.2.

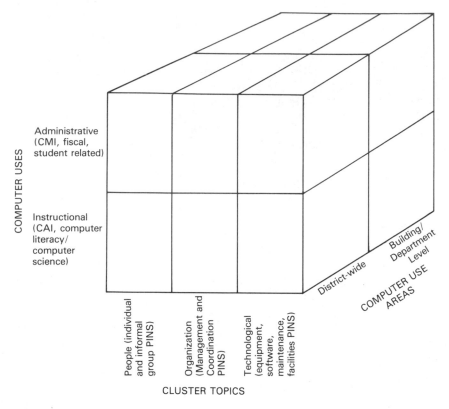

COMPUTER USES

Administrative (CMI, fiscal, student related)

Instructional (CAI, computer literacy/ computer science)

People (individual and informal group PINS)

Organization (Management and Coordination PINS)

Technological (equipment, software, maintenance, facilities PINS)

CLUSTER TOPICS

District-wide

Building/ Department Level

COMPUTER USE AREAS

FIGURE 12.5   Policy Analysis Using Computer Use/PIN Cluster Matrices   Adapted from Gray, P. J. (1984). The use of policy analysis in setting district policy on microcomputers. *Educational Leadership*, 42 (2), 76.

Data collection, analysis, and synthesis would then be conducted by knowledgeable school and district staff or by outside consultants with respect to conditions in the district regarding each cell in the matrix. The questions formulated for each PIN cell help provide direction about what specific procedures should be instituted. Once essential information has been compiled on the identified PINS, alternative policy options would be prepared. To be effective, these alternatives should include needed resource information on staffing, funding, logistical and scheduling activities, facilities, roles and relationships, equipment, materials and supplies, and other requirements. Once these policy analysis steps have been completed, the district superintendent and key staff have the information needed to submit a draft computer policy to the board of education for their approval. The end result would be a decision to adopt or revise the draft policy (Gray, 1984).

TABLE 12.2 Examples of Question Development in Using the PIN Process of Policy Analysis*

PIN TOPICS	POLICY/FRAMEWORK QUESTIONS	OPERATIONAL PLANNING QUESTIONS
I. Organizational Issues: A. Fiscal	• Should the district purchase, lease, or contract with a network to initiate administrative/instructional computer services? • What percent of the district's budget should be allocated for computer services (equipment, software, facilities, maintenance, training, etc.)	• What are the advantages and disadvantages of purchasing equipment versus leasing or buying services under a network arrangement? • What strategies might be used to finance the purchase of microcomputers for classroom use? • What costs are presently incurred in (1) teaching computer science/computer literacy courses, (2) using computer-managed and computer-assisted instruction programs, (3) scheduling students, doing attendance accounting, grade reporting, and student record keeping, (4) conducting the business operations of the district, and (5) maintaining and replacing equipment. • What are the estimated costs of purchasing computers compared to the lease or network utilization options in terms of maintenance, facility arrangement, staff training, software, etc.? • What is the anticipated life of the hardware considered for acquisition? How should it be amortized?
B. Management and Coordination	• Should control of the computer resource be centralized, decentralized, or distributed? • What phasing-in strategy should be implemented for the district's computer plan? • How should the computer resource be evaluated as to effectiveness? • Should the district subscribe to an educational network or national data bases to permit accessing and retrieving relevant information?	• What strategies and time lines are needed to implement a program of administrative and instructional use of computers? • What strategies should be introduced to encourage female students to use computers?

259

TABLE 12.2 Examples of Question Development in Using the PIN Process of Policy Analysis (continued)

PIN TOPICS	POLICY/FRAMEWORK QUESTIONS	OPERATIONAL PLANNING QUESTIONS
	• How should community support be fostered to promote the instructional use of computers? • What procedures should be adopted to catalog, process, and inventory computer hardware and software used in the district? • How should resources be allocated to ensure equal access and use of computers by students? • What role will other educational service agencies and groups have in the district framework and plan? • What precautions should be taken to assure private information will be kept confidential?	
C. Instructional Uses	• What roles will computers have in the school, e.g., computer-assisted instruction, computer literacy, computer programming? • Should all students meet minimum computer competency requirements? • How will the instructional role of teachers change with increased computer use? • Should computer literacy be taught at all grade levels or delimited to a specific grade level?	• What kind of social problems are being introduced into schools along with computers? • How can the district ensure equity in computer use, especially higher-level and creative uses? • What are reasonable rules and guidelines for student computer use? • Is there a special need for a "computer literacy" curriculum? • What are appropriate educational goals and curriculum materials for computer literacy? • How can the teacher overcome the constraints of using individually oriented computers in the context of a group-based instructional organization? • What curricular areas are best served by computer instruction? • What provision will be made for advanced students?

II. Technological Issues:

A. Hardware Acquisition and Maintenance

- What criteria/guidelines should be established for hardware acquisition?
- Should a single computer system be used for both instructional and administrative purposes?
- What strategies should be used in dealing with computer vendors?
- Should a mix exist as to using microcomputers, minicomputers, and mainframes for administrative and instructional use?
- How will computer-assisted instruction be integrated into the existing curriculum?
- What procedure will be employed to assess whether students have met minimum computer-literacy requirements?
- What successes/failures have been experienced by other districts or schools using specific hardware under a purchase, lease, or network arrangement? How reliable has been the equipment?
- What maintenance warranties and assistance will vendors provide in installing and servicing leased equipment?
- What size machine and/or memory are required to run the desired administrative and instructional software?
- What staff training is provided under a purchase, lease, or network arrangement?
- What expansion options exist under the alternative of acquiring computer services?
- What benefits would be gained by having microcomputers linked to a minicomputer or mainframe?
- How many classroom computers are needed to meet the proposed instructional goal?

B. Software Issues

- What procedures should be instituted to locate, evaluate, and acquire software?
- Should the district get involved in courseware/instructional software development?
- Should a district software library be established?
- What should district policy be respecting copyright issues for teacher-developed and -purchased software?
- What types of software best serve administrative computing needs—general purpose, task specific, or integrated packages?
- Will the software under consideration enable district/school computer goals and objectives to be met?
- How best can the results of software evaluation be disseminated?
- Is the recommended software program educationally sound?

TABLE 12.2 Examples of Question Development in Using the PIN Process of Policy Analysis (continued)

PIN TOPICS	POLICY/FRAMEWORK QUESTIONS	OPERATIONAL PLANNING QUESTIONS
		• Are district users in compliance with software license and copyright agreements? • Procedurally, how can computer-assisted and computer-managed programs be integrated with other instructional activities?
C. Facilities (housing, furniture, ergonomics, security issues)	• What is the best arrangement for housing computers? • What security precautions should be taken?	• Should instructional computers be housed centrally, in individual classrooms, or in departments? • Should local area networks (LANs) be introduced?
III. People: A. Staff Development Issues	• What should be the overall plan for staff development? • What knowledge do teachers, counselors, administrators, and office staff need in order to use computers? • How can state computer-literacy certification requirements be met? • What personnel should conduct and evaluate faculty/staff training and what type of follow-up aid will be needed?	• Will computer resource people be trained to function as building coordinators? • What should be the nature of computer training required of teachers, counselors, administrators, and office staff? • What arrangements will be made to assure faculty/staff are released to receive classroom and hands-on computer training?
B. Staffing Issues	• How will the computer resource be supervised? • What provision will be made for providing support personnel?	• Who will be responsible for district coordination, building coordination, and providing technical assistance? • Who will teach the computer science and computer-literacy courses?

*Adapted from Williams, R. C., Bank, A., & Thomas, C. (1984). The school district role in introducing microcomputers: A contingency planning approach. *Educational Technology, 24*(12), 41.

APPLYING THE POLICY ANALYSIS APPROACH

Three major PIN areas identified are: organizational, technological, and people oriented. To illustrate how policy analysis works, four technological PINS or problem concerns—computer acquisition, maintenance, location, and networking—are discussed. Relevant questions pertaining to these problems are presented in Table 12.2. The steps of data collection, analysis and synthesis, and the identification of alternative policy options with their implications have yet to be done. Sources of information are vendors, other districts' experience with the problem, consultants, and published material on the problem's issues/needs. The resource information presented for each of the PINs discussed should enable policy makers to assess which alternatives available to them are best for their circumstances.

Computer Acquisition

A district either initiating administrative and instructional computer services or expanding the service has the option to buy, lease, or enter into a network arrangement. The possibility also exists to purchase microcomputers for instructional use, yet lease a mainframe computer to handle administrative applications. Resource information on the advantages and disadvantages of these options is presented in Table 12.3. Factors that impact on which option to choose are district/school policy, goals, size of the district, and projected costs to operate the desired computer services.

To determine the costs associated with the acquisition options, school administrators should obtain quotations from vendors based on the school district's specifications. Next, they should check the quotations to determine who pays for such items as (1) the service repair manual, (2) staff training, (3) documentation, (4) after-sales user support for setting up the equipment, demonstrating data formatting, data recovery, and so on, (5) updates on hardware and software versions, (6) warranties, and (7) trade-ins (credits) to upgrade or expand. Costs need to be determined on a short-term and long-term basis, with a review conducted annually to assess how well the services will meet immediate and projected needs. In the final analysis, every effort should be made to obtain the information needed to assure the acquisition choice provides the best computer services possible (Splittgerber & Stirzaker, 1984).

Computer Maintenance

There is a hidden cost to computers. Once the customary ninety-day warranty expires, maintenance costs can be expensive. Obsolescence of microcomputers that are no longer manufactured or have been replaced by new and better models also create the problem of how to maintain them.

In formulating district policy, decision makers must opt for one of the following maintenance alternatives after the warranty expires.

TABLE 12.3 The Advantages and Disadvantages of Computer Service Options*

COMPUTER SERVICE OPTIONS	ADVANTAGES	DISADVANTAGES
Purchase arrangement	• Special school discounts up to 40 percent may be obtained. • An additional discount may result through a state-negotiated contract. • Software, peripherals, and maintenance costs are more readily negotiated. • Buying from the same vendor facilitates the upgrading of equipment.	• No tax write-off is possible when equipment becomes obsolete. • Loss of purchasing power results when trading in depreciated equipment for new hardware. • Poor service and maintenance may result if the vendor is unreliable.
Lease arrangement with another school district, college or university, business or computer manufacturer	• No additional costs are incurred when equipment depreciates. • A district is able to take advantage of upgraded equipment when a new lease is negotiated.	• During the length of the lease (typically two years) the district usually pays for the equipment. • Services may be paid for those not yet on line. • Programming changes necessitating a negotiation of the lease may result in delays in continuous service, confusion, and additional costs. • A penalty is imposed if the lease is cancelled before the expiration date. • Maintenance costs are paid whether needed or not.

| Network arrangement with several districts or involvement in a statewide or regional network (Examples are the Board of Cooperative Educational Services or COLES concept and the Minnesota Educational Computing Corporation or MECC) | • Financial savings can result when districts share the costs of equipment and software and may be greater than under a purchase or lease option.
• Standardization of software and data reporting is simplified. Some networks already gather basic data on school expenses using the *Federal Financial Accounting Handbook II.*
• Each district shares in making decisions about developed short- and long-term plans.
• The potential is great to obtain more services than would be possible if a district operates independently. | • Consensus may not occur among districts when planning and process decisions need to be made.
• Local control and autonomy is lost.
• Sensitive data may not be secure.
• Fear exists that a federally controlled system might be instituted. |

*Based on Splittgerber, F. L., & Stirzaker, N. A. (1984). Guidelines for financing school district computer services. *School Business Affairs, 50*(3), 32, 80–81.

The "Wait and See" Option. An extended warranty would not be negotiated, on the hope breakdowns would be minimal. Districts choosing this option assume all the risk and repair costs. If equipment breakdowns are excessive, repairs may be prohibitively expensive. Costs range between $45 and $100 per hour.

The "Play It Safe" Option. Districts, to protect themselves, would negotiate with a dealer or manufacturer through a vendor for an extended service contract. The costs associated with these contracts range from $100 to over $300 per year per machine dependent upon vendor, system configuration, and whether the service is on-site, carry-in, or next-day repair. As a rule of thumb, users can expect maintenance costs to run about 1 percent per month for the total dollar outlay a district expends on computer hardware. For a district owning 100 microcomputers, one year's maintenance contracts can run from $10,000 to over $30,000. This represents a heavy demand on the computer budget.

The Preventive "Go it Alone" Option. This alternative suggests that districts would institute both a preventive maintenance program to keep their peripherals and computers working and an in-house maintenance program. Preventive measures, compiled from several sources (Chion-Kenney, 1985b; Levin, Miyake, & Olivas, 1985) include:

- Consult with other districts about the track record of a given computer and its peripherals before buying or leasing.
- Limit the hardware mix. The acquisition of different computers can compound the service problem.
- Avoid placing microcomputers in areas subjected to extremes in temperature. The range of 60 to 80°F is ideal.
- Assure that each microcomputer's air inlets and outlets are not obstructed. Ventilation outlets need to be cleaned periodically.
- Reduce the risk of electromagnetic interference by not placing computers and storage devices near magnetic equipment such as library security systems, audio and video tape degaussers, and even telephones.
- Train staff members to conduct simple technical maintenance procedures.
- Combat static electricity by installing static-free carpeting or by spraying on an ion-free liquid or spray on the carpet once or twice a day.
- Keep food and drink away from computers.
- Limit the number of times computers are turned off and on during the day.
- Refrain from placing computers in dusty areas such as near chalk blackboards.
- Swap identical parts to check for defective parts.

The in-house maintenance program requires the district to train individuals to do the needed repairs. Training courses are available from most computer manufacturers. Once an in-house program is up and operating, total repair costs are less than under the other options. The Houston Independent School District, for example, reported its $250,000 operating expenses per year were about 10 percent of what it would have been had a contract been made with outside servicers (Chion-Kenney, 1985b).

Computer Location

The major policy decision respecting the location of computers is in the instructional area. Mainframe computers used for administrative purposes are routinely located in a separate room that should meet such requirements as having static-free flooring, controlled temperature and humidity, soundproofing, and indirect lighting (MacKenzie, 1984). Differences of opinion have existed as to where microcomputers used for classroom instruction should be located. Location options have been classrooms, libraries, computer laboratories, rotating microcomputers between rooms, and dispersing the machines around the building. Analyses by the John Hopkins Center for Social Organization of Schools (Becker, 1984b) found that where schools located their microcomputers had an impact on how they were used. Specifically, it was found that computer location affected (1) the amount of time machines were used by teachers and students, (2) the proportion of the student body using the computers, (3) the degree to which above average students compared to average or below average students had access to the computers, (4) how enthusiastic students using computers were toward schoolwork, (5) the emphasis placed on computer-assisted instruction compared to computer programming and computer literacy, and (6) the breadth of computer use across the different possible computer applications. The location that seemed to have the greatest affect on the extent and variety of school microcomputer use was the computer lab. Microcomputers located only in classrooms, the most popular placement, resulted in less use but more equitable use among students of different achievement levels.

The trend toward locating school microcomputers in labs is not without its critics. By having to send their students to the lab at appointed times, teachers are confronted with adjusting their schedules to that of the central lab. Reacting to this practice and how it might affect teacher acceptance of microcomputers, *Educational Technology* (1985b) editorialized:

> We fear, then, that school administrators, in the name of efficiency of operations, may be about to jeopardize the microcomputer revolution in education by turning the micro into yet one more nonflexible, hard-to-get-at, domineering instructional medium. It need not happen, of course, but it is very likely to happen unless educational leaders take heed now and begin to think about the full implications of what they are doing (Technically Speaking 1985b, p. 6).

Other drawbacks (Fisher & Finkel, 1984) of locating all the microcomputers in one place under the supervision of one person are: (1) there exists the risk of developing a microcomputer "priest" who will not permit the lab to be used by students and teachers unless he/she is present, (2) this plan may cater to only the "smart kids" who take math, and computer hackers, (3) a "territorial" situation develops when one department, typically the math department, has responsibility for the lab, and (4) the setup is incompatible with the ways most teachers wish to use computers for computer-assisted learning (CAL). Teachers seem to want more flexibility in their instructional use of computers, such as scheduling small-group activities that are short in duration and may be the result of a spur-of-the-moment decision. Under a centralized lab approach, teachers would be obliged to plan in advance to schedule the lab for the entire class for an entire period.

School districts that have the resources may wish to have separate labs for computer science/computer-literacy instruction and other uses such as business education instruction in addition to placing stand-alone units in classrooms. When resources are limited, Fisher and Finkel (1984) suggest administrators should carefully consider the instructional consequences of both approaches before settling on either.

Computer Networking

Computer networking has become a popular movement in educational institutions. Currently, it has been estimated that 15–30 percent of the nation's computer-using schools have networks, with educators at twice as many schools considering the installation of networks (Spain, 1984). As the districtwide computer policy is formulated, planners should carefully assess whether a recommendation for networking should be made. One alternative is to limit network participation to a commercial/educational network (Chapter 3). Local area network (LAN) options are to network all microcomputers located in school computing labs and/or those computers housed in administrative offices. Another option for districts having both microcomputers and a mainframe would be to implement a distributed processing system by networking these two types of computers. Minicomputers, similarly, can be networked to a mainframe. The recommendation to install any of these types of networks should be consistent with the administrative/instructional objectives of the district plan.

The cheapest and simplest network to implement is the subscription commercial/educational network. It would only require a modem to access the network, software like Crosstalk or P.C. Talk, and a microcomputer. The benefit of participating in a commercial/educational network is that information may be accessed and retrieved from national data bases and communication can be facilitated with fellow educators outside the district. Communication options are computer conferencing, electronic mail, and electronic bulletin boards.

Before determining whether to install a local area network or not, school officials need answers to such questions as: What is a LAN? What are its benefits? What pitfalls may be encountered in operating a LAN? What questions should vendors be asked about their networking systems? and What LAN choices are there? Respecting a distributed processing network, information should be collected by planners as to what it is, its purposes, benefits, and problems.

What Is a LAN? A local area network, as the name implies, is limited to a single site such as an instructional computing lab, an administrative office, or faculty offices located in a building. The heart of a LAN is a host computer whose disk drive powers the system. A LAN links together all the microcomputers in any of these locations to promote sharing and to facilitate communication. Users on a LAN are able to share printers, modems, a hard disk drive, and network-licensed software. Information can also be communicated between the networked microcomputers.

Benefits of a LAN that have been touted are cost effectiveness, increased control over hardware and software, promotion of shared information, enhancement of computer-assisted instruction, and increased storage capacity.

- Cost Effectiveness. The multiuser capability of a network helps reduce costs because (1) users share expensive peripherals such as a hard disk, letter-quality printers, and graphic plotters, (2) disk drives do not need to be purchased for each linked microcomputer, and (3) application software can be shared on the network, thus eliminating the need to purchase duplicate copies of the same program for all users. One district claimed this benefit resulted in a near 20 percent savings in software costs compared to a non-networked system (Adams 1984).

- Increased Control Over Software and Hardware. Software control is obtained by reducing the number of application and documentation diskettes to keep track of individual users and the time expended by them in loading and unloading boot and program disks. In a non-network school computing lab, for example, teachers spend considerable time getting students to load correctly a disk to boot up a program or they are faced with doing it themselves. With networked machines students are able to access the program simultaneously from the system file with just a few simple keystrokes. Hardware control is obtained using a print server. This feature frees users from physically having to wait in line for the computer with the printer to be free. By holding the print jobs electronically in the order they are received, the user can either continue working at the computer or engage in other activities.

- Promotion of Shared Information. One way this may be accomplished is to have messages sent electronically using electronic mail software (Chapter 3). Another way is the accessing of student information stored on a school's administrative network by authorized users. This capability enables administrators, counselors, and secretaries to enter, view, edit, update, and process information vital to their respective school responsibilities.

- Enhancement of Computer-Assisted Instruction. Managing the computer environment and helping teachers individualize the learning experiences of each student can be facilitated by the use of network-compatible computer-managed instruction packages. Teachers may monitor students' work electronically and send on-line messages to their screen. Flexibility is also provided whereby some students can do remedial, makeup, or enhancement work individually at their computers while the teacher gives special attention to other students. In an advanced network all students may be permitted to use one computer-assisted instruction (CAI) software program at the same time or to access different CAI programs to allow independent work.
- Increased Storage. A network having a hard disk provides greater storage capacity for student files.

Pitfalls of a LAN. As identified by users and observers of computer networks (Spain, 1984; Green, 1984; Judd, 1984; Smith & Kauffman, 1985), the pitfalls include lack of an accepted standard for networking, lack of support from third-party vendors, lack of network-compatible programs, difficulties in networking different brands of computers, electrical disturbances, heavy network demands, the risk of breaching private or confidential files, and hidden costs and time delays.

- Lack of an Accepted Standard for Networking. This absence has impeded the adaptation process necessary to get software programs running on a network. Though software publishers may have adapted a program for general network use, the peculiarities of each network frequently necessitate that the program be tailored to the demands of the system.
- Lack of Support from Third-Party Vendors. Few microcomputer manufacturers have developed networks for their machines due to the proliferation of third-party vendors in the network market. This can create problems for the purchaser, who is dependent on the vendor being knowledgeable about the characteristics of the machines to be networked.
- Lack of Network-Compatible Software Programs. Software publishers have moved slowly to market network versions of their administrative and instructional software. Reasons restricting this move are (1) loss of revenue when only one versus many copies of a program is sold to networking schools, and (2) the concern over unauthorized copying. To combat this piracy, publishers have instituted a matching serial number system. For the software to run, its serial number must match that of the network's hard disk. The seriousness of the software problem is underscored by the fact that less than 20 percent of the 1000 or so publishers currently marketing educational programs have agreed to license their products for network use. For those that do, their selling price is generally two to three times the normal price (Green, 1984). A recent survey of thirty-nine major software publishers (Williams & the editors of *EL*, 1985) found that 51% of them permitted at least some of their unprotected programs to be used on a network provided that educators checked with them first.
- Network Incompatibility and Mixed Computer Brands. Most network systems on the market are limited to linking only common brand microcomputers. This can create a problem for the district that has multiple brands. For those manufacturers who offer the capability of networking mixed brands, increased installation costs can be expected by a district.

- Electrical Disturbances. Power failures and electrical surges can cause a network to shut down, affecting user documents. Preventive measures, though, are available to compensate for this risk.

- Heavy Network Demands. The number of microcomputers that are networked can affect the efficiency and operation of a system. To be efficient, a network should have at least ten microcomputers. When the number increases to thirty or more, problems may occur due to the demand placed on the system. If appropriate software is not available a system may "crash" when all users are using the system simultaneously. Another problem that has occurred in computing labs is the speed it normally takes to load each machine is seriously reduced when all students access a program simultaneously.

- Security Breaches. Networks increase the risk of users gaining access to private, confidential files. Assurances should be had that a network under consideration has an effective file- and record-locking security system. Such a system would restrict file opening, reading, deleting, or adding of information to authorized users.

- Hidden Costs and Time Delays. Though networking has made rapid strides, problems in installing and getting the system to operate correctly can and have been experienced. School districts would be well advised to remember Golub's Laws of Computerdom (Groobey, 1972). Administrators should recognize that the process of installing and operating a network can be difficult, time consuming, frustrating, and expensive. Summarizing this process are Golub's Law 1 and its three corollaries. They are:

Law 1. No major computer project (network) is ever installed on time, within budget, with the same staff that started it, nor does the project (network) do what it is supposed to do. . . . It is highly unlikely that yours is going to be the first. . . .
   Corollary 1. The benefits will be smaller than initially estimated if estimates were made at all.
   Corollary 2. The system (network) finally installed will be installed late and won't do what it is (fully) supposed to do.
   Corollary 3. It will cost more, but it will be technically successful. (pp. 28–29)

Questions to Ask a Network Vendor. Preliminary questions (Forman, 1983; Judd, 1984; Darrow, 1984) planners should ask themselves are: Is the network focus to be administrative, instructional, or both? If administrative, it should be determined whether an interface with a district minicomputer or mainframe is needed. Once it has been concluded what the focus will be, answers from vendors should be sought for the following questions.

- Is the network a hard disk or floppy disk system? Will it serve multiple locations as well as a single location? Does it operate via a phone line or by coaxial cable wiring? How is the system configured—as a star, daisy chain, or drop line arrangement? The type of configuration dictates whether the system will continue to function notwithstanding one unit malfunctioning. The star and drop line are of this type. The daisy chain configuration has had the limitation of causing the system to be inoperative if one computer in the chain broke down. This is attributable to having each microcomputer wired in a series to the host computer. The star network has each machine connected in a starlike or radial pattern to the host computer. The parallel wiring of each microcomputer to the host computer's main cable via junction bases characterizes the drop line configuration. Knowing that a network may break down, vendors should furnish information on what happens to data stored on the system when this occurs.

- What kinds of service and support are offered purchasers? Will the names of other school districts who have purchased the system be available to assess user reactions to the system? What evidence can be presented to indicate the reliability of the system? Are provisions made for expanding and upgrading the system? Is the network supported by ongoing development?

- What is the maximum number of units the network will support? What is the maximum distance allowed between units or what is the greatest distance from one end of the network to the other? Answers to these questions will tell whether it is possible to network microcomputers located in different rooms.

- Does the network support BASIC and all other programming languages needed to be used? Will the network support microcomputers from different vendors as well as printers and other peripherals? How much mass storage will the system handle? Can the host computer be available for general use or must it be delimited to the system's control functions? The nature of these questions implies that networking is complicated, suggesting that district representatives asking the questions be reasonably knowledgeable about the use of computers.

Local Area Network Choices.   Network systems catering to school districts are offered by some twenty-one vendors (Table 12.4). Though Apple computers rank first, followed by IBM PCs in the number of microcomputers in the schools, most vendors appear to direct their network systems toward the PC. Over 70 percent of the systems are IBM PC-oriented, with almost one-fourth of the vendors being able to network Apple II and IIE computers. The requests of business offices to network their machines probably accounts for this trend. Two-thirds of the network systems are limited primarily to connecting only one brand of microcomputer. Radio Shack's Network 2, 3, and 4 and IBM's PC Network are two manufacturers producing a system for their own product. Apple Computer, Inc., offers its Apple Bus system, but it seems directed toward the business office and is limited to networking only Macintosh and Lisa computers. At present, few of these machines are in the public schools.

Distributed processing is the term used to refer to the networking of microcomputers or minicomputers to mainframes to take advantage of their separate strengths. The concept as defined by Foster (1983) is "the processing of information by several computers tied together through a network so it is possible to find the information that is desired by addressing any of the computers in the network" (p. 14). The benefit of such as system is that it serves to meet both school and central office information needs. At the local level, each school would be able to use its microcomputers to utilize a student information system, edit data, register

TABLE 12.4 Microcomputer Network Systems Offered by Vendors

NETWORK	COMPUTERS	MANUFACTURER'S NAME/ ADDRESS/TELEPHONE
ARC net	IBM PC Card compatibles, Datapoint	Datapoint Corp. 9725 Datapoint Dr. San Antonio, TX 78284 800/344-1123
CSI Switch	Commodore 64 or VIC 20	Educational Computer Specialists P. O. Box 6688 Stateline, NV 89449 800/821-1972
B25 Cluster Cable	Burroughs B25	Burroughs Corp. Burroughs Place Detroit, MI 48232 313/972-7000
3Bnet	3B Series, AT&T Computers, IBM PC	AT&T 222 Broadway New York, NY 10038 212/669-2584
Ethernet	Xerox Star Series, IBM PC	Xerox Corp. 701 S. Aviation Blvd. El Segundo, CA 90245 213/536-7000
Ether Series	IBM PC and compatibles	3COM Corp. 1390 Shorebird Way Mountain View, CA 94043 415/961-9602
Local Net	IBM PC and compatibles	Sytek, Inc. 1225 Charleston Rd. Mountain View, CA 94043 415/966-7300

273

TABLE 12.4 Microcomputer Network Systems Offered by Vendors (continued)

NETWORK	COMPUTERS	MANUFACTURER'S NAME/ ADDRESS/TELEPHONE
Microhost Instructional System	Apple II, IIe; IBM PC	Computer Curriculum Corp. 1070 Arastradero Road Palo Alto, CA 94304 800/982-5851
Multi Link	IBM PC and compatibles	Davong Systems, Inc. 217 Humboldt Ct. Sunnyvale, CA 94089 408/734-4900
Net/One	IBM PC and compatibles	Ungermann-Bass, Inc. 2560 Mission College Blvd. Santa Clara, CA 95050 408/1496-0111
Netware Series	IBM PC and other MS-DOS	Novell, Inc. 1170 N. Industrial Park Dr. Orem, UT 84057 800/453-1267
Network 816	Apple II series or Atari; Apple or Atari floppy disk drive	Wolsten Computer Devices 99 Washington St. East Orange, NJ 07017 201/678-0008
Omninet	Apple and Apple compatibles; Corvus Concept; DEC Rainbow; IBM PC/XT	Corvus Systems 2100 Corvus Drive San Jose, CA 95124 408/599-7000
Plan 3000	Apple II series; Apple II, IBM PC, and compatibles	Nestar Systems, Inc. 2585 E. Bayshore Rd. Palo Alto, CA 94303 415/493-2223

PC Network	IBM PC	IBM Entry Systems Division P.O. Box 1328 Boca Raton, FL 33432 800/447-4700
PC Net	IBM PC and compatibles; IBM DOS 2.0 hard disk drive	Orchid Technology 47790 Westinghouse Dr. Fremont, CA 94539 415/490-8586
Personal Mini	Televideo PC IBM PC: other MS-DOS	Televideo Systems 1170 Morse Avenue Sunnyvale, CA 94086 408/745-7760
Radio Shack Network 3	Radio Shack Models III or IV (host requires Model IV); Model IV floppy disk drive	Radio Shack 1400 One Tandy Center Fort Worth, TX 76102 817/390-3832
Schoolbus	Apple II or IIe, Profile or Corvus hard disk drives, or 5¼-inch floppy disk drive.	Apple Computer 20525 Mariana Ave. Cupertino, CA 95014 408/973-3706
User net	Sperry PC; other MS-DOS	Sperry Corp. P. O. Box 500 Blue Bell, PA 19424
Velan	Apple II e/e, IBM PC/PC Jr., Macintosh	Velan, Inc. 530 Oak Grove Avenue Menlo Park, CA 94025 415/322-2828
Wicat Network	WICAT	Wicat Systems, Inc. 1875 South State St. Orem, UT 84057 801/224-6400

275

students, track attendance, and print reports. By feeding this information to the central office mainframe, a district student data base can be maintained. District summary reports on enrollment, attendance, grading, and so on can be compiled for distribution to the schools. The mainframe computer would also service the individual schools by preparing the master schedule, teacher schedules and loads (Kauffman, 1983).

Problems pertaining to central office versus local school control prompted Foster (1983) to recommend the development of a district policy to resolve this issue. The policy would (1) cover the maintenance and sharing of information between school and central offices sites, (2) specify who would be responsible for collecting and maintaining network information, and (3) indicate who would have rights of information access and the right to update information.

Resource information is essential for school decision makers as they are faced with making a decision on whether or not to support a policy recommendation to network their district's computing labs, administrative offices, and/or microcomputers and mainframes. The approach taken to collect the needed information should be done systematically, incorporating elements taken from the material presented herein. Doing so should assure that the decision rendered is backed by hard evidence on what a vendor's network system will or will not offer and whether the price to be paid will ensure the expected outcomes. As Green (1984) states, "If your school (or district) plans to install a network, you'd be wise to venture into it with eyes wide open" (p. 77).

SUMMARY

Decisions made by school officials regarding computers may result from inaction. Typically, they are made with information. The information, though, may be dated and incomplete. What is needed is information that generates viable options and clarifies choices. That is the purpose behind the various policy approaches presented in this chapter. Once operating computer policies exist, school districts can be assured that their program has reached maturity.

GLOSSARY

Application software. Programs written to meet the needs of users. In the educational setting it includes instructional and administrative software that tells the computer to perform specific tasks.

ASCII. An acronym for *A*merican *S*tandard *C*ode for *I*nformation *I*nterchange. Pronounced "as-key," it is a computer code that converts letters, numbers, and symbols into electric pulses (bits). As a standard code, it enables different computers to talk to each other.

Bit. A term derived from *bi*nary digi*t*. In print it refers to a "1" or "0," meaning a one bit or a zero bit. A bit is the smallest unit of code that a computer can read. Usually bits are in groups of eight, with each group standing for a letter, number, or symbol.

Boot. The process of getting a computer ready to work or the loading of all the instructions a computer needs before it starts working on a program.

Byte. The amount of storage taken up by the computer's representation of a single character, for example, a letter, symbol, or number. A byte contains eight bits in different combinations of 0s and 1s. Since many thousands of bytes may be stored, the term *kilobyte* is used.

Centralized data processing. The situation in which the computer resource is located in a central area, serving all segments of an institution, agency, or business.

Central processing unit. The CPU contains the memory, control, and arithmetic units of a computer, which permits it to carry out essential and controlling tasks.

Characters. Individual letters or numbers that make up a given field of a document.

Computer-assisted instruction. The use of the computer to provide individual instruction in the form of drill and practice, tutorials, and simulations in different subject areas.

Computer-assisted testing. A support tool for the instructional program which helps instructors plan, construct, score, analyze, and interpret tests.

Computer conferencing. The linking of microcomputers at various locations by telecommunications to permit individuals with a common interest to conduct a conference through the use of their machines.

Computer information system. A hierarchal system that feeds operational information to middle managers and top administrators. It embraces the data-processing systems that generate the raw data used in the management information system and the decision support system.

Computer-managed instruction. The procedure used to manage the instructional process by assisting instructors in diagnosing instructional needs, testing and monitoring student achievement, prescribing learning activities, and matching instructional materials to teaching/learning objectives.

Commercial networks. Networks such as ED-LINE, CompuServe, The Source, Special-Net, and BESTNet/TechNet that have such features as electronic mail, bulletin boards, computer conferencing, and data bases which are made available to subscribers. Subscribers need a computer terminal, a telephone line, modem, and a communication card to permit their computer to send and receive data. The modem acts as a bridge between the local terminal and the remote network computer.

Curriculum management programs. Computer management programs designed to monitor a student's progress toward specified (locally and/or publisher determined) curriculum goals.

Cursor. A small light on the computer screen that shows where the next keystroke will appear. By pressing the appropriate arrow keys, the cursor may be moved up or down the screen or to the left or right of a word, character, or space.

Data bank. A huge source of information that a computer can tap into with the right password and equipment. To access a commercial data bank like The Source using a microcomputer, a modem is needed which will change the computer signals to telephone signals and vise versa.

Data base. A collection of organized information recorded on records held in files that are stored on a computer disk or tape. In schools, data bases on students and employees are common.

Data-base managers or data-base management systems (DBMS). Computer software programs designed to organize and maintain information that is contained in a data base.

Data-processing system. The system that generates the day-to-day or operational information of an institution, agency, or business. Typical systems are payroll, personnel, and student information.

Decentralized data processing. The condition under which each department in an institution, agency, or business controls its own processing needs.

Decision support system (DSS). The system used by top managers to make decisions and formulate policy. It utilizes projection and simulation procedures to predict trends and simulate future conditions based on predetermined assumptions.

Disk. An electronic storage device with a magnetic recording surface for recording programs or data. Types used by microcomputers are: floppy disks, hard disks, and Winchester disks. The floppy diskette consists of a round vinyl disk enclosed within a plastic cover to protect it from damage when handled by a user. The most common size is the 5 1/4-inch diskette, which may be single or double sided, with the latter having more storage capacity. A hard disk is made of a rigid material like aluminum, with a magnetic coating. It can hold from ten to one hundred times the amount of data that can be stored on a floppy diskette. The Winchester is actually a hard disk designed to store from six to ten times more data than a standard floppy diskette; it is sealed inside a Winchester disk drive.

Disk drive. A device that puts computer data onto a magnetic disk and later reads it back into the computer's memory.

Disk operating system (DOS). The link between the application programs and the computer and its peripheral devices. Its function is that of a general manager, coordinating the hardware and the application software to make sure everything runs smoothly. Well-known microcomputer systems are: MS-DOS, Apple DOS, and CP/M.

Distributed processing. The procedure reflecting how data can be transferred ("uploaded") to a central mainframe or minicomputer for processing, with the results returned or "downloaded" to an in-house computer.

Documentation. The manuals and instructions provided for individuals to orient them to the use of any purchased hardware and/or software.

Electronic bulletin boards. Bulletin boards typically found on commercial networks that store information for subscribers on job openings, calendar of events, announcements, legislation, and so forth.

Electronic calendar. Software that enables the computer to set up an appointment schedule containing dates, times, expected participants, and space for comments.

Electronic filing. The storage of information on floppy disks, hard disks, or tapes.

Electronic mail. The name given the procedure of sending messages by computer from one person to another person by transmitting them over hard wires or telephone lines.

Electronic spread sheet. An all-purpose problem-solving tool having built-in functions for calculating relationships and analyzing information. It performs such functions as creating, revising, formatting, file handling, and printing. Used in financial forecasting and "what if" analyses.

Ergonomics. The adaptation of machines and other elements of the working environment to enable individuals to work at optimum efficiency.

Files. A collection of *records* that consist of a number of *fields* that are constructed by different *characters*.

Formatting. How text may be positioned on the display monitor or on printed paper in terms of line spacing, print size, etc.

General-purpose software. Programs such as data-base managers, electronic spread sheets, and word processors that allow a user flexibility to customize to fit local needs.

Hardware. The physical components of a computer system, for example, disk drives, display monitor, central processing unit, keyboard, printers, and modems.

Input. The preparation and entry of information into a computer. This may be done in a number of ways, such as typing instructions at a keyboard, transferring data from a tape or disk, or having another computer call it on the phone.

Integrated software. A single program that combines several general-purpose software programs, or programs with an operating system that permits the transfer of data between compatible programs.

Kilobyte (K or KB). A measure of how much information a computer can store. One kilobyte equals 1,024 bytes where a byte equals eight bits or eight tiny impulses of electricity. A 32K microcomputer has very little memory compared to the 128K or 256K computers that are more common today.

Local area network (LAN). Computers delimited to a restricted area like a computer lab, administrative office, or building that are linked together for purposes of sharing peripherals and software and to facilitate communication between users.

Mainframe. A large computer that can operate at an ultra-high speed and store millions of bytes or units of information.

Management information system. Information derived from the data-processing systems that is used by middle managers to focus on relationships among data and/or where discrepancies occur between actual and expected outcomes. Direction and control of the educational or business enterprise is enhanced as a consequence.

Megabyte (MB or M-byte). One million bytes or one million sets of electric pulses (bits). Hard disks, which have more storage capacity than floppy disks, may have a 5, 10, or larger megabyte storage capability.

Microcomputer. A small but complete computer having an input unit like a typewriter keyboard. It has the capability of being networked with other computers.

Minicomputer. A computer whose memory size and processing speed fall between that of a mainframe and microcomputer. Due to the range in size, cost, and capability, it has become more difficult to define what a minicomputer is.

Modem. Derived from *mo*dulator-*dem*odulator. A device that changes computer code into signals that can travel over telephone wire and vice versa. Two types of modems exist: direct-connect modems which use wire connections to send and receive, and the acoustical coupler, which sends and receives signals directly through the mouthpiece and earpiece of the phone.

Office automation. A new way of using old ways, principles, equipment, and technology to help people manage information. Its ultimate goal is the development of an information network that integrates all information support tools in an office.

Output. Records and reports produced by a computer that contain meaningful information for the user. Also, output devices such as display monitors, printers, and tapes.

Password. A code determined by users to protect their computer records. If the correct password is not given, the computer will deny access to the stored files.

Peripherals. Extra equipment, such as a printer or modem, that one adds to the basic computer.

Piracy. The unlawful copying, distribution, or sale of software protected by copyright laws.

Program. Designed, written, and tested routine of computer instructions.

RAM or *random-access* memory. The computer's "working" or "temporary" memory, sometimes called the read/write memory. When the computer is on, anything in RAM can be changed, but RAM goes blank when the power is turned off. This necessitates making a backup copy on tape or disk to avoid the risk of losing one's work. A computer's RAM has limits, which means programs that require 128K will not run on a 64K computer, for example.

Record. A collection of data-related fields pertaining to a particular individual, thing, transaction, or event.

Run In BASIC, the computer command to carry out or execute a set of instructions; the term used to indicate that an application software program is executing.

Save. A command to the computer to transfer one's work from the display screen to a disk or tape. This process avoids having work lost once the machine is turned off.

Software. Computer programs, including compilers, operating systems, and user or application programs. The program may be stored on a disk or tape but may also be printed out on computer paper. User software may be task specific, general purpose, or integrated.

Stand-alone. Microcomputer workstations that operate independently; not networked.

Student information system. A computerized method of managing student and school records, for example, personal data, health information, grades, courses, attendance, and test scores. Other features include grade reporting, scheduling, and the generation of student educational plans.

Task-specific software. Programs prestructured to do a specific task like attendance accounting, student scheduling, or grade reporting.

Telecommunication. Communicating at a distance whereby a computer message may be transmitted by telephone, telegraph, satellite, or radio signal. It facilitates teleconferencing, computer conferencing, the use of electronic mail, and the accessing of commercial data bases.

Tickler files. Electronic reminders of meetings, deadlines, and organizational activities that affect a user.

Time-sharing. The sharing of a central processing unit by several users, usually with the use of terminals. These terminals may be in different rooms or different cities.

Word processors. Word-processing software programs that include such features as editing, screen formatting, print formatting, and the compact storage and flexible retrieval of documents; individuals who do word processing; a text-editing typewriter.

REFERENCES

ABERNATHY, S. M., & PETTIBONE, T. J. (1984). Computer literacy and certification: What states are doing. *T.H.E. Journal, 11*(4), 117-119.

Across the nation. (1985). *The School Administrator, 42*(5), 5.

ADAMS, D. R., WAGNER, G. E., & BOYER, T. J. (1983). *Computer information systems: An introduction.* Cincinnati, OH: South Western Publishing Co.

ADAMS, J. A. (1984). Networked computers promote computer literacy and computer-assisted instruction. *T.H.E. Journal, 11*(8), 95-99.

ALBERTE-HALLAM, T., HALLAM, S. F., & HALLAM, J. (1985). *Microcomputer use: Word processing, spreadsheets, and data bases.* New York: Academic Press.

ALTER, S. L. (1976). How effective managers use information systems. *Harvard Business Review, 54*(6), 97-104.

ANDERSON, L. W., & VAN DYKE, L. A. (1972). *Secondary school administration* (2nd ed.). Boston: Houghton Mifflin.

ARMBRUSTER. A. (1983). Ergonomic requirements. In H. J. Otway & M. Pelu (Eds.), *New office technology: Human and organizational aspects.* London: Ablex.

BAHNIUK. M. H. (1983). More than just a word processor. *American School and University, 56*(1), 42, 44, 46, 48, 50, 53.

BAKER, F. B. (1978). *Computer-managed instruction: Theory and practice.* Englewood Cliffs, NJ: Educational Technology Publications.

BARBOUR, A. (1984). Computing in America's classrooms 1984. *Electronic Learning, 4*(2), 39-41, 100.

BARBOUR, A. (1986). Computer coordinator survey. *Electronic Learning, 5*(5), 35-38.

BARCOMB, D. (1981). *Office automation: A survey of tools and techniques.* Bedford, MA: Digital Press.

BARKER, B. H., PENNINGROTH, G., & ROGERS, G. F. (1980). The registration process at Lindberg High School from arena vs. computer scheduling. *NASSP Bulletin, 64*(434), 114-116.

BARRETT, B. K., & HANNAFIN, M. J. (1982). Computers in educational management: Merging accountability with technology. *Educational Technology, 22*(2), 9-12.

BASS, R. V., & MAROUS, A. (1983). Fixed asset reporting. In F. L. Dembowski (Ed.), *Administrative uses for microcomputers: Vol. 1. Software* (pp. 79-85). Park Ridge, IL: Research Corporation of the Association of School Business Officials of the United States and Canada.

BEACH, R. H., & LINDAHL, R. A. (1984). The hidden costs of training your staff. *Electronic Learning, 3*(7), 30.

BECKER, G. (1984). Software copyright looks fuzzy, but is it? *Electronic Education, 4*(2), 18-19.

BECKER, H. J. (1983). *School uses of microcomputers* (Reports from a National Survey, No. 1). Baltimore: Center for Social Organization of Schools, Johns Hopkins University.

BECKER, H. J. (1984a). *School uses of microcomputers* (Reports from a National Survey, No. 4). Baltimore: Center for Social Organization of Schools, Johns Hopkins University.

BECKER, H. J. (1984b). *School uses of microcomputers* (Reports from a National Survey, No. 5). Baltimore: Center for Social Organization of Schools, Johns Hopkins University.

BECKER, H. J. (1986). Our national report card: Preliminary results from the new Johns Hopkins survey. *Classroom Computer Learning, 6*(4), 30-33.

BENDER, M., & CHURCH, G. D. (1984). Developing a computer applications training program for the learning disabled. *Learning Disabilities: An Interdisciplinary Journal, 3*(8), 91-102.

BENDERSON, A. (1983). Computer literacy. *Focus*. Princeton, NJ: Educational Testing Service.

BENNETT, R. E. (1982). Applications of microcomputer technology to special education. *Exceptional Children, 49*(2), 106-113.

BENNETT, R. H. (1981). Humanizing student scheduling. *NASSP Bulletin, 65*(443), 120-121.

BENSEN, D. (1983). Microcomputers and transportation management. In F. L. Dembowski (Ed.), *Administrative uses for microcomputers: Vol. 1. Software* (pp. 105-108). Park Ridge, IL: Research Corporation of the Association of School Business Officials of the United States and Canada.

BLACKHURST, A. E. (1983). Using microcomputers to manage student records. *TEASE, 6*(3), 164.

BLASCHKE, C. L. (1984). *SLATE*. Falls Church, VA: Educational Turnkey Systems.

BLOCK, J. & ANDERSON, L. (1975). *Mastery learning in classroom instruction*. New York: Macmillan.

BLOOM, B. S., et al. (Eds.). (1956). *Taxonomy of educational objectives: Handbook I. Cognitive domain*. New York: McKay.

BOCK, A. (1983). Microcomputers with school business applications. *School Business Affairs, 49*(5), 46, 60.

BORK, A. (1985). *Personal computers for education*. New York: Harper & Row.

BOZEMAN, W. C. (1979). Computer-managed instruction: State of the art. *AEDS Journal, 12*(3), 117-137.

BOZEMAN, W. C. (1984). Strategic planning for computer-based educational technology. *Educational Technology, 24*(5), 23-27.

BRADY, H. (1985). School districts singled out on piracy charges. *Classroom Computer Learning, 6*(2), 14.

BROWN, N. P. (1982). CAMEO: Computer-assisted management of educational objectives. *Exceptional Children, 49*(2), 151-154.

BUDOFF, M., THORMANN, J., & GRAS, A. (1984). *Microcomputers in special education*. Cambridge, MA: Brookline Books.

BURKE, A. L. (1982). *CAI source book*. Englewood Cliffs, NJ: Prentice-Hall.

Buyer's Guide/Word Processing. (1984). *Personal Software, 2*(7), 130-140.

CAMPBELL, R. F., & LAYTON, D. H. (1969). *Policy making for american education*. Chicago: Midwest Administration Center, University of Chicago.

CAMPBELL, R. F., CORBALLY, J. E., & NYSTRAND, R. O. (1983). *Introduction to educational administration* (6th ed.). Boston: Allyn & Bacon.

CANDOLI, I. C., HACK, W. G., RAY, J. R., & STOLLAR, D. H. (1978). *School business administration: A planning approach* (2nd ed.). Boston: Allyn & Bacon.

CANDOLI, I. C., HACK, W. G., RAY, J. R., & STOLLAR, D. H. (1984). *School business administration: A planning approach* (3rd ed.). Newton, MA: Allyn & Bacon.

CARNINE, D., & SILBERT, J. (1979). *Direct instruction reading*. Columbus, OH: Charles Merrill.

Case history workbook, computerized accounting saves district $200,000 a year. (1983). *School Business Affairs, 49*(8), 48, 58.

CECILIA, J. L. (1983). Microcomputers: A powerful energy management tool. In F. L. Dembowski (Ed.), *Administrative uses of microcomputers: Vol. 1. Software* (pp. 128-137). Park Ridge, IL: Research Corporation of the Association of School Business Officials of the United States and Canada.

CHAPIN, J. (1977). *An administrative summary of the Madison Metropolitan School District's E.S.E.A. Title III Computer Managed Instruction Program*. Unpublished manuscript.

CHION-KENNEY, L. (1984). State officials report their intention to expand role in computer policy. *Education Week, 4*(8), 10.

CHION-KENNEY, L. (1985a). Computer sales fall but not in schools. *Education Week, 4*(39), 1, 15.

CHION-KENNEY, L. (1985b). The "hidden" cost of computers. *Education Week, 4*(23), 27-28.

CHIRLIAN, B. (1982). *The tenderfoot's guide to word processing*. Beaverton, OR: Dilithium Press.

CHURCH, G. D., & BENDER, M. (1985). School administration and technology: Planning educational roles. *Educational Technology, 25*(6), 21-24.

COHEN, E., & COHEN, A. (1983). *Planning the electronic office*. New York: McGraw-Hill.

Computer courses widespread in education schools, OERI survey finds. (1986). *Teacher Education Reports, 8*(3), 6-7.

Computers. (1985). *Education Week, 5*(13), 6.

Compuview. (1983). *School Product News, 22*, 45.

COOGAN, B. (1983). Getting started with microcomputers: Which central office jobs are "computer priorities"? *Electronic Learning, 2*(6), 30, 32.

COOK, J. W. (1982). Minimum competency testing: North Boone style. *NASSP Bulletin, 66*(454), 45-48.

CORBETT, J. J., DUNN, R. C., LALTA, R. F., & LEHMAN, R. A. (1982). Principals are key to effective use of computer technology. *NASSP Bulletin, 66*(454), 109-115.

CORNISH, E. (1984, December 9). Computers offer big benefits for education. *The Salt Lake Tribune*, p. F16.

CORY, S. (1984). A four-stage model for full implementation of computers for instruction. *Independent School, 43*(4), 51-54, 57-58.

CRANER, J. (1983). The electronic spreadsheet. In F. L. Dembowski (Ed.), *Administrative uses for microcomputers: Vol. 1. Software* (pp. 86-89). Park Ridge, IL: Research Corporation of the Association of School Business Officials of the United States and Canada.

CRAMER, J. (1984). Controversy "mystifies": N.E.A. reviewed. *American School Board Journal, 171*(11), 33.

CUMMINS, C. (1984). School districts enter the computer age: The student information system. In C. D. Martin & R. S. Heller (Eds.), *Capitol-izing on computers in education—Proceedings of the 1984 Association for Educational Data Systems Annual Convention* (pp. 411-416). Rockville, MD: Computer Science Press.

DARROW, M. (1984). Shopping for networks. *Classroom Computer Learning, 5*(2), 77.

Data processing. (1979). *School Business Affairs, 45*(1), 15-16.

DEARDEN, J. & NOLAN, R. L. (1973). How to control the computer resource. *Harvard Business Review, 51*(6), 68-78.

DELF, R. M. (1982). How to shop for a student information system. *American School and University, 54*(12), 18, 20.

DEMBOWSKI, F. L. (1984a). Desired features of user friendly software. *School Business Affairs, 50*(11), 58-60.

DEMBOWSKI, F. L. (1984b). Microcomputer hardware/software for the school business office. *School Business Affairs, 50*(5), 14, 64.

DEMBOWSKI, F. L. (1984c). The microcomputer and transportation. *School Business Affairs, 50*(4), 16, 48-49.

DENNIS, J. R., & KANSKY, R. J. (1984). *Instructional computing: An action guide for educators*. Glenview, IL: Scott Foresman.

Department of Elementary and Secondary Education. (1980). *Checklist to determine the need* for and the adequacy of a school district's data processing program. Jefferson City, MO: Author.

Department of Health, Education and Welfare. (1967). *Principles of public school accounting*. Washington, D.C.: U.S. Government Printing Office.

DIERDORFF, W. H., & SMITH, J. (1984). Microcomputer program answers "what if" questions. *School Business Affairs, 50*(7), 48-49, 60.

DREHER, M. J., & SINGER, H. (1984). Making standardized tests work for you. *Principal, 63*(4), 20-24.

DUANE, J. (1985, May-June). Changing trends in instructional computer curriculum. *On Line—Utah's Computer Journal*, pp. 6-7, 19.

DURKIN, D. (1985, August 4). Focus on teaching, not testing educators told. *Deseret News*, p. B8.

Educational Research Services, Inc. (1982). *School district uses of computer technology*. Arlington, VA: Author.

ELMORE, R. (1979-1980). Backward mapping using implementation analysis to structure program decisions. *Political Science Quarterly, 94*(4), 601-616.

EL survey: Educators look to alternate funding sources. (1984). *Electronic Learning, 3*(6), 14.

ELY, D. W. (1977). *Data processing systems used in educational institutions during 1977* (Research Bulletin No. 2). Chicago: Research Corporation of the Association of School Business Officials.

EMDAD, A. (1984). Electronic publishing: Using new technologies in education. In J. H. Tashner (Ed.), *Improving instruction with microcomputers* (pp. 166-169). Phoenix, AZ: Oryx Press.

ENGLADE, K. (1984). Look for the union label on the computer software in your classroom. *American School Board Journal, 171*(11), 30-32.

ESTES, N., & WATKINS, K. (1983). Implications of the micro for educational administrators. *Educational Leadership 4*(1), 28-29.

EVEN-TOU, S. (1984). Small computers take over giant jobs. *American School and University, 54*(4), 8-10, 13, 16, 18, 20-21.

Fifteen million students in U.S. use a million computers. (1986, January 11). *Salt Lake Tribune*, p. A5.

FINKEL, L. (1983). When is a pirate a thief? *Electronic Learning, 3*(2), 26, 28.

FISHER, G., & FINKEL, L. (1984). The computer lab: Where it helps and where it doesn't. *Electronic Learning, 4*(2), 52.

For your information: Computers in the schools. (1982). *Education Times, 3*, 8.

FORMAN, K. (1983). Networking saves $$ for New York school district. *Electronic Education, 3*(1), 62-63.

FOSTER, F. (1983). Distributed processing in a school setting. *AEDS Monitor, 22*(3, 4), 14-15.

FRANKEL, P., & GRAS, A. (1983). *The software sifter: An intelligent shopper's guide to buying computer software*. New York: Macmillan.

FREDENBURG, P. B. (1983). Analysis of negotiating salary schedules. In F. L. Dembowski (Ed.), *Administrative uses for microcomputers* (pp. 90-99). Park Ridge, IL: Research Corporation of the Association of School Business Officials of the United States and Canada.

FREEMAN, R. J. (1982). An innovative student data system. *AEDS Journal, 16*(1), 16-43.

FRIESE, J. C. (1981). Menu, personnel, money management. *School Business Affairs, 47*(12), 24-26.

FRIESE, J. C. (1981). Personnel, money management. *School Business Affairs*, 47(12), 24-26.

GALITZ, W. O. (1980). *Human factors in office automation*. Atlanta, GA: Life Office Management Association.

GANGEL, D. M. (1983). Administrative uses of micros, "lopsided." *Electronic Education, 2*(8), 32-33.

GARDNER, J. (1965). *Self-renewal: The individual and the innovative society*. New York: Harper & Row.

GARRISON, W. A., & RAMAMOORTHY, C. V. (1970). *Privacy and security in data banks*. Austin, TX: Electronics Research Center.

GERHARD, M. (1971). *Effective teaching strategies with the behavioral outcome approach*. West Nyack, NY: Parker Publishing.

GIBSON, C. F., & NOLAN, R. L. (1974). Managing the four stages of EDP growth. *Harvard Business Review*, 52(1), 76–88.

Give computers to administrators first, researcher urges. (1984). *Report on Education Research*, 16(5), 4.

GLOSSBRENNER, A. (1984). *How to buy software: The master's guide to picking the right program*. New York: St. Martin's Press.

GOLZ, W. C., JR. (1984). Integrated facilities management and fixed asset accounting. *School Business Affairs*, 50(1), 32–45.

GOODSON, B. (1984). Software report: Are computer managed instruction programs worth the trouble? *Electronic Learning*, 4(1), 8.

GORTON, R. A., & MCINTYRE, K. E. (1978). *The effective principal: Vol. 2. The senior high school principalship*. Reston, VA: The National Association of Secondary School Principals.

GORTON, R. A. (1980). *School administration and supervision: Important issues, concepts, and case studies* (2nd ed.). Dubuque, IA: William C. Brown.

GORTON, R. A. (1983). *School administration and supervision: Leadership challenges and opportunities* (2nd ed.). Dubuque, IA: William C. Brown.

GRAY, P. J. (1984). The use of policy analysis in setting district policy on microcomputers. *Educational Leadership*, 42(2), 72–77.

GRAYSON, L. P. (1984). The overview of computers in U.S. education. *T.H.E. Journal*, 12(1), 78–83.

GREEN, E. J., & REDMOND, G. H. (1957). Comments on a general theory of administration. *Administrative Science Quarterly*, 2(2), 240.

GREEN, J. O. (1984). Straight talk about local networks. *Classroom Computing Learning*, 5(2), 72–77.

GRIFFITHS, D. E. (1959). *Administrative theory*. New York: Appleton.

GRISDALE, G. A. (1985, April–May). *Large district administrative services*. IBM School Executive Conference, Atlanta, GA.

GRONLUND, N. (1981). *Measurement and evaluation in teaching* (4th ed.). New York: Macmillan.

GROOBEY, J. A. (1972). Maximizing return on EDP investments. *Data Management*, 10(9), 28–32.

GROSSNICKLE, D.R., & LAIRD, B.A. (1982). Planning for the microcomputer: Innovation insurance may help. *NASSP Bulletin*, 66(455), 60–63.

GUBA, E. G. (1984). The effects of definitions of policy in the nature and outcomes of policy analyses. *Educational Leadership*, 42(2), 63–70.

GUILBEAU, J. J. (1984). Micros for the special education administrator. Profile: A Louisiana district's network of special educators. *Electronic Learning*, 3(5), 43.

GUSKY, R. R. (1985). *Implementing mastery learning*. Belmont, CA: Wadsworth.

HALLARD, J. J., SMITH, E. R., & REESE, D. (1983). *The electronic office: A guide for managers*. Homewood, IL: Dow Jones Irwin.

HANSEN, T., KLASSEN, D., & LINDSAY, J. (1978). The impact of computer-based information systems upon school and school district administration. *AEDS Journal*, 12(1), 1–10.

HARDING, B. C. (1982). Taming the paper tiger. *American School and University*, 54(5), 108–109.

HASLEDALEN, D. W. (1978). Personnel systems. *AEDS Monitor*, 16(11, 12), 4–5.

HEATH, B., & CAMP, W. G. (1984). *Microcomputers in small business management*. Columbus, OH: The National Center for Research in Vocational Education.

HEBENSTREIT, J. (1983). Training for future office skills. In H. J. Otway & M. Pettu (Eds.), *New office technology, human and organizational aspects*. London: Ablex.

HENTSCHKE, G. (1975). *Management operations in education*. Berkeley, CA: McCutcheon.

HERZLINGER, R. (1977). Why data systems in non-profit organizations fail. *Harvard Business Review*, 55(1), 81–86.

High schools find use of electronic cards by students boost security, attendance. (1984, December 30). *Deseret News*, p. 12A

HOFMEISTER, A. (1984). *Microcomputer applications in the classroom*. New York: Holt, Rinehart & Winston.

HOLBROOK, B. (1984, August 18). On the fasttract. *Deseret News*, p. 6C.

HOOVER, T., & GOULD, S. (1982). Computerizing the school office: The hidden cost. *NASSP Bulletin, 66*(455), 89–91.

HSU, T., & NITKO, A. J. (1983). Microcomputer testing software teachers can use. *Educational Measurement: Issues and Practice, 2*(4), 15–18, 23–30.

HUGHES, L. W., & UBBEN, G. C. (1980). *The secondary principal's handbook.* Boston: Allyn & Bacon.

HUGHES, L. W., & UBBEN, G. C. (1984). *The elementary principal's handbook* (2nd ed.). Boston: Allyn & Bacon.

HUNTER, M. (1970). Tailoring your teaching to individualized instruction. *Instructor, 79*(7), 53–63.

HUNTINGTON, F. (1983). The microcomputer in the administrator's office. *AEDS Journal, 17*(1, 2), 91–97.

HUSSAIN, K. M. (1973). *Development of information systems for education.* Englewood Cliffs, NJ: Prentice-Hall.

Information and Instructional Services. (1984). *SIS student information system.* Salt Lake City, UT: Utah State Office of Education.

INGERSOLL, G. M., & SMITH, C. B. (1984). Availability and growth of microcomputers in American schools. *T.H.E. Journal, 12*(1), 84–87.

JARRETT, D. (1982). *The electronic office: A management guide to the office of the future.* London: Altershot, Hantz & Gower.

JOINER, L. N., VENSEL, G. ROSS, J. D., & SILVERSTEIN, B. (1982). *Microcomputers in education: A non-technical guide to instructional and school management applications.* Holmes Beach, FL: Learning Publications.

JONES, B. L. (1983). Selecting microcomputer software: Administration. In F. L. Dembowski (Ed.), *Administrative uses for microcomputers: Vol. 1. Software* (pp. 32–37). Park Ridge, IL: Research Corporation of the Association of School Business Officials of the United States and Canada.

JORDAN, K. F. (1969). *School business administration.* New York: Ronald Press.

JUDD, R. C. (1984). Network for education. *Educational Computer, 4*(1), 18–19, 47.

KACANEK, P. (1984). Spreadsheets and pupil enrollment projections. *Electronic Learning, 4*(2), 26, 28.

KANTGLEHNER, J. (1983). Computerizing custodial services. *School Business Affairs, 49*(2), 38, 48.

KATZAN, H., Jr. (1982). *Office automation: A manager's guide.* New York: American Management Association.

KAUFFMAN, F. H. (1983). Distributed processing and computer networking at Broward County—A status report. *AEDS Monitor, 22*(3, 4,), 16–18.

KELLY, L. L. (1979). Student self-scheduling—Is it worth the risk? *NASSP Bulletin, 63*(424), 84–91.

KENISTON, D. C. (1983). (1983). Determining custodial staffing needs. In F. L. Dembowski (Ed.), *Administrative uses of microcomputers: Vol. 1. Software* (pp. 100–103). Park Ridge, IL: Research Corporation of the Association of School Business Officials of the United States and Canada.

KISER, C. (1984). Educators' guidelines for administrative microcomputer systems. In D. Martin & R. S. Heller (Eds.), *Capitol-izing on computers in education/proceedings of the 1984 Association for Educational Data Systems Annual Convention* (pp. 435–439). Rockville, MD: Computer Science Press.

KLAUSMIER, H. (1977). IGE in elementary and middle schools. *Educational Leadership, 34,* 330–336.

KOHL, H. (1985). Classroom management software: Beware the hidden agenda. *Classroom Computer Learning, 5*(7), 19–21.

KRAHN, K., & HUGHES, B. (1976). Benefits of computer class scheduling. *NASSP Bulletin, 60*(396), 106–108.

KRAUSS, L., & MACGAHAN, A. (1979). *Computer fraud and countermeasures.* Englewood Cliffs, NJ: Prentice-Hall.

LANDERS, T. J., & MYERS, J. G. (1977). *Essentials of school management.* Philadelphia: W. B. Saunders.

LEAHY, P. E. (1983). General use of microcomputers for school management. In F. L.

Dembowski (Ed.), *Administrative uses for microcomputers* (pp. 8-15). Park Ridge, IL: Research Corporation of the Association of School Business Officials of the United States and Canada.

LECHNER, H. D. (1984). Computers: Why do executives use only partial computer ability? *California Business, 19*(9), 174.

LEIBLUM, M. D. (1982). Computer-managed instruction: An explanation and overview. *AEDS Journal, 15*(3), 126-142.

LEUSSLER, D. (1976). School eager to share self-scheduling details. *NASSP Bulletin, 60*(399), 117-118.

LEVIN, D. (1984). This ingenious computer program makes school bus maintenance reliable and cost effective. *American School Board Journal, 171*(11), 36-37.

LEVIN, J. A., MIYAKE, N., & OLIVAS, J. (1985). Computer Rx. *Electronic Learning, 5*(1), 55-57.

LEWIS, C. (1983). *Managing with micros.* Oxford, England: Basil Blackwell.

LIKERT, R. (1961). *New patterns of management.* New York: McGraw-Hill.

LYNN, L. E. (1985). Integrated software a versatile management tool. *Principal, 64*(3), 44-46.

MACKENZIE, D. G. (1984). Give your computers a room of their own and a home they can love. *The American School Board Journal, 171*(9), 40-41.

MACRAE, D., Jr. (1979). Concepts and methods of policy analysis. *Society, 16*(6), 17-23.

MANDEL, S. L. (1984). *Computer data processing and the law.* St. Paul, MN: West Publishing.

Market Data Retrieval. (1984). *Microcomputers in schools 1983-84.* Westport, CT: Author.

MARTIN, E. G. (1981). Microcomputer applications to special education administration. *AEDS Monitor, 19*(10-12), 5, 30.

MCCALEB, R. B. (1982). *Small business computer primer.* Beaverton, OR: Dilithium Press.

MCCUTCHEON, J. W. (1986). A spreadsheet will crunch your A computer gradebook. *Tech Trends, 31*(1), 26, 39.

MCGINTY, T. (1984). West Virginia: A plan to link every school. *Electronic Learning, 4*(3), 26-27.

MCGINTY, T. (1985). Tracking truants with automatic dialers. *Electronic Learning, 4*(4), 24, 26-27.

MCISAAC, D. N., & BAKER, F. B. (1981). Computer-managed instruction system implementation on a microcomputer. *Educational Technology, 21*(10), 40-46.

MILLER, C. (1984a). Relational data base managers. *Personal Software, 2*(8), 97-98, 100-101.

MILLER, C. (1984b). Word processing software. *Personal Software, 2*(7), 125-129.

MILNER, S. D. (1980). How to make the right decisions about microcomputers. *Instructional Innovator, 25*(6), 12-19.

MIMS, M. T. (1984). Computer competencies for school administrators (Doctoral dissertation, North Texas University, 1983). *Dissertation Abstracts International, 44*(5), 2379A.

Mind sets: What is it that keeps educators from learning how to use the computer? (1985, May-June). *On Line—Utah's Computer Journal,* pp. 10-11.

MITCHELL, R. E. (1982). Tomorrow's school office today. *American School and University, 54*(8), 30, 35.

MORGAN, J. (1983). Cincinnati schools data base. *Electronic Learning, 3*(1).

MORT, P. R., REUSSER, W. C., & POLLEY, J. W. (1960). *Public school finance* (3rd ed.). New York: McGraw-Hill.

MOURSUND, D. (1985). *The computer coordinator.* Eugene, OR: International Council for Computers in Education.

National Association of Secondary School Principals. (1975, March). School Attendance and Absenteeism. *The Practitioner.*

NAUMER, J. N. (1984). *Media center management with an Apple II.* Littleton CO: Libraries Unlimited.

A new era for management. (1983). *Business Monitor,* pp. 50-58.

NEWMAN, P. (Ed.). (1983). *The Associated Press pocket guide to buying a home computer.* New York: Associated Press and Dialogue Systems.

News briefs. (1986). *School Tech News, 3*(7), 2.

NOONAN, L. (1983). Computer literacy for administrators. *AEDS Monitor, 22*(1, 2), 5-8.

ODDEN, A., & ODDEN, E. (1984). Education, reform, school improvement, and state policy. *Educational Leadership, 42*(2), 13-19.

O'DRISCOLL, P. (1980). A local option for test scoring. In C. D. Martin & R. S. Heller (Eds.),

Capitol-izing on computers in education—Proceedings of the 1984 Association for Educational Data Systems Annual Convention. Rockville, MD: Computer Science Press.

O'KEEFE, L. (1984). *Integrated spreadsheet software.* New York: McGraw-Hill.

PARKER, J. (1973). A student centered scheduling model. *NASSP Bulletin, 57*(369), 47–52.

PATTERSON, J. L., & PATTERSON, J. H. (1983). *Putting computer power in schools: A step by step approach.* Englewood Cliffs, NJ: Prentice-Hall.

PATTIE, K. (1985). Copyright abuse: No need for lawsuits. *Tech Trends, 30*(7), 39–40.

PENNINGTON, J. R. (1984). Word processing and teacher evaluation. *Electronic Learning, 3*(6), 66, 68.

PETERSON, F., & K-TURKEL, J. (1984a, April 8). Can you guess the extent to which computers have invaded our lives? *Deseret News,* p. M5.

PETERSON, F., & K-TURKEL, J. (1984b, June 24). Business computers. *Deseret News,* p. M5.

PETERSON, F., & K-TURKEL, J. (1984c, August 19). Software companies employ "licenses" in attempt to rob buyers of right to alter product. *Deseret News,* p. M3.

PETERSON, F., & K-TURKEL, J. (1985, May 26). Hard disks are becoming increasingly beneficial. *Deseret News,* p. M3.

PETERSON, F., & K-TURKEL, J. (1986, February 2). Latest spreadsheets incorporate helpful new wrinkles. *Deseret News,* p. M7.

PHARIS, W. L., & ZAKARIYA, S. B. (1979). *The elementary school principal-ship in 1978: A research study.* Arlington, VA: National Association of Elementary School Principals.

PITNER, N. J. (1979). Satisfaction often eludes the workaholic superintendent. *Executive Education, 1,* 18–20.

POGROW, S. (1982a). Microcomputerizing your paper work: Part II. Scheduling and attendance. *Electronic Learning, 2*(2), 20, 22, 24, 26–27.

POGROW, S. (1982b). Microcomputerizing your paper work: Part III. Financial management. *Electronic Learning, 2*(3), 34, 36, 40–42.

POGROW, S. (1983a). *Education in the computer age: Issues of policy, practice and reform.* Beverly Hills, CA: Sage Publications.

POGROW, S. (1983b). Integrated software for administrators. *Electronic Learning, 3*(1), 42, 44, 46.

POGROW, S. (1983c). The perfect marriage integrated word processing and data base management programs. *Electronic Learning, 3*(3), 26, 28, 30, 32, 110–111.

POGROW, S. (1984a). Buying a scheduling program. *Electronic Learning, 3*(5), 30, 32, 34–35.

POGROW, S. (1984b). Finance packages for the central district office. *Electronic Learning, 2*(8), 32, 34, 36.

POGROW, S. (1985). The state-of-the-art in educational administration software. *T.H.E. Journal, 13*(4), 72–74.

PORTER, A. C. (1983). The role of testing in effective schools. *American Education, 19*(1983), 25–28.

POTTER, D. A. (1977). *Software objectives for the administrative network.* Address presented to the International Data Corporation Conference. (1972).

Privacy and computers (A Report of a Task Force). (1972). Ottowa, Canada: Departments of Communication and Justice.

Professional computing word processing programs for the IBM personal computer. (1983, March). *The Seybold Report, 1*(2), 1–31.

PROUTY, J. W. (1983). *From word processors to workstations: Insights into automation.* New York: American Management Association.

RADIN, S., & GREENSBERG, H. M. (1983). *Computer literacy for school administrators and supervisors.* Lexington, MA: D.C. Heath.

RAIMONDI, S. L. (1984). Electronic communication network. *Educational Technology, 46*(2), 39–41.

RAMPY, C., WHITE, D. J. D., & ROCKMAN, S. (1983). Computers in the schools: 21 critical issues for policy decisions. *Educational Technology, 22*(8), 20–23.

RAUCHER, S. M. (1984). Office automation—Planning for implementation. *AEDS Monitor, 23*(1,2), 8–10.

REBORE, R. W. (1984). *A handbook for school board members.* Englewood Cliffs, NJ: Prentice-Hall.

REINHOLD, F., & CORKETT, K. (1985). Mandates: EL's fifth annual survey of the states. *Electronic Learning, 5*(2), 25–26, 31.

RIESDESEL, C. A., & CLEMENTS, D. H. (1985). *Coping with computers in the elementary and middle school*. Englewood Cliffs, NJ: Prentice-Hall.

ROBERTS, J. M. E. (1978). *Implementation of innovations in educational organizations and instruction*. New York: Research for Better Schools.

ROGERS, E. M. (1984). Foreword. In F. Williams & V. Williams, *Microcomputers in elementary education* (p. xii). Belmont, CA: Wadsworth.

RUBIN, L. (1984). Formulating educational policy in the aftermath of the reports. *Educational Leadership, 42*(2), 7-10.

RUST, A. O., & JUDD, F. J. (1984). Redistricting is less torturous when a computer does the nitty-gritty for you. *The American School Board Journal, 171*(3), 35-36.

SALISBURY, A. R. (1971). Computers and education: Toward agreement on terminology. *Educational Technology, 11*, 35-40.

SAVER, C. W. (1983). Data switching. *American School and University, 56*(2), 32-38.

SAX, G. (1974). *Principles of educational measurement and evaluation*. Belmont, CA: Wadsworth.

SCHUFORD, R. S. (1983). Word tools for the IBM personal computer. *Byte, 8*(5), 176-319.

SCHULTZ, K. A., & HART, L. C. (1983). Computers in education. *Arithmetic Teacher, 31*(4), 36.

SCOFIELD, A. (1983). Computerized food services management. In F. L. Dembowski (Ed.), *Administrative uses for microcomputers: Vol. 1. Software* (pp. 117-124). Park Ridge, IL: Research Corporation of the Association of School Business Officials of the United States and Canada.

School policies fail to cope with micros? (1984). *School Tech News, 2*(1), 1.

SERBIAN, A. L. (1983). Computer literacy levels and attitudes toward computers of California site administrators (Doctoral dissertation, University of the Pacific, 1983). *Dissertation Abstracts International, 44*(10), 2947A.

SHATEN, N. L. (1982). Building the schedule: breaking from the mold of traditional thinking. *NASSP Bulletin, 66*(451), 91-95.

SHAW, L. C. (1980). Budgeting in 1980. *Datamation*, p. 129.

SHOA, R. C. (1984). Enrollment forecasting: What methods work best? *NASSP Bulletin, 117*(1), 53-58.

Sixth Annual Survey of School Board Members. (1984). Fill yourself in: 97% of you will back computers with bucks. *American School Board Journal, 171*(1), 28-29.

SLOAN, C. A., & YUDEWITZ, G. J. (1983). Using this forecasting process to take the mystery out of your financial future. *American School Board Journal, 170*(8), 33-34.

SMITH, B. R. (1981). *The small computer in small business*. Brattleboro, VT: Stephen Green Press.

SMITH, R. M. (1981). *Improving instructional management with microcomputers* (Goal Based Educational Program Occasional Paper No. 1.). Portland, OR: Northwest Regional Laboratory.

SMITH, R., & KAUFFMAN, D. (1985). Before you choose a network, consider . . . *Electronic Education, 4*(6), 25, 27-28.

SNIDER, W. (1986). Study views computers in independent schools. *Education Week, 5*(20), 4.

Software piracy puts big dents in revenue. (1985, February 17). *Deseret News*, p. M7.

SPAIN, T. (1984). Networking pie in the sky or icing on the cake. *Electronic Learning, 4*(2), 48-51.

SPG electronic networking. (1984). *Instructional Innovator, 29*(1), 6-7.

SPIVAK, H., & VARDEN, S. (1981). Classrooms make friends with computers. In J. L. Thomas (Ed.), *Microcomputers in the school* (pp. 52-53). Phoenix, AZ: Oryx Press.

SPLITTGERBER, F. L., & STIRZAKER, N. A. (1984). Guidelines for financing school district computer services. *School Business Affairs, 50*(3), 30, 32, 80-81.

SPROULL, L., & ZUBROW, D. (1981). Standardized testing from the administrative perspective. *Phi Delta Kappa, 62*(1981), 628-631.

State policies affect electronics learning. (1985). *T.H.E. Journal, 12*(7), 30.

Staying in charge. (1983). Boca Raton, FL: International Business Machines.

STEINBERG, E. R. (1984). *Teaching computers to teach*. Hillsdale, NJ: Lawrence Erlbaum.

STERN, R. A., & STERN, N. (1982). *An introduction to computer and information processing*. New York: Wiley.

STRASSMANN, P. A. (1985). *Information payoff*. New York: The Free Press.

STRONGE, J. H., & TURNER, J. H. (1983). Computer scheduling: Is it worth the effort? *Electronics Education, 3*(1), 56-57.

STULTZ, R. A. (1982). *The word processing handbook*. Englewood Cliffs, NJ: Prentice-Hall.

STURDIVANT, P. (1984). Courseware for schools: Present problems and future needs. *AEDS Monitor, 23*(12), 25–27.

SWARTZ, T. F., SHULLER, S. M., & CHERNOW, F. B. (1984). *Educator's complete guide to computers*. West Nyack, NY: Parker Publishing.

TALAB, R. (1985). Look both ways before you copy software. *Tech Trends, 30*(2), 28–30.

TALLEY, S. (1983). Selection and acquisition of administrative microcomputer software. *AEDS Journal, 17*(1,2), 69–82.

Technically speaking. (1984a). *Educational Technology, 24*(6), 6.

Technically speaking. (1984b). *Educational Technology, 24*(16), 6.

Technically speaking. (1985a). *Educational Technology, 25*(1), 6.

Technically speaking. (1985b). *Educational Technology, 25*(2), 6.

TELEM, M. (1982). CMI and the MIS—An integration needed. *AEDS Journal, 16*(1), 48–55.

TELEM, M. (1985). The school computer administrator. *Educational Technology, 25*(7), 12–15.

TEMKIN, K., & SHAPIRO, P. (1983). Computerizing your annual purchasing. In F. L. Dembowski (Ed.), *Administrative uses for microcomputers: Vol. 1. Software* (pp. 38–43). Park Ridge, IL: Research Corporation of the Association of School Business Officials of the United States and Canada.

The educational administrator's survival guide to administrative uses of microcomputers. (1984). Tallahassee, FL: Florida Department of Education.

The National Software Testing Center. (1984). *The rating's book: Spreadsheets*. Wynnwood, PA: Software Digest.

The Sector Report: Special education technology in Utah. (1985). *The Special Educator, 5*(7), 7–9.

TIDWELL, S. B. (1974). *Financial and managerial accounting for elementary and secondary school systems*. Chicago: The Research Corporation Association of School Business Officials.

TILWICK, R. L. (1975). Student self-scheduling: An unintentional deception. *NASSP Bulletin, 59*(381), 114–117.

Training lack seen undermining use of micros? (1985.) *Soft Tech News, 3*(2), 3.

TRUETT, C., & GILLESPIE, L. (1984). *Choosing educational software*. Littleton, CO: Libraries Unlimited.

United States Department of Agriculture. (1984). *Automated school food service system*. Alexandria, VA: Author.

United States Office of Education. (1973). *Handbook II financial accounting: Classification and standard terminology for local and state school systems, revised*. Washington, DC: U.S. Government Printing Office.

Up front—Chopping information down to size. (1983). *Electronic Learning, 3*(1), 27.

Utah school district guide for self-evaluation of school business functions (1983). Salt Lake City, UT: Utah State Office of Education.

VAN EGMOND-PANNELL, D. (1981). *School food service* (2nd ed.). Westport, CT: AVI.

VIET, S. (1983). Viet on computer software: What makes a data base management system ticket the kind you need. *Computers and Electronics, 21*(7), 22.

VIGILANTE, R. P. (1983). Decision making in software acquisition. In F. L. Dembowski (Ed.), *Administrative uses for microcomputers* (pp. 15–31). Park Ridge, IL: Research Corporation of the Association of School Business Officials of the United States and Canada.

WAGNER, W. (1983). Microcomputers and the management of instruction. *Educational Computer, 3*(6), 46–47, 71.

WALKER, D. F. (1984). Computers in schools. *Education Brief*, p. 9.

WALL, F. E. (1976). Student self-scheduling works well for us. *NASSP Bulletin, 60*(397), 99–103.

WALL, F. E. (1979). Class schedules—Computer "loaded" or student scheduled. *NASSP Bulletin, 63*(427), 93–97.

Wall Street Journal. (1984, Sept. 11), Volume CXI, No. 50.

Want to cut paperwork 50%? Here's an answer. (1986). *School Tech News, 3*(6), 8.

WEINTRAUB, W. (1986). Computer piracy and the myth of computer innocence. *The School Administrator, 43*(4), 8–10.

WELDY, G. R. (1979). *Principals: What they do and who they are*. Reston, VA: National Association of Secondary School Principals.

WESTIN, A. F. (1967). *Privacy and freedom*. New York: Atheneum.

WHITE, G. T. (1984). Micros for the special educator, how to use a computer to keep up with special education law. *Electronic Learning, 3*(5), 29-40.

WILES, J., & BONDI, J. L. (1983). *Principles of school administration*. Columbus, OH: Charles E. Merrill.

WILLIAMS, A. T. (1984). *What if . . . ? A user's guide to spreadsheets on the IBM PC*. New York: Wiley.

WILLIAMS, C., & the Editors of EL. (1985). Untangling the copyright issues. *Electronic Learning, 5*(3), 46, 51, 78.

WILLIAMS, R. C., BANK, A., & THOMAS, C. (1984). The school district role in introducing microcomputers: A contingency planning approach. *Educational Technology, 24*(12), 37-42.

WILLIAMS, W. L., & LE CESNE, T. (1985). Getting the picture: Graphs and charts by computer. *Electronic Learning, 4*(5), 40-44.

WILLIS, J. W., JOHNSON, L., & DIXON, P. N. (1983). *Computers, teaching and learning*. Beaverton, OR: Dilithium Press.

WOOD, C. L., NICHOLSON, E. W., & FINDLEY, D. G. (1979). *The secondary school principal*. Boston: Allyn & Bacon.

ZAIDEN, D. J. (1975). The paper work explosion. In R. S. Minor & C. W. Fetridge (Eds.), *The Dartnell office administration handbook* (5th ed., p. 517). Chicago: The Dartnell Corp.

ZUK, D. A., & STILWELL, W. E. (1984). Taming the beast: A comprehensive model for the implementation of microcomputers in education. *Education, 104*(4), 377-384.

RESOURCES

SOFTWARE DIRECTORIES

Administrative: School Emphasis

An Administrator's Guide to Microcomputer Resources (1983)
The National Center for Research in Vocational Education
National Center Publications, Box F
1960 Kenny Road
Columbus, OH 43210
800/848-4815 or 486-3655

The Administrator's Guide lists computing periodicals, selected organizations, a sampling of software vendors, and an annotated bibliography on microtechnology in education, $6.50

The Administrative Systems/Program Directory (1986)
C/VEG Publications
Santa Clara County Office of Education
100 Skyport Drive, Mail Code 236
San Jose, CA 95115
408/947-6756

The Administrative Directory covers systems/programs that deal with scheduling, transcripts, attendance, reporting, grading, and finances, $7.00.

Microcomputers in Small Business Management (1983)
The National Center for Research in Vocational Education
National Center Publications, Box F
1960 Kenny Road
Columbus, OH 43210
800/848-4815 or 614/486-3655

This publication includes a listing of business software for Apple, IBM, and TRS-80 microcomputers by type of function that may be used by schools, evaluation criteria for business and educational software, and software evaluation and rating forms, $6.50.

Microcomputers and Word Processing Programs: An Evaluation and Critique (1985)
CUNY Research Foundation, Box BG
Instructional Resource Center
City University of New York
535 E. 80th St. New York 10021

This 191 page guide includes a critical survey of 20 word processing programs. It also discusses word processing in writing courses identifying special techniques and potential problems for different types of students, $5.00.

Micros for Managers: A Software Guide for School Administrators, Revised Edition
J. R. Little, P. E. Mackey, and L. J. Tuscher, editors
New Jersey School Board Association
315 West State Street
P.O. Box 909
Trenton, NJ 08605
609/695-7600

For each of the over 300 administrative software programs listed, descriptive information is provided on cost, features, system and peripheral requirements, user references, locations of product reviews, availability of demo software, and estimated processing time. Purchase cost is $25.00 plus $3.00 for handling and shipping.

General Purpose

Educational Software Directory, a Subject Guide to Microcomputer Software (1982)
Libraries Unlimited
P.O. Box 263
Littleton, CO 80160
303/770-1220

For each of the over 900 software programs for use in grades K–12, descriptive information on cost, hardware, format, subject area, grade level, and features is provided. The directory price is $27.50

IBM Personal Computer Educational Software Directory (1984)
Electronics Communications, Inc.
Suite 220
1311 Executive Center Drive
Tallahassee, FL 32301

Educational software in the directory is listed under sixteen categories, including administration, teaching aids, and word processing, that directly relate to school management tools. Copies provided free upon request.

Instructor's Computer Directory for Schools (1985–86 Edition)
Instructor Books
P.O. Box 6177
Duluth, MN 55806
800/346-0085

The directory includes a management category that describes administration, classroom, library, and special education programs. The cost is $9.95 plus shipping and handling.

Queue Educational Software Catalog (1986)
Queue, Inc.
5 Chapel Hill Drive
Fairfield, CT 06432
800/232-2224; from Connecticut, Alaska, Hawaii, and Canada call 203/355-0908

The *Queue Catalog* editions are free and contain software listings for the Apple, Atari, Commodore, IBM, Amiga, and TRS-80 computers. School administration software programs are listed dealing with business applications, attendance, and computer-managed instruction.

Radio Shack TRS-80 Sourcebook (4th ed.)
Contact local Radio Shack dealer or:
Radio Shack Education Division
400 Atrium, One Tandy Center
Fort Worth, TX 76102
817/390-3832

Teacher/administrative software for scheduling, attendance, and test scoring to be used on various Radio Shack microcomputers are listed in the *Sourcebook*.

Swift's Educational Software Directories
Sterling Swift Publishing Co.
7901 South IH-35
Austin, TX 78744
1/800/428-8071

Administrative software applications are featured in the Apple Corvus ($26.60), Apple IIe ($33.26), and IBM ($26.60) directories. Twenty-five percent discount applied on purchases.

T.E.S.S. The Educational Software Selector (1986)
EPIE Institute
P.O. Box 839
Water Mill, NY 11976
516/283-4922

The *Selector* offers a comprehensive listing of microcomputer software, including administrative and guidance software, at a cost of $54.00.

The Software Catalogs
Menu
1520 S. College Ave.
Fort Collins, CO 80524
1/800/843-6368 or 303/482-5000

Catalogs published of interest to educational administrators are: *Software Catalog: Microcomputers* ($95.00 for two volumes), *Software Catalog: Minicomputers* ($125.00), and *Software Catalog: Business Software* ($35.00). Educational software is included in the first two catalogs, while business software that may be considered for use in the schools is contained in the latter. This catalog provides details on over 5000 business programs for all major microcomputers, minicomputers, and mainframes. Included are descriptions of the "big five" accounting programs, data-base managers, and word processors.

SOFTWARE GUIDES/EVALUATION FORMS

Research on Evaluation Program
Northwest Regional Educational Laboratory
300 S. W. Sixth Avenue
Portland, OR 97204
503/248-6800

Nine guidebooks have been published by Northwest Lab pertaining to evaluation per se and general-purpose software. The three software guides are:

No. 3: *Microcomputers: Word Processing*
No. 7: *Microcomputers: Data Base Management Software*
No. 9: *Microcomputers: Spreadsheet Software*

Also available from the lab is the "Review of Administrative Application and Instructional Management Software" form. It was created with input from administrators and software producers and revised after field testing.

SOFTWARE PREVIEW/REVIEW RESOURCES

The Digest of Software Review: Education
School and Home Courseware, Inc.
301 West Mesa, Suite F
Fresno, CA 93704
209/431-8300

Though the emphasis is on listing courseware evaluations, the *Digest* does include reviews on administrative/classroom management programs. The subscription cost for nine issues published during the school year is $147.50.

Evaluations of Educational Administrative Software
Ed-Ad Systems
P.O. Box 22801
Tucson, AZ 85706

This book by Stanley Pogrow presents evaluations of student management systems, district-level financial management systems, word processing, data-base systems, spread sheets, and general financial-management systems programs.

SECTOR
Special Education Technical On-line Resources
Exceptional Child Center
UMC 68
Utah State University
Logan, UT 84322
801/753-7973

SECTOR offers the following services: (1) evaluation forms and software management reviews, (2) a resource file of specialized hardware and software for the handicapped, and (3) a computerized data bank of over 500 articles of potential interest to computer-using educators. Two items of interest are *The Quick Guide to Resources in Special Education Technology* and the SECTOR evaluation forms, which may be used for evaluating computer-managed instruction, computer-assisted testing, and individual education programs. The *Guide* ($15.00) lists and describes over 250 organizations, producers, software programs, publications, and networks in the field of special education.

Software Preview Centers

Electronic Learning, a computing journal, has published a listing of preview centers throughout the country in its January (Vol. 3, No. 4) and February (Vol. 3, No. 5) 1984 issues. Presented is a two-part directory by state of all local and regional noncommercial centers open to educators for previewing instructional and, in many instances, administrative/management software. Part I of the "National Directory of Software Preview Centers" included all locations in states west of the Mississippi, while the February or Part II issue covered all remaining states with the exception of Wisconsin and the District of Columbia.

Software Report Cards

Infoworld
530 Lytton Avenue
Palo Alto, CA 94301
415/328-4602 or
1/800/544-3712 outside Pennsylvania
to obtain back issues of *Infoworld*

Reviews, collected from weekly issues of *Infoworld*, are available free to subscribers. General-purpose and educational software are featured.

PUBLICATIONS

Educational Computing Journals/Newsletters Addressing Administrative Applications and Issues

AEDS Journal and AEDS Monitor
Association for Educational Data Systems
1201-16th Street, NW
Washington, DC 20036
202/822-7845

The *Journal* publishes four issues per year for $32.00, while the *Monitor* has six issues at $28.00. Administrative computing articles are featured regularly.

American School Board Journal
National School Boards Association
1680 Duke Street
Alexandria, VA 22314

The *Journal* periodically includes computer articles that address administrative issues, $38.00/12 issues.

American School and University (AS & U)
Education Division
North American Publishing Company
401 N. Broad Street
Philadelphia, PA 19108
215/238-5300

Published monthly at $40.00 per year. The annual May issue of *AS & U* is a "Who's Who Buyer's Guide and Directory" that contains information on computer hardware, software, furniture, and supplies.

Classroom Computer Learning
Peter Li, Inc.
19 Davis Drive
Belmont, CA 94002
415/592-7810

Though directed toward the classroom teacher, this publication now features "The Administrator's Eye," which examines issues and trends of interest to school administrators. Its August 1984 (Vol. 5, No. 1) issue featured a "Directory of Educational Computing Resources" listing hardware and software resources and information on fund raising. The January 1986 issue (Vol. 6, No. 4) included a "Buyer's Directory" listing firms offering management, administrative, classroom, testing, grading, and word-processing software.

Computers in Education
Pergamon Press, Inc.
Maxwell House
Fairview Park
Elmsford, NY 10523
914/592-7700

This quarterly publication ($40.00 per year) is international in scope and reports on current applications of computers in education, educational administration, and current research.

Computers in the Schools
The Haworth Press, Inc.
28 East 22nd Street
New York, NY 10010
212/228-2800

Featured in this quarterly publication ($26.00/individuals; $32/institutions) are articles on instructional and administrative applications, software and hardware, and research in the field.

The Computing Teacher
International Council for Computers in Education (ICCE)
University of Oregon
1787 Agate Street
Eugene, OR 97403
503/686-4414

Software reviews, computing problems, and suggestions for teaching about computers are typical of articles printed in *The Computing Teacher*, $21.50/9 issues.

Educational Computer
Edcomp, Inc.
P.O. Box 535
Cupertino, CA 95015
408/988-0135

Educational Computer includes software reviews and application articles on microcomputer technology in the classroom, administrative offices, for the handicapped, and current trends in the field, $25.00/10 issues.

Educational Technology
140 Sylvan Avenue
Englewood Cliffs, NJ 07632
201/871-4007

Articles featuring computer-managed instruction, administrative planning for the use of computers, and editorials on various aspects of microcomputer technology in the schools makes this publication of interest to school administrators, $49.00/12 issues.

Electronic Education
Electronic Communications, Inc.
1311 Executive Center Dr., Suite 2201
Tallahassee, FL 32301
904/878-4178

School administrators and educators are oriented in issues of *EE* to the uses of technology in the schools, new products, trends, and developments in the field. Free issues are provided to qualified educators, otherwise $18.00/8 issues. Special "Software Buyer's Guide" reviews on administrative software were featured in 1983 and 1984, for example, "Administrative Aids Software" (Vol. 3, No. 1, September 1983); "Teaching Aids and Word Processing Software" (Vol. 3, No. 2, October 1983); and "Administrative Software" (Vol. 3, No. 6, March 1984).

Electronic Learning
Scholastic Learning
730 Broadway
New York, NY 10003
212/505-3000

Articles appealing to school administrators have appeared regularly in issues of *Electronic Learning*. Topics have included "Computing in America's Classrooms," "The Hidden Costs of Training Your Staff," "Computer Coordinator Survey," "Buying a Scheduling Program," and "Microcomputerizing Your Paper Work." Software reviews on administrative/management programs also appear, $19.00/8 issues.

Microcomputer Digest
201 Route 516
Old Bridge, NJ 08857
201/679-1877

Digest appeals to school administrators, claiming that they would have to subscribe to dozens of periodicals to obtain the same information provided in one of their issues. $29.95/11 issues.

NASSP Bulletin
National Association of Secondary School Principals
1904 Association Drive
Reston, VA 22091

NASSP Bulletin regularly features articles accenting microtechnology in the schools pertaining to scheduling, acquisition, computer-managed instruction, issues, and trends. Membership dues in NASSP are $85.00 which includes the *Bulletin*; otherwise, $40.00/9 issues.

Principal
National Association of Elementary School Principals
1615 Duke Street
Alexandria, VA 22314
703/684-3345

Principal has a feature entitled "Computer Station" that addresses administrative uses of computers. The January 1986 issue contained a special report on "Computers in the Schools," $20.00/5 issues.

The School Administrator
American Association of School Administrators
1801 North Moore Street
Arlington, VA 22209
703/528-0700

The School Administrator periodically includes articles on computerization in the schools. Membership dues in AASD includes the $5.00/11 issues subscription cost.

School Business Affairs
Association of School Business Affairs
1760 Reston Ave., Suite 411
Reston, VA 22090

School Business Affairs caters to school business officials and regularly has featured articles on the computerization of transportation and food services and the business office.

The School Microcomputer Bulletin
Learning Publications, Inc.
5351 Gulf Drive
Holmes Beach, FL 33510
813/778-6818

The SMB focuses on printing articles that seek to promote administrative/instructional applications. $28/10 issues.

School Tech News (NASSP Edition)
Education News Service
P.O. Box 1789
Carmichael, CA 95609

The *News*, which publishes seven issues per year ($32.95), contains news briefs, conference reports, and research findings on computers that have direct implications for school administrators.

SIG Bulletin
International Council for Computers in Education (ICCE)
Special Interest Group for Educational Administrators
1787 Agate Street
Eugene, OR 97403
503/686-4429

The *SIG Bulletin*, published quarterly, features nontechnical articles that address the use of microcomputers in the public schools. Of interest to administrators are articles on networking, general-purpose software, and computer education issues.

T.H.E. Journal
P.O. Box 992
Acton, MA 01720
617/263-3607

Published ten times per year, *T.H.E. Journal* presents a variety of articles on such topics as trends in computerization in America and other countries and examples of successful use of microcomputers by schools and colleges. Reports on upcoming events and new hardware and software releases are tied to an inquiry service card which may be used to obtain additional information. Qualified educators may receive free issues of the publication; otherwise, $29.00/10 issues.

INDEX